Yours sincerely
Richard Fjader

THE BIG GAME OF AFRICA

BY

RICHARD TJADER

WITH MANY ILLUSTRATIONS FROM
PHOTOGRAPHS BY THE AUTHOR

D. APPLETON AND COMPANY
NEW YORK AND LONDON
1910

COPYRIGHT, 1910, BY

D. APPLETON AND COMPANY

Published November, 1910

Printed in the United States of America

TO

MY DEVOTED WIFE

THIS VOLUME IS
DEDICATED

CONTENTS

CHAPTER VII

THE AFRICAN OR CAPE BUFFALO

CHAPTER VIII

LEOPARDS AND CHEETAHS

CHAPTER IX

THE AFRICAN RHINOCEROS

CONTENTS

LIST OF ILLUSTRATIONS

LIST OF ILLUSTRATIONS

THE BIG GAME OF AFRICA

CHAPTER I

BRITISH EAST AFRICA

BRITISH EAST AFRICA being not only the best country in the world for big game hunting, the size of the animals, and the multitude of the different species considered, but also of all big game countries by far the healthiest and most easily reached, I shall in the following chapters deal exclusively with that country, its climate, topography, seasons, game, and natives.

Barring the low and unhealthy coast belt on the Indian Ocean, where no game worth shooting exists (with the exception of elephants, having small tusks of comparatively poor quality, buffaloes, with not nearly as fine heads as their upland kinsfolk, and the beautiful sable antelope), the greater part of the Protectorate has a healthful climate. But the sable antelope, which many hunters class as the finest of the antelopes, exists in British East Africa, alas! only on and around the Shimba Hills, not very far from Mombasa. Yet even this stately antelope develops here horns that cannot be compared with those from other inland places, as, for instance, German East Africa and farther south.

From the narrow coast belt the Uganda Railroad begins to climb the inland plateaus and soon reaches an altitude of 1,830 feet at Voi, 5,250 feet at Matchakos, and

5,450 feet above the level of the sea at Nairobi, the government headquarters, and now, in spite of its youth, the most important town in the Protectorate. From Nairobi the climb continues, and at beautiful Lake Naivasha the station lies at an altitude of 6,230 feet, while at a place on top of the Mau escarpment the railroad reaches its highest point. A large signboard is placed here on the north side of the railway with the inscription: "Summit; altitude 8,320 feet." From here the country gradually falls away toward the great Victoria Nyanza, where the Kisumu railway station lies at an altitude of only 3,650 feet.

The rainfall of British East Africa naturally varies considerably, as the country differs so widely in altitude and general aspect. The latest statistics show an average rainfall of 14.78 inches at Kismayu, on the coast, 73.93 inches at Molo railroad station, from over 80 inches at Kericho down to 38.86 at Nairobi; but on the big mountains, like the Aberdare range, Mount Elgon, and the magnificent, snowclad Kenia, the rainfall sometimes even exceeds 100 inches a year.

The best and most popular hunting grounds lie to the northeast, north, northwest, and southwest of Nairobi at altitudes varying from 4,500 to 7,000 feet, and can, therefore, with ordinary precautions, be said to be perfectly healthy. Take, for instance, the great Athi plains, northeast of Nairobi. There large herds of zebra, hartebeest, Grant's and Thomson's gazelles may still be seen even from the railroad, with occasional glimpses of the lion, rhino, eland, and giraffe. Here the hunter seldom sees a mosquito, and if he always has the water boiled before drinking it, and is careful not to sit around in wet clothes in the evening, he has no reason to fear any attack of malarial fever.

The only insects that are bothersome on these plains are the ticks, with which the sportsman becomes literally covered from morning to night. Fortunately these ticks, although extremely disagreeable, do not seem to cause any "tick fever," as the dangerous Uganda ticks do. Another very unpleasant experience that many have had on these plains is to be attacked by the hardly noticeable little sand fly, or "funza," the special trick of which is to work its way in under some toe nail, and there, without the knowledge of the toe's owner, deposit a great number of eggs. As soon as this is done, itching generally sets in, and a slight inflammation becomes noticeable, which instantly should be followed by an "operation," generally performed to perfection by the Swahili "boys," who, with a needle, dig out the flea and scoop out the eggs, which otherwise, if hatched, would cause serious trouble, and sometimes even loss of the toe.

By being careful to wash my feet every evening, never to walk around, even on the tent's ground cloth, with bare feet, and using pajamas with "stocking extensions," I fortunately escaped this unpleasant experience. But some people I met, who had been hunting on these plains, had tales of misery to tell about their contact with the "funza." An American hunter, whom I saw in Nairobi, late in 1909, told me that he had not been able to walk properly for several weeks after such an "attack," as the "operation" had been performed rather late, and perhaps not as thoroughly as necessary.

3

As there is nothing in the way of game on these plains that the hunter may not secure more easily, and that with better horns and finer manes in other, much healthier places, there is no necessity to hunt here, where the animals are much more shy than almost anywhere else in the Protectorate, because so often molested by people from near-by Nairobi. Besides this, there is very little genuine " sport " in such hunting, or, let me say, killing of game on the Athi plains, for hunting in its true sense includes skillful and difficult tracking and stalking, of which there can be no question here. Let me explain without exaggeration how most men " hunt " on these plains.

With a couple of gun bearers and a few porters to carry the meat and trophies back to camp, the newcomer starts out from his camp generally not very early in the morning. Soon he sees in front of him a herd of zebra and hartebeest, often feeding together. They are calmly grazing at a distance of six to seven hundred yards. As there are no trees for cover, not even an ant-hill to stalk behind, he simply marches on, making straight for the animals. Suddenly, one of the more watchful hartebeests notices him and, as at a word of command, the whole herd swings around and faces him for a moment, the zebra looking particularly pretty, as their shining black and white stripes alternately appear in the sunlight or the shadow.

There are still over five hundred yards to the herd, and carefully the hunter pushes on. The next moment, however, the herd turns with jumps and all kinds of queer antics, and off they go at a gallop for a couple of hundred yards or more. Then they stop, some begin to graze again, while one or two seem to be keeping a sharp lookout for

4

the queer-looking, two-legged intruders. After this maneuver has been repeated a few times, the "sportsman" may succeed in getting up to within two or three hundred yards and, being disgusted with the chase, begin to empty his magazine at the herd in the attempt to bring down some of the animals. A young German lieutenant with whom I traveled back from Africa in 1910 told me unblushingly that he in such a way, and by firing not less than one hundred and ten shots, had one day on the Athi plains killed only three animals—one zebra, one hartebeest, and one Grant's gazelle! But he did not tell me how many unfortunate animals he may have wounded more or less severely! This he was naïve enough to call "great sport."

One of the most interesting hunting trips is the Kenia-Laikipia tour. Laikipia is a high plateau at about 7,000 feet altitude, mostly well watered from lovely streams, running down from Kenia and the Aberdare Mountains, and having a climate as nearly perfect for a hunting trip as it is possible to imagine. Only during the noon hours, from eleven to two, the sun is rather hot, the plateau lying exactly on the line of the equator, but the heat is not strong enough to prevent a healthy man from enjoying the following up of his prey even during that time. The rest of the day, both mornings and afternoons, is ideal.

The tour to this plateau can from Nairobi be comfortably made in from four to six weeks, but there is game enough, as to quantity as well as to the value of the trophies, to warrant the spending of two months or more in these beautiful regions. The mosquito is practically unknown, there are no ticks of any kind, the "funza" is nonexistent, and the water of the very best.

5

If the hunter starts out from Nairobi, going by way of the government station Fort Hall, he can begin his shooting within an hour after he has left the hotel in Nairobi with his " safari," for all along the route are seen the zebra, Coke's hartebeest, Grant's and Thomson's gazelles, many of the smaller antelopes, and sometimes even wildebeests. Then when, near Fort Hall, the Tana River is reached, the safari may follow that stream down for an hour or two to some fine camping grounds among large mimosa trees, and here the sportsman will be able to shoot hippos and crocodiles to his heart's content.

Then continuing the northward march, the caravan passes the fort, or " boma," the native name for all military and government stations, where the hunter generally pays his respects to the Provincial Commissioner, who may require him to show his game license and the special permit to proceed farther, as the Kenia-Laikipia is one of the " closed " districts, for which such a permit is a necessity. From the boma the safari proceeds along a fairly good native path, which in a few days' time leads up among the foothills of the magnificent, snowclad Kenia, which rears its domelike peak over eighteen thousand feet high. Now the sportsman may at any time come across fresh elephant tracks, or meet with buffalos, eland, bush buck, with luck, even the coveted bongo, impalla, water buck, and in a day or two more with the beautiful oryx beisa, wild dogs, possibly giraffes, plenty of rhinos, lions, and leopards, while higher up on the foothills the hunter may bag with ease his allowed number of the beautiful colobus and other fur monkeys, if monkey killing does not seem to him too much like " murder." So day after day the party may go on, finding big game everywhere, including the Grevey's zebra in the country northwest of Kenia and near the lovely river Guaso Narok at its junction with the Guaso Nyiro, to the north of which junction the northern game reserve begins. Turning thence upstream on the right bank of the Guaso Narok, the path takes the safari back again toward civilization, returning to the railroad by another also very interesting route.

On this beautiful Laikipia plateau there are scattered a good many Masai villages, or " manyata," where it is possible to obtain fresh, fine milk for trade goods, such as " Americano " (a kind of unbleached muslin), brass wire, glass beads, or, nowadays, also for money. All along the river to the north, at a distance varying from half a mile to two miles from the river bed, there are large plains, extending from rather abrupt bluffs from the river valley for miles and miles inland, dotted here and there with single good-sized trees, or clumps of the thorny mimosa.

These highlands seem to be the favorite play and feeding grounds of countless rhinos, which, if one is carefully observing the wind, and using some cover, can be approached to within thirty yards and less before they either run away or else, like the Chinese, take exception to being photographed and stared at, and with " puffs " and " snorts," with lowered horns and uplifted tails, charge down on the intruders. On these plains, where often also eland, oryx, and giraffes are seen, I once met not less than eleven rhinos within one hour, mostly in pairs of male and female or female and young. I was fortunate enough to secure some good photographs of them, but although not

7

intending to shoot any at that time, I finally had to kill a charging bull, whom I had given a chance to save his life by " changing his mind," until he was within ten yards of my camera. What happened then will be later described in the chapter on rhinos.

Following the Guaso Narok farther up, the path leads to a very large swamp, formed by the river and all overgrown with papyrus. Toward the northwest end of this swamp is a Protestant American mission station, where in 1909 Mr. and Mrs. Barnett and two fellow-laborers were doing a splendid work among the Masai people. They were highly commended by the British Commissioner of that district for their untiring efforts for the betterment of the natives.

At the extreme western end of this large and, strange enough, not unhealthy swamp, lies the government boma Rumuruti, where Mr. Collyer, a most able and kind-hearted official, in 1909–10 represented the British Government in the Laikipia Masai reserve. By the time this appears in print, the Masai of this reservation may have been already shifted away to join the rest of their tribe in the southern Kedong Valley and the Sotik and Loita plains, and the Laikipia plateau opened up for white settlements. This would mean, as everywhere else where the white man settles, the diminishing, and finally the complete disappearance, of the big game from the district.

From Rumuruti there are three paths to take. One goes in a north-northwest direction down toward Baringo, a lake swarming with crocodiles and hippos, but as this is one of the most unhealthy parts of British East Africa,

8

the before-named districts either in regard to healthfulness of climate or variety and abundance of game.

British East Africa is supposed to have four different seasons: December, January, and February, the *dry, hot* season, the East African summer; March, April, and the half of May, the *heavy rainy* season; end of May to September, the *long dry*, or "winter" season, and then again October and November the "*small rains*." But the seasons have for the last years been most irregular. The only really unpleasant months to be out on safari in British East Africa are March and April, when there is pouring rain everywhere and almost every day.

The height of the nowadays quite fashionable shooting season is from October to February, when it is safe to say that dozens of hunting parties are out in the field; but the pleasantest time for shooting trips is, without question, from May to October, when comparatively few hunters are in the land, owing to the social summer seasons in Europe and America. During that time it is much cooler, and the sportsman is not so likely to run across another safari when in the field. It is then also much easier to secure good porters, guides, and horses than at the height of the season, when "everybody" comes. I myself have tried both seasons, and should I go back again would certainly choose *our* summer for the sojourn in British East Africa.

The game laws of British East Africa have recently been materially changed, and are now not as liberal to the hunter as in the years gone by. For thorough information I have copied below the exact rendering of the new law of December, 1909, as recorded in the *Official Gazette*.

Only such paragraphs as deal directly with the sportsman who visits the country for shooting are included; all other matter is omitted:

GAME LICENSES

16. (*a*) The following licenses may be granted by a Provincial Commissioner or a District Commissioner or by such other person as may be authorized by the Governor on the behalf, that is to say:

> A Sportsman's License.
> A Resident's License.
> A Traveler's License.
> A Landholder's License.

(*b*) The following fees shall be paid for licenses: For a Sportsman's License, 750 rupees;[1] for a Resident's License, 150 rupees; for a Traveler's License, 15 rupees; and for a Landholder's License, 45 rupees.

(*c*) A Sportsman's License, a Resident's License, and a Landholder's License shall be in force for one year from the date of issue. A Traveler's License shall be in force for one month from the date of issue.

18. A Sportsman's License and a Resident's License, respectively, shall authorize the holder to hunt, kill, or capture animals *of any of the species mentioned in the Third Schedule*, but *not more* than the number of each species fixed by the second column of that schedule.

24. (*a*) A Provincial or District Commissioner may, on the application of the holder of a Sportsman's or Resident's License, grant *a Special License* authorizing such person to hunt, kill, or capture either one or two elephants as the application shall require and as shall be specified

---

[1] There are exactly *three* rupees to *one* dollar of United States currency.

14

therein. Such Special License shall not authorize the holder to hunt, kill, or capture any elephant having tusks weighing less than thirty pounds each.

(*b*) There shall be paid for such Special License the fees following:

For a license to hunt, kill, or capture
one elephant .... 150 rupees.
For a license to hunt, kill, or capture
two elephants .... 450 rupees.[1]

33. No license granted under this ordinance shall entitle the holder to hunt, kill, or capture any animal or to trespass on private land without the consent of the owner or occupier.

First Schedule

Animals not to be hunted, killed, or captured by any person except under Special License:

Elephant, giraffe, greater kudu bull (in the District of Baringo), greater kudu (female), buffalo (cow), Neumann's hartebeest in the area (2) of this schedule; eland in the following areas:

(1) An area bounded on the south by a line drawn from Kiu Station due east to the western boundary of Machakos Native Reserve to a point where the Athi River enters the said reserve, thence by the Athi River to a point due north of Donyo-Sabuk, thence by a line drawn direct to Fort Hall, on the north by the Nairobi-Fort Hall main road, on the west by the Uganda Railway.

(2) The Rift Valley south of Lake Baringo.

(3) Guas Ngishu plateau south of the Nzoia River.

---

[1] It is also provided for that if the sportsman takes out this Special License to kill two elephants, but fails to do so, the government refunds him three hundred rupees, but not more.

THE BIG GAME OF AFRICA

Roan (female), roan (male), in areas (1) and (2) of this schedule, sable (female), rhinoceros (on the northeast side of the Uganda Railway and within ten miles thereof between Sultan Hamud and Machakos Road Station), vulture (any species), owl (any species), hippopotamus (in lakes Naivasha, Elmenteita, and Nakuru), fish eagle.

SECOND SCHEDULE

Animals, *the females of which* are not to be hunted, killed, or captured when accompanying their young, and the young of which are not to be hunted, killed, or captured except under Special License:

Rhinoceros, hippopotamus, all antelopes and gazelles mentioned in any schedule.

THIRD SCHEDULE

Animals, a limited number of which may be killed or captured under a Sportsman's or Resident's License:

Buffalo (bull), 2; rhinoceros, except as provided in the First Schedule, 2; hippopotamus, except as provided in the First Schedule, 2; eland, except as provided in the First Schedule, 1; zebra (Grevey's), 2; zebra (common), 20; oryx (callotis), 2; oryx (beisa), 4; water buck (of each species), 2; sable antelope (male), 1; roan antelope (male), except as provided in the First Schedule, 1; greater kudu (male), except as provided in the First Schedule, 1; lesser kudu, 4; topi (in Jubaland, Tanaland, and Loita Plains), 8; Coke's hartebeest, 20; Neumann's hartebeest, except as provided in the First Schedule, 2; Jackson's hartebeest, 4; Hunter's antelope, 6; Thomas's kob, 4; bongo, 2; palla, 4; sitatunga, 2; wildebeest, 3; Grant's gazelle, four varieties, typicus, notata, Bright's, and Robertsi, of each, 3; Waller's gazelle (generuk), 4; Harvey's duiker, 10;

16

Isaac's duiker, 10; blue duiker, 10; Kirk's dikdik, 10; Guenther's dikdik, 10; Hinde's dikdik, 10; Cavendish's dikdik, 10; Abyssinian oribi, 10; Haggard's oribi, 10; kenya oribi, 10; " suni " (*Nesotragus moschatus*), 10; klipspringer, 10; Ward's reed buck, 10; " Chanler's reed buck, 10; Thomson's gazelle, 10; Peter's gazelle, 10; Soemmerring's gazelle, 10; bush buck, 10; bush buck (Haywood's), 10; colobi monkeys, of each species, 6; marabout, 4; egret, of each species, 4.

Fourth Schedule

Animals, a limited number of which may be killed or captured on a Traveler's License:

Zebra, 4. The following antelopes and gazelles only: Grant's gazelle, Thomson's gazelle, Jackson's and Coke's hartebeest, palla, reed buck, klipspringer, steinbuck, wildebeest, paa (*Medoqua* and *Nesotragus*), oryx beisa, bush buck, Waller's gazelle, topi (in Jubaland, Tanaland, and Loita Plains).

Five animals in all, made up of a single species or of several; provided, however, that not more than *one of each* of the following may be shot on one license:

Grant's gazelle, palla, wildebeest, oryx beisa, bush buck, Waller's gazelle, topi, Jackson's hartebeest.

Fifth Schedule

(GAME RESERVES)

(Caravans with guns are not even allowed to pass through these.—Ed.)

1. The Southern Reserve.

An area bounded by a line following the right bank of the Ngong River from the railway line to the edge of the

Kikuyu Forest, along the edge of the forest to a beacon at the point where the M'bagathi River leaves the forest by a line of beacons to the Survey beacon on the Ngong hills (Donyo Lamuyu), thence to Mt. Suswa by a line of beacons and from Suswa due west to the Mau escarpment, which it follows south to the Guaso Nyiro and by the left bank of that river to the German frontier.

Thence following the German frontier to the Tsavo (Useri) River.

By the left bank of the Tsavo River to a beacon at the point where the Ngulia and Kyulu hills approach the river. Thence following the foot of the eastern slopes of Kyulu hills to the Makindu River, which it follows to the Uganda Railway.

From the Makindu River the line follows the railway to the Ngong River.

2. The Northern Reserve.

Eastern Boundary

Starting from the ford at " Campi ya Nyama Yangu " on the Northern Guaso Nyiro River, the boundary follows the eastern slopes of the following hills:

Mt. Koiseku, Mt. Kalama, Mt. Lololugi, Mt. Wargies (Table Mountains), Mt. Leo, Mt. Endata, Mt. Kulal.

From Mt. Kulal by a line northeast to Mt. Moille, thence following the eastern slopes of this mount and Mount Seramba, Mt. Loder Moretu, and Mt. Kul.

From Mount Kul to a beacon on the western side of Mt. Marsabit.

Northern Boundary

From the beacon on the western side of the Mt. Marsabit by a straight line west to Mt. Nyiro.

BRITISH EAST AFRICA

Western Boundary

From Mt. Nyiro following the foot of the Laikipia escarpment to the Mugatan River.

Thence in a direct line to the junction of the Guaso Nyiro and Guaso Narok.

Southern Boundary

Thence following the left bank of Guaso Nyiro to the ford at " Campi ya Nyama Yangu."

(See map.)

CHAPTER II

THE CARAVAN OR " SAFARI "

SAFARI is a Ki-Swahili word, which is commonly used not only for designating the caravan itself, meaning thereby all the people who serve as headmen, gun bearers, porters, etc., but it also means traveling by any other means than by railroad or steamer. If it is said, for instance, that anyone is " out on safari," it conveys the idea that the person in question is out on a trip with porters, oxen, mules, horses, or donkeys; in one word, moving about the country living in his tent. " Safari," therefore, is one of the first words the traveler learns of the useful Ki-Swahili language, the *lingua franca* of the whole East and Central Africa. In fact, I have heard hunters say that they were surprised to find this language so serviceable to them even far in the interior of the Congo Free State. On account of this great usefulness of the Ki-Swahili language, there will be a chapter at the end of the book devoted to the rudiments of grammar, words, and phrases most necessary for the hunter, who would be independent of irresponsible and often inefficient interpreters, and who also wishes to get his information about the game and paths at *first hand* from the natives of the different tribes. This is often of the greatest importance to the sportsman.

THE CARAVAN OR "SAFARI"

As soon as the hunter arrives at Nairobi he will at once set about getting his safari ready, unless he has made his arrangements beforehand through some of the Nairobi agents or, as they call themselves, "safari outfitters." This is, of course, the most convenient way, saving quite a little personal work, trouble, and a few days of time, but costing considerably more than when the sportsman fits out his caravan himself. One of the largest safari out-fitters in Nairobi advertises that people in employing them "save trouble and expense." Once I tried this firm, being in a great hurry to get off to the jungle, but found that, although I saved some "trouble," the "expense" was much larger than if I had arranged for everything myself.

Of course, the hunter going into the country for the first time without some knowledge of the Ki-Swahili language, and with little time at his disposal, but plenty of "cash on hand," does best in letting some firm fit him out with everything, making the agreement that the firm in question shall supply everything at the lowest local retail cost, and then charge five per cent commission on the total expenditure. Another, but more expensive, way of doing the same thing is to agree on a certain fixed sum per month for so many men, horses, or mules, as the case may be, including all expenses, but the reader may be absolutely sure that the "certain fixed sum" in this case is so "fixed" that the safari outfitters, at all events, profit largely thereby.

To give the intending sportsman an idea of what an ordinary, average safari in British East Africa may cost him per month, I shall here give a few extracts from my own carefully kept accounts during three different expeditions into the interior. A single sportsman needs, to be perfectly comfortable and for a three- or four-months' shooting trip, about forty men in all, although he may get along with less. This will cost him about as follows:

1 headman	wages per month,			$14.00
2 gun-bearers (for both).......	"	"	"	25.00
4 askaris (for all).............	"	"	"	16.00
1 cook	"	"	"	10.00
1 personal "boy," or butler....	"	"	"	9.00
1 syce, or horse boy...........	"	"	"	5.00
30 porters at $3.34 each........	"	"	"	100.00
Food for all 40 men...........		"	"	30.00
Extra expenses for occasional guides, etc........				21.00
Total for all men, wages and food..........				$230.00

Besides this monthly expense there is an initial outlay, according to the government regulation, requiring for each man one blanket, a jersey, and a water bottle, amounting to about $1 to $1.50 per man according to quality, or, say, in all about $60 for the forty men. Then, in most cases the hunter has to supply the headman, gun bearers, cook, and "boy" with a suit of khaki clothes, coat and trousers, which cost about $3 the suit. This would add to the initial expense another $15. A good horse costs about $200, more or less, and a fair, strong riding mule from $100 to $150, while good donkeys can be had from $14 to $18. These animals are sold again at the end of the safari, realizing, if in good condition, about sixty to eighty per cent of their original cost.

The "askaris" are a kind of native soldier, whose duty it is to look after and help the men during the march, to pitch the owner's tent, as well as to watch at night in turns around the camp fire, and they are, therefore, really indispensable for his comfort and safety in the jungle.

Adding all these expenses up, and allowing for " additional extras," such as railway trips, and the hunter's own food supply, a *four months'* safari, during which time the sportsman, with ordinary luck, will be able to secure most of the big game of East Africa, will cost approximately:

40 men's regulation outfit..........once for all,	$60.00
5 men's khaki suits .... " " "	15.00
40 men's wages and food.......... " " "	960.00
A good riding horse............... " " "	200.00
Possible extras.................. " " "	215.00
Total expense for four months............$1,450.00
Possible return from sale of horse........ 150.00
Total expense.....................$1,300.00

The price of the hunting license must be added to this expense, and from the beginning of 1910 this will cost the sportsman $250, giving him, as we have already seen, a certain amount of different kinds of animals, with the exception of elephants. If he wants to kill one elephant he has to pay an additional $50, and if he desires a license to shoot a second elephant he has to pay a further additional fee of $100, so that the total price of the general license, including the right of killing or capturing two elephants, amounts to $400.

Therefore, if the safari is carefully looked after, a four months' trip, including the above-mentioned licenses and all expenses, would not need to cost more than about $1,700, and may be run for even much less than that.

The reason why one man for a long jungle trip needs as many as forty men, which would give him about *thirty porters* for carrying loads, and possibly only twenty of these would carry food, is that in most of the outlying districts, where the best game is to be had, no food or " posho," as the porters' food is generally called, can be obtained locally, and forty men will eat just about one load of posho of sixty pounds each day. This again would only carry the safari along for less than a month, but within that time the hunter probably passes by some East Indian's store, or a native village, where it is possible to buy the needed loads of posho. And besides this, at the start each man may carry his own food for six to eight days in a small muslin bag, which is added to his load. Then, if much game is secured, it is possible to feed the men on smaller rations of posho, so that twenty loads of posho, for instance, would in such a way be sufficient for four or five weeks, within which time the sportsman is now reasonably certain of being able to buy food locally in almost any place in British East Africa.

If, however, the hunter desires to go very far off from inhabited country, he can arrange for the posho in another way—by taking, say, only twenty men in all, just enough to have them carry the camp outfit, guns, and a few loads of food, and then use twelve donkeys to carry the rest of the men's posho. As each donkey carries from one hundred and twenty to one hundred and fifty pounds, and only feeds on the grass, it is possible, in such a way, to be out from fifty days to two months without buying fresh supplies. If rations are cut down, when meat is very plentiful, it may be possible to be away

CAMP OF THE TJADER EAST AFRICAN EXPEDITION, 1906, AT SOLAI, B. E. A.

THE ADVANCE GUARD OF THE CARAVAN CROSSING A RIVER ON THE WAY TO SOTIK.

even for two months and a half or more with such an outfit.

On my first expedition to East Africa I engaged a great many more men than most hunters need. At times I had over one hundred porters in my caravan, and on one of our trips the number rose to one hundred and seventeen. The reason for this was that I was collecting specimens for the American Museum of Natural History in New York City. When I informed the director of the museum of my intention to go out to Africa on a hunting trip, and that I was also willing to use the opportunity to enrich the collection of the museum, he volunteered to give me letters of introduction to British officials to secure special permits for me in the field. He also gave me one of the best preparators of the institution, Mr. Herbert Lang, who acted as our official photographer and taxidermist, and to whose faithfulness, skill, and untiring efforts much of the success of the expedition was due. The museum further supplied most of the curing materials, special skinning knives and other things needed for the work in the field. When a scientific expedition goes out into the jungle to collect specimens for preservation in museums, it needs a great deal more curing material, special drying boxes for bird skins, traps for smaller mammals, etc.

Then, again, the scientist, when he secures an animal, not only takes off the head and the skin of head and neck for trophies, as the mere sportsman generally does, but has to conserve the whole skin of the beast. But not only that, in a great many cases he also desires to bring home the leg bones, as well as the ribs and sometimes the whole chest, without cutting the ribs apart, and all the rest of the skeleton. This again necessitates a great many more porters than the ordinary hunter needs. Thus, for instance, it required forty men to carry the skin and skeleton of my largest rhino from the place where he fell to the camp, where the skin was cut thin and prepared, whereas if this rhino had only been taken as a trophy two men could easily have carried anything that the sportsman would have liked to take home with him. My first trip to East Africa has several times been mentioned in the annals of the museum as the " Tjader East African Expedition." About one third of its actual expenses were afterwards contributed by the American Museum of Natural History, which received the greater part of the collection, or somewhat over four hundred specimens of mammals, reptiles, and birds. The rest of the " spoil," besides a couple of dozen trophies which I kept for myself, was presented to the Royal Swedish Academy of Science in Stockholm.

In getting the safari together it is often of great importance to take porters of different tribes, such as the Wa-Swahili, the Wa-Nyamwezi, the Wa-Kamba, and the Wa-Kikuju, as they are then not so apt to try any conspiracy or mutiny of any sort, which hunters have sometimes had to contend with; and it is also possible to get more work out of the men by playing one tribe off against another, for they all want to show that *their* tribe is better than any other. This worked very well indeed when I sometimes had to make exceptionally long and hard marches over difficult territory and waterless tracts of the country.

The porters generally like to start out very early in the morning, long before the sun rises, so as to be able to cover the day's march of some fifteen to twenty-five miles before the heat of the noon hours. In such a case, as soon as camp is made, and firewood and water brought in, most of the men have the whole afternoon for rest and play, if they are so bent, and the hunter a fine chance to bring some additional game to bag, after the greatest heat of the day is over. To gain this point, I have often started the safari as early as 3.30 and 4 A.M., particularly if we had moonlight, or else a few minutes after five, when the eastern sky begins to show signs of the morning light. If one can use a well-defined path, the early morning march is very pleasant, but it may otherwise be dangerous, and particularly so in dense bush country, where a lion or rhino may be lurking around, and suddenly take exception to having his own territory invaded.

I remember one early morning on the beautiful Laikipia plateau, when we had left camp before 4 A.M., and the whole caravan of some hundred and fifteen men was slowly moving along the northern banks of the beautiful Guaso Narok River, going downstream through rather thick bush, how suddenly one of the men right behind me half whispering said:

"Bwana, naona vifaru viwili mbele karibu," or, in English, " Sir, I see two rhinos near by in front."

As I tried to peer through the bush in the half dark, the bright moon having disappeared for a moment behind some rather thick clouds, I saw one large and one half-grown rhino, only some twenty yards off, standing in a little open space, at the edge of which our path wound its way. They were evidently a mother with her young, and therefore very " unsafe " indeed. Having already had

27

to shoot more rhinos than allowed on my license only to
protect our lives, and it being too dark anyway to take
careful aim, I stopped, with one of the gun bearers, to
stand guard while the caravan passed by on the other side
of some bush. The men had been told to walk as quietly
as they could. As the porters marched .very closely together, it did not take them perhaps more than two minutes
to pass the little opening on which the rhinos stood. During this time the old female " sniffed " and " puffed " and
tossed her head, evidently scenting the men, but unable
to make up her mind whether to charge or not, while the
youngster continually changed his position from one side
of his mother to the other. Finally, as the last man had
passed, I retreated carefully, " covering " the mother with
my gun, until she was out of sight. The caravan porters
seem, as a rule, to have very little personal courage, for
twice afterwards, when a rhino charged down on us in
front, a great many of the men far behind, and out of
immediate danger, threw down their loads and stampeded
for the nearest cover like so many frightened cattle!

It is of great importance for a successful safari to have
an experienced and efficient headman, who understands
how to handle his people, for if he does not know how to
make himself respected and instantly obeyed, the whole
caravan is soon demoralized. The best thing to do then
is to " degrade " the headman and select the best askari
to take his place. I was once forced to take this measure.
It worked very well, indeed, as the askari whom I made
headman turned out to be a splendid " captain," and everything went on beautifully after the change.

When a hard day's march is done, and the hunter has

succeeded in bagging some coveted trophies, it is a great pleasure to sit down near the big camp fire, after a good but simple dinner, and let the men perform their war dances, sing and chant, and tell their very often interesting stories, until the oncoming darkness reminds the sportsman that it is time to "turn in" to gather new strength for the morrow's adventures and possible hardships.

CHAPTER III

ALMOST since time immemorial the lion has been called the " King of beasts." Most writers of natural history still bestow this high title upon the big feline, largely on account of its generally majestic appearance, courage, and fierceness of its character. Yet a good many prominent African hunters do not share this opinion, and have from experience learned that the lion is not so " noble " and " fearless," except when wounded or cornered, as it is cowardly and mean. From my own limited experience in lion hunting, I side with the latter, and think that for many reasons the elephant is much more worthy of the exalted title.

The lion is the only representative of the large cat family which grows a mane, covering often not only head, neck, and shoulders, but sometimes also fully half of the back and chest. The mane of the African lion differs a great deal in size and color. Contrary to the general opinion, the lion of the Old World also carries a mane, although perhaps not of the average size of that of the African lion. Another and rather queer characteristic of the big feline is a large, strange-looking tuft of hair at the end of its tail, which very often at the extreme point carries a small horny appendage, surrounded by a brush of coarse hair. Much has been said and written about the reason for this kind of " horn " on the lion's tail, and some have thought that it served as a goad, with which the lion provokes itself to fury, when it lashes its flanks with the tail, as it often does when angry. With the exception of the smaller or larger mane of the male, the hair of both lion and lioness is very short and close. Its color varies from light yellowish brown or tawny to dark brown, turning, in the manes of some old males, into an almost perfect black. The skins of young cubs are almost invariably plainly spotted, which is often the case in full-grown young lionesses. The manes begin to make their appearance first during the third year, and a lion's age is estimated anywhere from thirty to fifty years.

Lions vary a great deal in size and weight. Measured, as a rule, from the tip of the nose to the very end of the tail, Indian lions have been found as long as eight feet ten inches, whereas the famous lion and elephant hunter, Mr. F. C. Selous, gives records of specimens of lions he had shot in South Africa which measured respectively ten feet six inches, ten feet nine inches, and eleven feet one inch. The largest lion I have ever shot measured ten feet two inches from the tip of the nose to the end of the tail, the tape line being laid along the curve of the body before skinning. The height at the shoulders of full-grown specimens also varies from three feet to three feet six inches, and I have heard of a lion shot in German East Africa which stood fully three feet nine inches high, but this is probably rather extraordinary. Still more does the weight of full-grown lions vary, and not only the size of the beast, but its general condition makes a great difference in this respect. Lionesses have been found weighing from three hundred pounds to four hundred and twenty-five pounds, and full-grown males tip the scales at four hundred and fifty pounds and more, one of the largest on record having weighed five hundred and eighty-three pounds. This was an unusually large male lion, in the prime of life, killed in the Orange Free State, in 1865, in a locality where game was very abundant. That specimen, therefore, was in splendid condition.

The lion inhabits at present not only the greater part of Africa, from the Cape Colony in the south to Abyssinia and the northern parts of the Sahara Desert in the north, but it is also found in many places in southwestern Asia, where it still occurs in certain parts of Mesopotamia and Arabia, as well as in northwestern India. It is now more and more rarely seen in the latter locality, and it is only a question of a few years when the beautiful beast will have been completely exterminated within the limits of India. In ages past, and even within historic times, the lion was found in southeastern Europe, in such countries as Roumania and Greece, and bones and skulls of prehistoric lions, of unquestionably the same species, have been found as far north as Germany, the British Isles, and France.

In South Africa lions are now very scarce in the districts south of the Orange River, where the white man with his modern firearms has almost exterminated the big cat. In other parts of Africa, however, it is almost absolutely certain that where large herds of game are still to be found, there the lion also abounds. On the other hand, in places where there is a scarcity of game, one

YOUNG LION WALKING TOWARD THE CAMERA.

LIONESS KILLED ON THE ATHI PLAINS.

rarely finds the great feline, the appetite of which seems tremendous. It is said by prominent African hunters, and corroborated by the natives themselves, that, where game is plentiful, an adult lion kills a good-sized animal almost every night. In places where it has not been much shot at, the lion sometimes hunts even in the daytime, if it, for some reason, failed to secure its prey the night before. This I myself firmly believe, for the first lion I ever killed had just slain a zebra, which it was devouring, when a good Winchester bullet, at close quarters, intercepted the meal; and this happened about ten o'clock in the morning of a perfectly bright day and right on the Athi plains, only a few miles from Nairobi.

As a rule the lion hunts just after sunset, when it can more easily stalk its prey unobserved. Its favorite food seems to be zebra meat, but any good-sized antelope will do just as well if, for any reason, a zebra cannot be secured. There have been instances, although they are probably very rare, where a lion has stalked even a full-grown buffalo, but only extreme lack of other food would make the lion bold enough to attack such a powerful animal, which certainly has many times over the strength of the lion.

On the foothills of Kenia I was once told by some Wandorobo, the wildest and most primeval natives of British East Africa, who also are, as a rule, the best trackers and pathfinders in the jungle, that they had once witnessed a fight between a lion and a full-grown buffalo cow. The lion had just sprung upon its calf and killed it, when the infuriated mother suddenly appeared on the scene, and, with lowered horns, rushed at the murderer of its "baby" with such speed that, before the lion could jump up, it was caught on the horns of the buffalo and tossed many feet into the air. No sooner had the lion touched the ground than the angry mother was at it again, and although the big cat succeeded in cutting some terrible gashes on the neck of its assailant with its claws, and actually bit off half its nose, yet it was finally crushed to death by the horns of the buffalo. As soon as the lion was dead the cow stood bleeding and trembling over the dead body of its offspring, until the cruel but delighted Wandorobos shot it with their poisoned arrows, and so put an end to its sufferings.

When the lion kills big game single-handed it does it generally in the following way: It first stalks its prey, until it is so close that a few mighty leaps will bring it up alongside the same. Then it suddenly seizes the victim's nose with one of its mighty paws, while with the other it catches hold of the back of the animal, and so in an instant pulls the head sideways and downward with such force as almost invariably to break its neck at once, or else gives the beast a tremendous bite at the back of the head, which instantly kills it. Sometimes the lion begins its meal by tearing its prey open, first drinking the blood and eating heart and lungs, before it begins on the rest of the body, but it often prefers starting with the hind-quarters.

Very often the lion simply lies in hiding near some water hole or drinking place in a stream, near enough to reach its prey with a single mighty swoop. It seems very strange that herds of zebra, for instance, will night after night go down to the very same watering place to drink, where they frequently have had the excitement of losing one of their " comrades." Someone has said that the animals seem to understand that, as soon as one of them has been killed, the others are safe for that night at least, and so they often continue to drink and feed as if nothing at all had happened. I have also noticed that in the early morning the animals seem to have no dread whatsoever of the lions.

Once on a march over the Sotik plains with the whole caravan, the second gun bearer stopped me and, pointing a little to the left, said: " Bwana, tasama simba wawili huko " (" Sir, look out, there are two lions over there.") Turning in that direction, I first only saw a number of Coke's hartebeest and some smaller gazelles quietly feeding, and did not believe that the gun bearer could be right. As he insisted that the lions were there, I took the strong field glasses and saw, to my amazement and joy, three full-grown lions, stretched out on the ground, not fifty yards away from the nearest antelopes, which must have passed even much closer to the lions, judging from the way they were feeding!

Were the antelopes perhaps intelligent enough to know that the lions, having had their " fill " during the night, would not attack them in the daytime? Or could they have known that lions after a hearty meal are unable to run fast enough to catch an antelope? This is indeed a fact, for I had soon bagged the largest of the trio, a splendid, black-maned lion, which was too full to run very fast and long, its stomach being filled with zebra meat, bones, and pieces of striped skin. It may be remarked here that neither lion, leopard, nor cheetah seems to be able to run very fast for any length of time. For a few dozen paces they go with great speed and in long leaps, but then their wind seems suddenly to give out, and they fall into a heavy gallop, or canter, when an ordinary riding pony will soon outdistance them.

One of the most interesting and at the same time sure ways of hunting lions is to have a man gallop after them on horseback until the lion, unable to escape any longer, suddenly stops and turns on its pursuer, giving the sportsman an excellent chance to shoot his trophy at close quarters. On one of the first days of my sojourn on the Sotik and Loita plains I had two very interesting lion hunts in this way, the account of which I here copy from my diary:

". . . After marching with the whole caravan for about five hours this morning, we came up to a rather high point in the plains, where we rested for a few moments, and where I looked around with my field glasses to see if I could detect something that looked like a watering place, for it was now evident that our Masai guide had not told us the truth about the distance to the nearest water. With the glasses I now plainly saw three lions a little to our left and about a thousand yards off. One looked unusually large and had a very black mane, while the two others seemed to be either young males or possibly a maneless male and a female. I was very anxious to bag one of these lions, particularly as they lay right in the line of our march, so I dispatched my brave 'lion chaser,' Asgar, to gallop away with the hunting pony to hinder the biggest lion from running away, until we could come up.

" Now followed the most exciting and interesting chase

that I have ever witnessed! As soon as the three lions saw the horse, they all ran off in different directions, Asgar following the big black-maned one, and evidently gaining on him with every second. My gun bearers and I followed on the run, as fast as we could possibly go. When Asgar came within about fifty yards of the lion, it suddenly stopped, viewed him for a few seconds, and then turned with a roar and rushed at him. Asgar instantly whirled his horse around, and galloped off toward us, with the lion close behind him. After a few leaps the lion saw that it was impossible to catch the horse, so it gave up the chase and turned around to run away. At the very same moment Asgar also turned and galloped after the lion, and these scenes were repeated again and again, until finally the lion was completely tired out, and was brought to bay near a half-dried-out stream.

"As we approached the place, Asgar pointed toward the lion with his whip, but I could only hear loud grunting from the other side of the little stream. Against the advice of my gun bearers, but bound on getting the lion at any cost, I crossed the river bed through the dense bush, to be faced the next second, to my unspeakable joy, by this magnificent 'king of beasts,' which showed its beautiful head above a little bush, only some thirty yards away from where I emerged from the stream. As it caught sight of me, it advanced up into the bush, exposing entirely its head and shoulders. Here it stood, majestically, switching its tail and giving a tremendous roar as a warning signal for me not to come any nearer.

"Just one look around assured me that my camera bearer had unfortunately again failed to follow me closely, and, seeing this, I fired with my excellent 11.2 millimeter Mauser rifle, hitting the lion square in the chest. It took three or four big leaps into the dense bush lining the little stream, and from there we now heard his loud grunting for a few seconds. My men wanted me to shoot into the bush at random, thinking I might hit the lion somewhere, but this seemed to me perfectly useless and cowardly, so I advanced cautiously, with the gun ready. Parting the bushes with my left arm, to be able to peer into the dense thicket, I finally caught sight of the ' fallen monarch,' breathing his last and stretched out on the ground. Now it was my turn to shout, and in a few seconds the rest of the men came around congratulating and saying that they had never before seen a lion with such a big mane. After having pulled it out from the bush, we found that it measured nine feet eight inches from the tip of the nose to the end of the tail, and so proved to be a large specimen with an unusually long and thick black mane. . . ."

On the following Tuesday morning we left camp long before daylight to see if we could find some more lions, and this day proved to be one of the most successful hunting days that I have ever had. Having arrived just after sunrise on a rather high elevation on the plains, from where we had an excellent view in all directions, I sat down on a big rock to examine the plains with the field glasses. To the east I saw six giraffes—three large ones, evidently a male and two females, and three young ones, the smallest of which was not much larger than an ordinary calf, except for the length of its neck. Between us and the giraffes was a herd of about thirty eland ante-

LARGE, BLACK-MANED LION KILLED ON THE SOTIK PLAINS, MAY, 1909.

SAME AS ABOVE.

Note the enormous size of the mane, the longest hairs of which measure seventeen inches.

lopes, calmly grazing. Farther to the north we saw countless numbers of zebra and antelopes of different kinds,
and toward the south and west, big herds of wildebeests
and other game. . . .

On the way back to the rock, whither we decided to return for another survey of the land, after I had bagged a
cheetah and a topi, I saw an unusually large white-bearded
gnu which I also secured, and when we finally arrived on
top of the hill again, I discovered two lions, due south from
us, both resting, and fully stretched out on the ground.
Now followed a still more interesting chase than the one a
couple of days before, as this lion was even more " gamey "
than the other.

" Repeatedly it turned and charged so suddenly and
quickly at the horse, that it looked as if it would catch
up with Asgar; but a few moments later the tables were
turned and we found Asgar chasing the lion. So it went
on for half a dozen times at least, until we succeeded in
coming so close to the lion that it caught sight of us.

" Instantly the beast made for me in a bee line. Before
the lion had come even within one hundred yards the
gun bearers begged me to shoot. But, enjoying the looks
of the beautiful oncoming beast with its enormous flut-
tering mane, I let it come, calling out to ' his majesty ' in
Ki-Swahili: ' Karibu mzee, karibu,' which means, ' Come
on, old man, come on.' And on it came! Oh, had my
camera bearer only been up beside me now, what a magnificent picture I should have obtained!

" Again the men begged me to shoot, but as I was sure
of my aim and my gun, I let the lion come on until within
thirty yards or less, when I fired, the bullet hitting squarely

39

between its shoulders, and down the lion went in an instant. I sprang forward, shouting for joy, when, to my utter surprise, the lion got up and, with a never-to-be-forgotten roar, rushed for me, now less than twenty yards off! Then the second bullet sent it to the ground again, never more to move! An examination of the trophy revealed to our great delight that this lion was even larger than the one killed before, measuring ten feet two inches from the tip of the nose to the end of the tail, and having a much larger and almost black mane. Everybody that saw this skin, including a government official who has examined over two hundred lion skins, seemed to think it one of the largest and most beautiful lions ever killed in British East Africa. . . ."

When big plains are traversed by rivers, or even dried-out water courses, where always a great many large trees and high grasses grow, one may be reasonably sure of finding lions or leopards, unless they have often been disturbed by hunters. In such places it is a good scheme to go in among the trees, up wind, to some point where one can see across the whole belt of bush, then screen one's self as well as possible, and send the men to beat the bush for a mile or so above. The lion will then generally run away from the beaters, down wind, but, fearing to be detected on the open plains, it will, as a rule, keep running between the trees and the bushes along the river or in the dry river bed. Then it is easily shot, as it passes the place where the hunter stands. If the lion, under such circumstances, is only wounded, it will almost invariably charge, and woe to the hunter who then fails to receive it with steady nerve and ready gun!

THE LION—KING OF BEASTS

The lion seems to hate the heat of the noonday sun, for it loves then to lie down in the thick bush, or in a cool swamp among the high papyrus, even often partly down in the water itself. It also loves to retreat into caves, well protected from the rays of the sun. In the hot lowlands and lower plateaus of East Africa the manes of the lions are exceedingly poor, a good many having practically no manes at all, while others have a short, tawny-colored mane—a poor trophy indeed. In the cooler regions, however, the manes are sometimes perfectly magnificent, covering the neck, more than half of the back, away down over the shoulders, and are dark brown to almost black in shade. The " black-maned " lion is regarded as the finest trophy, and comparatively few sportsmen are lucky enough to shoot such a one. People have even suggested that there are different species of lions according to their manes, but as lions with all sorts of manes, but otherwise perfectly alike, inhabit the same localities, this is entirely untenable.

It is when the lion gets too old to be able to catch game that it takes to " man-eating " and so becomes the terror of the natives in its district. In January, 1910, I met a government official, whom I had visited on my previous trip to Kenia, and who told me of some terrible experiences he had had with a man-eater since then. But before relating these, I must tell of an incident which happened on the way to this official's house.

We had just crossed a river, where we saw fresh lion tracks. As we emerged from the bank of the river, we found a great many Kikuyu beads, often worn by the men of the tribe, strewn on the ground. Not thinking of the fresh lion tracks, that we had seen below, my gun bearer jokingly remarked to me that perhaps two Kikuyu men had been fighting here, having torn off each other's beads. When I suggested that a lion might have killed a man here, he stoically said: " Labda, Bwana " ("Perhaps, sir)?" No sooner had we reached the little government forestry station, than we heard that the very evening before a man-eating lion had killed a Kikuyu on this very spot. But owing to heavy rains during the night, the blood marks and other possible signs of the struggle had been washed away.

This government official told me that it very probably was the same man-eater, an old lioness, which had killed a number of people in the district, finally growing so bold that it would come up to within a few yards of his own house to try to slay some of his workmen. One dark evening four of his men wanted to go to a spring about a hundred yards from his house to get some additional water. They were warned not to go by their employer, but said they would all take spears and torches, so that there would be no danger. They subsequently went, but none of them ever returned! The ferocious lioness succeeded in killing all of them, and dragged the bodies of two away into the dense bush, where a few days later their crushed skulls and a few bones were all that was left! In vain the official tried to shoot or trap the lioness, for fear of which his wife and baby for days never dared to leave the house. But finally one moonlight night, when a goat was tied close to the house and the bloodthirsty brute was in the very act of springing on its easy prey, it was killed by two well-aimed shots, fired from the open window, and so the district was ridded of a man-eater, which had slain over twenty people in a few weeks!

In spite of such not infrequent occurrences, and numerous accidents to lion hunters, it seems to me that the dangers of lion hunting are generally overestimated, for few African beasts are as easily killed as the lion, if hit either in head, neck, or chest. But, of course, the following up of a wounded lion or lioness in dense bush, or high grass, is a very dangerous undertaking, just as it would be to pursue wounded buffaloes, rhinos, leopards, and particularly elephants. With ordinary precautions, however, a man with a good magazine gun and steady nerve, and perhaps with a reserve gun of some bigger bore close at hand, runs very little risk of being killed or wounded by lions, unless he should attack a large number at the same time, or else lose his head and fail to make his shots tell.

A good many have been mauled or killed when hunting lions on horseback, as the movements of the more or less frightened horse make a steady aim and a good shot almost impossible. It was in this way a young settler, a Mr. Smith, in the Sotik country was very nearly killed, while I was out there in 1909. He had gone lion shooting on horseback with a friend of his, both being good shots and fearless men. They had succeeded in bagging a couple of lions, and as they were returning to Mr. Smith's farm in the evening, they came upon a lioness, which they wounded, but which they did not want to follow into the dense jungle, as the sun was just about setting.

The next morning, however, they rode out again to secure the wounded lioness, but before they anticipated any charge at all, she sprang upon Mr. Smith's friend, trying to tear him down from his saddle. Young Smith then fired at the lion, wounding it in the back. Instantly the lion let go his comrade, and made for Mr. Smith in mighty leaps. From his saddle he fired five times at the oncoming beast, yet without hitting any of its vital spots, and before his comrade had a chance to come to his rescue, the lioness tore him down from his saddle and horribly mauled him. Just as he had given up all hope, and the lioness was burying its terrible fangs in his leg, his badly wounded comrade succeeded in killing it by a well-aimed shot through the head at a few yards' distance.

As lions often go in pairs and groups of from eight to twelve, or sometimes even more, it may be very dangerous for a single man to attack such a large number of these powerful beasts. But, on the other hand, if the hunter is not far off and able to make every shot tell, and first kills the grown females, he will probably be able to master the situation. The well-known German traveler and explorer, Dr. Carl Peters, the founder of German East Africa, told me that he once, on one of his trips there, came upon a group of twenty-two lions, most of which were full-grown males and females. Being an absolutely fearless man and a good shot, he was able to kill five, the others running for cover in the bushes. Another sportsman, an American, killed six lions in less than two hours during the fall of 1909. An Australian hunter and settler told me last December that he went out in the fall of 1909 to shoot a lion which the night before had killed one of his oxen. But being confronted with eleven of these big felines, he quickly retreated without molesting the lions, some of which had already observed him, although they did not seem to mind him in the least.

According to my own limited experience with lions, having in all killed but six, and perhaps only seen seven or eight more, I must say that I do not admire their courage, unless they are both wounded and cornered. Five full-grown lions, which I once saw lying on some flat rocks, unfortunately jumped down and disappeared into the high grass before it was possible for me to fire. I then shot a few times into the moving grass in the hope that by possibly wounding one of them it might charge down on me, and so give me the chance of a shot at close quarters, but, alas! nothing of the kind happened.

Much has been said and written about the roaring of the lion, some holding the view that the lion only roars *after* it has killed its prey, and when wounded or cornered, and when prepared to charge. Others again affirm that the lion also often roars *before* it kills its prey. In localities where it has not been much disturbed by hunters the lion's roar may be heard at all times of the day. Personally, I am inclined to join the latter's opinion, for I have at least twice heard lions roar just after sunset, and in both cases I was in the position of knowing that they had not yet killed their prey. Lions often hunt in company with each other, and are then evidently roaring to confuse the game, and thus drive it in a certain desired direction, where other " quiet " lions lie in wait.

Once I was hunting on the Loita plains, and seeing a " donga "—i. e., a great many trees strung out along some water course—I decided to go through the same for some distance with the view of possibly putting up a lion or leopard among the bush. Going up wind, with some eight or ten of my men spread out in chainlike fashion behind me, I walked slowly and without making any unnecessary noise, so as not to scare away any beast, before I should have a chance of shooting. We thus walked along for about half an hour, only putting up a small cheetah, which I did not care to fire at for fear of frightening away some bigger game.

The little, partly dried-out stream was winding its way in constant turns, so that we often had to cross and recross the same. I was again just crossing one of these turns, with one of the gun bearers behind me, and at a place where all that remained of the stream, so formidable during the rainy season, was a big, stagnant pool, which, to judge from the maze of lion, antelope, and zebra tracks, was a favorite drinking place for all kinds of game. Suddenly, as I went down into the bottom of the river, and without a moment's warning, a big lioness, which was hiding in the bush on an islandlike projection in the bottom of the river, jumped out. With an angry grunt, and passing my right shoulder within a yard or two, she tried to make good her escape into a clump of thick bush which we had just passed.

Had the lioness jumped right upon me instead, her sheer weight would have almost crushed me against the hard river bottom; but as it was, I turned quickly, and with great rapidity fired at the running feline, the bullet crushing her pelvis. Before I had time to fire again, she had disappeared into the dark bush, from where she now ejected the most awe-inspiring roars. With gun cocked and ready, I advanced to within six or seven yards of the

THE LIONESS WHICH ALMOST KILLED THE AUTHOR.
Shot on the Sotik, 1909.

A FINE SPECIMEN.

thicket in spite of my men's trying to keep me back. Yet I could see nothing, so dense was the bush, and so fired in the direction of the roar. The shot was followed by still louder roaring, after which I heard a noise that made me think that the lioness in her fury was crushing the bush with her teeth. Again I fired into the bush, but this time the wounded lioness answered with a few short grunts, at the same time making a desperate effort to get out of the bush and charge. Now she exposed her chest and neck, and instantly another bullet silenced her forever.

We all went into the bush to drag the trophy out, and found, to our amazement, that the lioness in her anger and pain had crushed one of her own hind legs almost to pieces, having bitten twelve big holes in it, above and below the knee! This lioness was in her prime, with very large and beautiful teeth. The contents of her stomach showed that her last meal had consisted of zebra meat.

One of the most remarkable lion stories which I have ever heard, and which I know to be perfectly true, runs as follows: Some years ago a man-eating lion had killed a number of people near one of the stations of the Uganda Railroad. One day, as the Hindu station master, assisted by the switchman, was labeling packages on the station platform, this man-eater charged down upon them. The station master rushed headlong through the window into his office, but the switchman, whose retreat was cut off by the lion, climbed up on a telegraph pole. The station master, in his despair, now sent on the following telegram to headquarters at Nairobi: " Big lion patrolling platform. Switchman on telegraph pole. Send soldiers. My life almost gone."

Instantly three sportsmen made themselves ready to go down by the next train to the station to kill the maneater. They arrived there in the evening, and the private car in which they traveled was switched off at the station. They all now agreed that during the night they should take turns, so that one should always be watching, while the other two slept until the morning broke, when they expected to go out and look for the lion. That evening they probably had taken a little too much whisky, for they all went to sleep, including the unfortunate hunter, who with his loaded gun had sat down in the open door of the carriage to keep watch. The one, however, who did not sleep was the lion. For a little after sunset it bounded right into the car, snatched the sleeping watchman, and jumped out with him through one of the windows of the car, quickly disappearing with its unfortunate prey into the jungle.

It is a fact, although almost incredible, that the ill-fated hunters' comrades were either too frightened or too drunk, or both, to make any attempt at rescuing their friend, for they both shut themselves up in the car, and when they went out the next morning to look for the lion, they found only the skull and a few bones of their unfortunate comrade. This lion was subsequently killed, a good many glass pieces in its mane and back proving beyond a question that it had been the guilty one.

I heard this story for the first time while I was traveling on the Uganda Railroad between Mombasa and Nairobi on my hunting trip in 1906. A German officer who shared the same compartment had told me this story most dramatically, and, full of excitement and anticipated

48

adventures, I shouted: "If I saw a lion here, I think I would jump out of the train to get it." Imagine my surprise when the German lieutenant, pointing with his hand to the left of the track, answered: "There is one right here." Looking in that direction, I actually saw a large lion lying upon a zebra which he had killed, and whose hind quarter it was devouring, only some three hundred yards from the track!

Quicker than I can describe, I picked up my 50 x 110 Winchester, which I had near at hand, took a handful of cartridges out of the bag, and rushed out of the train, which had almost been brought to a standstill. In big bounds I made off for the lion, putting the cartridges into the magazine as I ran. Two English sportsmen thoughtlessly opened fire on the lion right from their car, and I could plainly hear the bullets whiz by as I was running, but they, fortunately, hit neither the lion nor me.

As one of their bullets hit the ground a few inches from the lion's nose, throwing sand and dust upon it, the big beast turned around as quick as a flash, and with a wild roar was ready to fling itself upon me. I had then come up within some twenty-five yards. Before the lion could spring, I fired at it, the bullet smashing the right shoulder and penetrating the heart, and with another roar it fell over.

As this was the first day I ever spent in the interior of Africa and the first shot I fired on African soil, the reader can imagine how happy I felt at having secured such a beautiful trophy. Strange enough, I found out three months later that the train had not stopped to accommodate me in any way, but that something had gone wrong with the engine at the very moment we saw the lion. The driver simply had to stop the train, and so gave me this exceptional chance of getting the lion.

One often hears people praise the courage of the natives, hunting the "king of beasts" only with their spears or bow and arrow, as compared to the white man and his modern rifles. But it is then generally forgotten that whereas the white man, as a rule, meets his antagonist alone, the natives invariably turn out in great number for this sport. If, for instance, a certain lion has repeatedly killed cattle or donkeys from a native village or "manyata," the warriors of that village will go out in a body to kill the marauder with their deadly spears, which they use with great skill and precision. The lion is located, surrounded and cornered, and then a rush is made for it *en masse* by the men, who spear it to death, but not often without a desperate fight, during which generally a few warriors are badly mauled, and sometimes killed, before the lion succumbs. An eyewitness of such a fray told me that when the fight was over, one warrior was dead and three or four badly wounded, while the body of the lion, with the spears sticking into it, resembled very much a huge yellow pin cushion.

Of all big game, I believe the lion is the most uncertain to secure. A man may for weeks and even months be in a regular "lion district," where he may hear them roar every night and see their fresh "kills" time and again, and yet never be able to sight a single one of these very wary and cunning beasts. In fact, an English settler not far from Naivaska told me that he had lived for over four years in British East Africa in a district much frequented by lions. He had often had cattle killed by the big felines, but never yet had seen a single lion, although he had tried a good many times to get a shot at one. Finally he succeeded with the unsportsmanlike method of poisoning some of them with strychnine.

Some people have killed lions by, for instance, shooting a zebra or larger antelope, the body of which is then left as it falls without being touched in any way by human hands. They then wait on a moonlight night from a nearby tree, or a temporary shelter, made by thorn bush, until the lion comes along, or else they return to camp and revisit the place of the kill before sunrise the following morning, before the lions generally leave their prey. Many more hunters, myself included, have again and again tried this in vain, only to find the carcass undisturbed, or else eaten by hyenas or jackals.

It is a well-known fact that the lion is just as fond of eating an already dead animal—even in a state of putrefaction—as it is of eating its own, fresh "kill." The old theory, although universally believed, that the lion only eats the meat of animals it kills itself, has by unmistakable evidence been proven to be entirely false. Another strange fact is that where lions abound in great numbers, large herds of game have existed for ages and still even increased, while the lion itself, although very seldom killed by another beast, never multiplies so much as to threaten the game with destruction, even in localities where the "king of beasts" has never been hunted by white men.

CHAPTER IV

THE ELEPHANT, THE GIANT OF THE FOREST

THERE are two different species of elephants—the African; and the Asiatic, or, as he is more generally called, the Indian. This latter species appears to be more closely related to the mammoth of past ages than the African elephant, particularly in regard to the shape of the head and the structure of the molar teeth. These are in the Asiatic, or Indian, elephant of much finer construction than the coarse molar teeth of his African cousins, with their larger plates and thicker enamel, proving that the African elephant is accustomed to live upon harder and more " substantial " food than the Indian, a fact that is borne out by all careful observers.

The heads of the two species differ so much that anyone who knows their characteristics at once distinguishes the one from the other. In the African species the forehead is much more convex, the base of the trunk wider, and the ears more than twice as large as those of the Indian elephant. The same is the case with the tusks, being in the latter much smaller in bulls, and practically nonexisting in females, while the African elephant of both sexes carries splendid tusks, weighing in the males sometimes two hundred pounds apiece, and more. The females have much thinner tusks, which, although of considerable length, seldom weigh over thirty pounds apiece. Of the two species, the African is also considerably larger, averaging fully two feet more in height than the Indian elephant, the same proportions existing if girth and weight. are considered.

In regard to their different dispositions, the Asiatic species is much milder and more timid. He is therefore more easily tamed and used for work or " show " than the African elephant, which, if enraged and charging, is one of the most terrific foes to encounter. He will then come on with raised head, with trunk generally held up in a kind of " S " form, his enormous ears standing out in right angles against the massive head, forming an expanse of ten feet or more. At the same time he will often emit short, shrill trumpet screams, that seem to make the very ground vibrate with their sound, as he " shuffles " forward, breaking down everything in his way!

No animal in the world is in reality more deserving to be called " King of Beasts " than the elephant, the giant of the forest. Not only is this mighty pachyderm by far the largest and strongest land animal, but probably also the most intelligent. It fears no beast. While the lion has to fear the elephant, the rhino, and sometimes even the buffalo, and these two latter probably each other, the elephant is absolutely without a rival. In fact, the native hunters say that as soon as elephants invade a certain locality, the rhinos invariably quit, evidently fearing for their safety.

It is perfectly wonderful to see with what " engineering skill " the many elephant paths are made, which ascend and descend the steepest mountain sides of, for instance, Mt. Kenia, the Aberdares, Kinnangop, and other places, The beasts not only seem always to find the best places for their paths, but understand also how to make them zigzag up the steepest grades, carefully avoiding any stones and rocks that are not absolutely solid and safe to step on. In the same way they understand how to make fine paths through the dense forest, where it would be almost impossible for any human being to go forward at all.

To cite only one example of how dense these forests sometimes are: A certain government forestry official, already referred to in Chapter III, saw my camp fires on one of the foothills of Mt. Kenia, just about three miles in a straight line from his house. He started out in the early morning, thinking that he could easily reach me before eight o'clock, and although doing his utmost to make as good headway as possible, he did not arrive until after twelve at noon, just in time to partake of my Sunday dinner, having had to cut his way through the jungle almost inch by inch, as there were no animal paths leading in the desired direction.

The elephant has a much more varied and luxuriant " table " than that of nearly all other wild animals, for his meals consist of branches and young shoots of certain trees, while of others he eats the bark only. He is very fond of bamboo leaves and twigs as well as of the young bamboo sprouts, before these open up. The forest giant probably also consumes a great deal of grass. In certain parts of the country, where he has been much hunted and where he spends the greater part of the time in the dense forest, or high up in the mountain, he makes nightly trips down to the plains.

The favorite haunts of the elephant in British East Africa to-day are either among the foothills or higher slopes of the before-named mountains, where the bamboo often grows in mighty forests, intermingled with large, deciduous trees, and occasionally cedars. I have myself found elephant tracks on Mt. Kenia at elevations of over 10,000 feet, far above the timber and bamboo line; and I have no doubt that natives tell the truth when they say they have known wounded elephants to go almost up to the very snow line, which here, under the equator, starts first at an altitude of some 15,000 feet.

Nothing in the way of big-game shooting can be compared with elephant hunting for the danger, excitement, and amount of real sport. No other hunting taxes to such an extent the best qualities of the sportsman. He has to use the greatest amount of precaution, judgment, strength, endurance, nerve and personal courage, strategy, and skill, if he desires to bring a fine trophy to bag, without wanting to bang indiscriminately at the first best elephant he sees hundreds of yards off without regard to its size or sex, as, alas! so many " sportsmen " do to-day. Two Russian noblemen whom I met in East Africa told me without hesitancy that they were going to take out licenses enough to kill three elephants each, this being possible under the old game laws in force until December, 1909, and that they would fire at the first elephant they saw, whether big or small, whether male or female, and that even if the tusks would be afterwards confiscated by the government for weighing less than sixty pounds together, they would simply buy back the ivory, and, as so many others have done, say that they had shot the elephants in " self-defense! "

As soon as an elephant track is found, three questions have to be satisfactorily answered before it is taken up and followed:

(1) Is the track fresh—i. e., made recently enough to be worth following?

(2) Is the track large enough to justify being taken up?

(3) Is the track made by a bull or a cow elephant?

The first question is comparatively easy to answer, for even a novice will soon see whether or not the track is a day old or more. This can be easily determined by carefully observing the leaves, branches, and grass which have been broken off and trodden down. If these, for instance, are perfectly withered and dry, it is reasonably sure that the track is at least twenty-four hours old; but if they have not had time to wither, and it is evident that the grass was pressed down *after* the dew had fallen, the track has been made late the previous night and, if large enough, is certainly worth following. Then by going a few hundred yards farther along, the hunter may find branches, torn off the trees recently enough for the leaves to be still fresh, and with the sap perhaps dripping from the broken limbs. This is a sure sign that the elephant has passed by only some ten to twenty minutes ago. Then when also fresh, " steaming " droppings are found, there can be no doubt that the elephant is very close at hand. To look at the droppings alone would not be sufficient, for if the elephant is trekking from one place to another, he may just have passed the place in question only half an hour ago, and yet it may be absolutely impossible to follow him up, if he has not stopped to feed here and there, for these huge beasts walk very fast, and may go on for thirty or forty miles before they stop again, if they have been disturbed.

Then, secondly, as to the size of the imprints of the feet, there is some difficulty in determining with absolute certainty if the animal is a large "tusker" or not. With elephants as with men, big feet are not always the signs of a very big and powerful "owner." Some elephants with very large feet have not had large tusks, and sometimes, strange enough, may carry only one tusk or no tusk at all, even in Africa. In Ceylon and India this is very often the case. Again, some exceedingly big tuskers have had remarkably small feet. But, as a general rule, a real big foot means an old bull, and so the sportsman measures at once the imprints in the ground after having been satisfied that the track is fresh enough to follow. If the diameter of the imprint of the forefoot, which is more of a circular form than the hind foot, is only twelve to fifteen inches, it is probably not made by a fine tusker; but if the distance across the imprint from front to rear is anywhere from eighteen to twenty-four inches or more, it is reasonably certain that the track has been made by some splendid old tusker, which very often goes by himself instead of mingling with the herd.

Somewhat more difficult to answer is the third question, as to whether the track has been made by a bull or a cow elephant. If by careful measurements its diameter is found to be eighteen inches or over and the tracks of the hind feet fairly rounded, they have without much doubt been made by a bull elephant. If smaller, and with the marks of the hind feet very much of an oval, almost pointed shape, it is reasonably certain that they have been made by a female elephant. As elephants often walk one behind the other in each others' steps, particularly when trekking, the imprint of the feet must be very carefully examined, for several animals may have used exactly the same track for some distance. This is, however, not very difficult to determine, for it is readily seen by the careful observer that the different imprints do not cover each other altogether.

Imagine that the fresh track of a good-sized bull elephant has been found! Before it is followed up, however, the direction of the wind must be carefully considered, for no animal seems to be able to scent a man as quickly and as far as the elephant. If the wind is " right " —i. e., blowing in the face of the one following the track— he may go on as fast as possible, yet taking good care not to break twigs or to make any other unnecessary noise. The accompanying gun bearers and others should be forbidden to utter a word as the party hastens on, carefully observing the track. As, strange to say, only a very few natives of British East Africa are really good trackers, the hunter is often entirely dependent on his own woodcraft and skill in this respect. Suddenly another elephant spoor may join the first one at an angle, then another and another, until soon there is a whole maze of tracks, in which the sportsman can find no trace of his old bull!

The new tracks may show that a whole herd of elephants, including a good many females and " babies," have trekked along, and from the unbroken trees along the broad " elephant road " it is easily understood that the herd has been disturbed, and is moving along quickly, without stopping to eat or rest. The hunter should now be looking around very carefully, as he hastens along on this " road," to find the track of the old tusker, hoping that he has left the herd again, as very often happens. But all in vain! The pursuit may have to be given up, and the party returns to camp, downhearted and discouraged.

The above had been my experience in 1909, when, on one dreary return march to the camp, having forgotten to take an emergency tent with us, one of the native trackers suddenly stopped and whistled faintly. Looking in his direction, I saw him nod to us to come on quickly. Before we reached him, however, we heard the cracking of the trees all around, and now only about eighty or ninety yards off we saw a little herd of twelve to fifteen elephants, big and small, but mostly females with their " babies," without a single big tusker. As the wind was blowing steadily from them to us, we noticed their very strong, peculiar smell, while they themselves were unable to scent us. After all our men had gathered, we told them to lie down and be absolutely quiet while I, with one gun bearer and the man carrying the camera, sneaked forward to try to secure at least some photographs of the herd at close quarters. As yet, we were altogether unobserved by the herd. Some of the " youngsters " ran playfully about, while others were eating the leaves from a tree, which one of the adult elephants had broken down for that purpose. One very small calf stood between his mother's hind legs, probably getting his meal of fresh milk, although from where we stood it was impossible to see the little fellow's head.

Nearer and nearer I stole with still more caution, for the wind had entirely died away, and, as is very usual in thick forests, is liable to spring up again in another direction. The forest was rather dense in this place, the big trees making the shadow so deep that a snapshot was almost impossible; but, trusting to good luck, I tried to approach the herd still nearer. Both my men began to feel uneasy at about forty yards from the elephants, but I simply ordered them to follow me as silently as possible. I must confess that my own heart beat a little faster than usual at the prospect of this wonderful opportunity of observing a herd of elephants from such close quarters, and I was fully aware of the danger of the undertaking.

I had told the "camera man" to walk next to me, followed by the gun bearer, who was one of the most courageous natives I have ever employed. We were making for a small elevation some twenty yards away from the herd, from which point I wanted to take the picture. I was at the time carrying the big .577 express rifle myself, and was just considering what stop to use, and how long exposure to give, when all of a sudden there was a commotion among the elephant herd, the wind having evidently changed its direction. Up went all the trunks in a kind of "S" form, while with outspread ears the forest giants began to trumpet furiously, so that the whole region reëchoed with their angry tones, a magnificent, never-to-be-forgotten spectacle! I turned around for my precious camera only to see the man, apparently without a thing in his hands, climbing a large cedar tree, a dozen or so yards away, while even my gun bearer, shouting, "Wana kuja" ("They are coming"), ran for another tree.

On they came! Two big, young bulls, both with small tusks but otherwise full-grown, led the charge, and when within some twenty-five yards of me I raised the gun and pulled the trigger. " Snap, snap! " That was all that followed, both cartridges failing to explode! As I broke open the gun as quickly as possible to put in two new shells, backing at the same time to gain a fraction of a second's time, I fell into a hole above my knees! Now the two charging bulls were perhaps within fifteen yards or so, and just as I raised the gun to fire again, a shot from the gun bearer rang out to my left. The nearest bull, hit in the shoulder by the powerful 11 millimeter Mauser, at once turned and ran away sideways to my right, followed by the others, all vanishing as quickly as they could, crushing through the bush in their wild stampede!

Not wanting to feel that my life had depended upon my gun bearer's shot, I tried the big gun again, this time aiming far above the fleeing monsters. Both shots went off with a tremendous roar, which made the elephants increase their speed still more. This showed to my satisfaction that had my gun bearer not returned and shot when he saw my plight, I could easily have killed both my antagonists at a few yards' distance. Examining the unexploded shells afterwards, I found that they had been carelessly loaded, although being bought from a reliable London firm, the percussion caps having been pushed in so far that the firing pin of the gun could not reach them.

On the following day we found another very large track of a single bull, which we with few interruptions followed for five whole days under the most trying circumstances. We had to cross over marshes, rushing mountain streams, up among the bamboo at more than 9,000 feet altitude, only to have to come down again into the valley below, until on the fifth day we saw from the appearance of the tracks and the untouched trees along his path that we would have to abandon the pursuit, the elephant outdistancing us more and more.

Another time we found fresh tracks of a very large single elephant on the western slopes of the Gojito Mountains, which we at once followed. From the amount of recently broken twigs and branches, and from the looks of the grass and flowers, trodden down by the big feet, we understood that the elephant had passed only about one hour ahead of us, and that he was moving along slowly. Therefore, after finding that the wind was " right," we pursued our prey as quickly as possible. The grass in the open places between the bushes and trees was fully twelve to fifteen feet high, so that it was impossible to see more than a few yards ahead, and I, therefore, sent a man up into a large tree along the track to reconnoiter. Quick as a squirrel he climbed up half the length of the tree and looked around. In another second he was down again, reporting a large bull elephant with big tusks " very near," which in the native language may mean anything from fifty to five hundred yards!

I saw a few paces in front of me a small single rock, and, climbing upon the same, got a good view of the monstrous pachyderm just as he swung around and began to return the same way he had come, at about two hundred yards' distance. As quickly as I could raise the big gun to my shoulder, I fired for his back, the only thing that showed above the grass. A few angry trumpetings announced that he was wounded, and with a rapidity that the reader would think impossible by such a big and clumsy beast as the elephant, he again whirled around and ran off toward the dense forest to our left. Before he had taken many strides, however, a second bullet crashed into his left side, followed by furious trumpeting for a moment, and then the giant disappeared, the high grass and bush hiding the beast completely from our view, as he ran toward the Gojito Mountain slopes, crashing down trees and bushes in his way.

Now followed a most wearying chase for hours, up and down hill, over streams and through jungles, which would have been almost impenetrable if we had not been able to follow in the tracks of the forest giant, who was bleeding profusely from the two wounds. It seemed as if our pursuit was almost useless, and soon the men had become so tired out that they begged me to give up the chase. I almost felt like doing this myself, and when we had come down to another little stream, I decided to take a rest there for a moment, while I could discuss with the men what would be the wisest thing to do.

As we sat down to rest, we heard the trumpeting of the elephant, and, looking up, saw on the mountain side, some five hundred yards away, the magnificent beast, his two large tusks glittering in the sunlight! This was the first time we had been able to see the whole size of the elephant, and not before that moment had I known that we had been tracking an unusually large " tusker." This sight gave us all new courage, and on we went, swifter than before, in his pursuit. After another half hour we had evidently come up a good deal closer to the elephant, and we all began to feel the earnestness of the situation, for nothing is more terrible to meet in " jungleland " than a wounded elephant.

Fortunately for us, the wind had been in our favor so far, so that the elephant had not been able to get our scent, and, as he himself made a great deal more noise than we, he could not even have heard us. A few moments later the elephant suddenly turned completely around, and now we had to follow him down the wind. We understood that from this moment we had to be doubly careful, for the elephant was now able to scent us as we came along.

We stopped for a moment to consult. I told all of the men to stay somewhat behind, and with only Mabruki, the gun bearer, and my Kikuju headman, Moeri, I took up the pursuit again, after once more having examined my elephant gun and seen that it was loaded with two steel-pointed bullets. So on we went again, slowly and carefully. We had not gone thus more than about five minutes before we suddenly were faced by the huge elephant, which had made a complete half circle. Turning back close to his own track, he had stood immovable for some time in the thick bushes, waiting for his pursuers to come along.

One of the most glorious sights met us! The elephant, larger in size than the well-known Jumbo, was almost upon us, when we caught sight of him! With his enormous ears spread out, measuring fully ten feet from tip to tip, and with his trunk bent up almost in an " S " form, he made a wild dash forward, charging down upon us most furiously. For a moment I thought of what I had often heard about the impossibility of killing an African elephant with a front head shot, but, as escape was impossible, I aimed

ELEPHANTS COMING THROUGH HIGH BUSH AND ELEPHANT GRASS, KISILI, 1909.

A SPLENDID TROPHY: A BIG BULL ELEPHANT KILLED NEAR THE GOJITO MOUNTAINS, 1906.

The head is now in the New York Zoölogical Park. It is said to be the largest mounted elephant head on record and weighs 1,750 pounds.

quickly for the center of his head in a line a little above the eyes, and pulled the trigger! Before the sound of the gun had died away, the forest giant lay dead at my very feet! I was so surprised at the quick execution of the bullet that I remained standing for a moment or two with the gun at my shoulder, ready to fire the second barrel if the elephant had moved again, but it was all over with him forever!

My two men had rushed right and left into the jungle, when the elephant charged. They and the other natives, previously left behind, now came up to congratulate me on having had so good luck. The reaction of the moment's nerve strain was tremendous. Just when the elephant charged down on us I was as calm as when writing these lines, and to that and my quick aim is due the fact that I live to tell the tale; but after it was all over, sitting down on one of the tusks of the fallen monarch, I felt quite dizzy for a moment, and noticed a slight tremor of the hands.

We soon had made a little clearing to enable me to make some good photographs of the dead elephant. Although my taxidermist, Mr. Lang, and a good many more men had been brought up from the camp, it was impossible for us to finish skinning the huge beast that day. We, therefore, left a number of men at the place to sleep overnight by the carcass, and to make a big fire to keep away the lions and leopards, which otherwise would have spoiled the skin.

The next day was the " glorious Fourth," and, as Mr. Lang volunteered to take the men up himself to the elephant and bring down the trophy, I decided to stay in camp and rest, as I had also a good deal of writing to do. The reader will perhaps bear with me if I here quote a few lines directly from my diary, written on this same Fourth of July, 1906: "Toward evening Mr. Lang and his men arrived with the elephant skin, head and feet, it looking very much like a big funeral procession as they all descended from the escarpment into the valley and slowly and carefully crossed the Meroroni River to the monotonous and doleful tunes of their native songs!

"Yesterday, as I for the last time looked around where the fallen elephant lay, solemn thoughts came to my mind. There stood, dead and bare, an enormous cedar tree, and almost at its very 'feet' lay, slain by human hands in an instant, and with a comparatively small bullet, the largest of the remnant of the mightiest of beasts! Looking at both, a great sadness fell over me and I went away silently toward camp in the light of the shining moon. . . ."

We found when measuring the elephant that his length was 24' 7"; height from the shoulders, 11' 4"; around the chest, 18' 7"; length of the trunk, 8' 6"; circumference of one of the front legs, 5' 2"; length of tusks, 7' 2"; and weight of same, 168 pounds.

. A few years later, when tracking elephants through high grass and partly dense bush in the Kisii country, we ran into a herd of about two hundred elephants of all sizes and ages, including two very large bulls. As we were trying to close in on them to get nearer to these splendid "tuskers," I noticed to my utter surprise that two of the young bulls *actually saw us* at over two hundred yards' distance! It is generally believed that the elephant is very nearsighted, but in this case they must have *seen* us, as we walked along, for they could *not possibly have scented us,* for a fairly strong wind was blowing from the herd in our faces. Neither could they at this time have *heard* us, for, walking along in the wide elephant tracks, we went too silently for them to have detected us, even if at much closer quarters.

These two bulls instantly gave the alarm, and the whole herd began to move down in our direction. I succeeded now in dropping one of the big tuskers, when, from the report of the gun, the whole herd suddenly stampeded, breaking down everything in front of them in their mad attempt to avenge themselves on their two-legged enemies. We could do absolutely nothing but remain where we stood, the elephant grass being so high, and the bush so dense that the big animals were now entirely hidden from view. Hearing how the herd came nearer and nearer, angrily trumpeting and making a terrific noise, as trees and bushes were crushed before them, some of my men broke away and ran. Suddenly a big elephant head shot out of the high grass right in front of us, but in the next instant the monster fell in a heap, with a bullet through its head from the small 6.5 millimeter Mannlicher rifle. I had exchanged the big .577 elephant gun for this excellent little weapon, the Mannlicher, having six shots to the other's two, without reloading. Unfortunately this elephant proved to be a female, and although the tusks were fairly long, they were afterwards confiscated by the government, as they did not together weigh sixty pounds. A few seconds later I again had to shoot in self-defense. This time it was a full-grown young bull with a pair of fine, although small, tusks weighing only forty-eight pounds. He also fell in his tracks, hit by two little Mannlicher bullets, only at some seven yards' distance from where we stood, which, fired in quick succession, had entered the center of his head.

Not quite so lucky was a German lieutenant, who in the fall of 1909 was out elephant shooting in the vicinity of the Kivu Lake, to the southwest of the Ruwenzori Mountains. He had, with a few black followers, run into a small herd of elephants, among which was one large bull, which he stalked for a few minutes. Suddenly the elephant got a whiff of his wind, and, without even being shot at, whirled around and charged down on his pursuer through the grass. Although the lieutenant fired not less than five shots into the big elephant's head, emptying his whole magazine, he failed to reach the deadly spot, the center of its brain. In the next instant the infuriated bull caught him up with his trunk and threw him high in the air. As soon as he fell to the ground the elephant rushed at him again, putting one of its big tusks right through the unfortunate hunter, who was subsequently crushed into an unrecognizable mass under its forefeet, while this whole tragedy was witnessed by his cowardly black trackers and hunters from nearby trees!

One of the most marvelous escapes ever recorded was experienced by the famous elephant hunter, F. C. Selous. It was in the early days, some thirty years ago, when Mr. Selous was elephant hunting south of the Zambezi River. He had shot several elephants one day, when on horseback, and was just returning toward camp, when he espied another big " tusker," which he wanted to bag. At this time Mr. Selous used a single-barreled breech-loading gun of very large bore. He jumped from his horse and fired at the big bull, aiming for his heart. The shot, having missed the deadly spot, made the elephant charge him at once. Mr. Selous had to fling himself upon his horse before he could put another cartridge in his rifle, and with the breech still open he tried to escape by galloping away, as he had done so often before. His horse was, however, so tired out after the hard work of the day that the elephant gained on him every second.

The last he could remember, Mr. Selous relates, was a terrific scream right over his head. The next moment he was knocked unconscious. When he regained consciousness he found himself in a rather peculiar position. He was actually lying *between the two tusks of the elephant,* with the blood of the latter pouring down upon him from a wound in the chest. Mr. Selous was saved only by the strange fact that the elephant, when trying to gore him with his tusks, missed him by an inch or so, and from the great impetus of the charge these buried themselves so deep in the ground that he had not succeeded in extricating them. Mr. Selous lay for a second perfectly quiet, thinking over what would be the best thing to do under the circumstances. Finally, seeing an opening between the elephant's front legs, he made a desperate effort to regain his liberty, squeezed through this " gate " and escaped. Strange to say, before Mr. Selous could get hold of his gun, which had been dropped some distance away, the elephant managed to extricate its tusks and disappeared, never to be found again.

It was my great privilege to be a fellow passenger with both Colonel Roosevelt and Mr. Selous when they, in April, 1909, went cut to Africa. Almost every evening after dinner Colonel Roosevelt, Mr. Selous, a few other fellow passengers and myself used to spend some time in telling our experiences as hunters in different parts of the world, and it was during these evening hours that we had the privilege of listening to the wonderful experiences of Mr. Selous, without a question the most successful lion and elephant hunter alive. Another of Mr. Selous's stories, of the truth of which we were all persuaded, ran about as follows:

" One evening shortly before he returned to his camp he saw a good-sized ' tusker,' at which he fired. With a crash the elephant went down, and was lying motionless on the ground, when Mr. Selous arrived on the spot. Being very much tired out, he sat down on the side of the elephant to take a much-needed rest, after which he decided to go home to camp for the night, it being too late to cut out the tusks that evening. Before leaving the fallen monarch, he cut off his tail to have something to show when he would arrive in camp. The next morning he sent some of his natives back to chop out the tusks, while he was going out in a different direction to look for other elephants.

" Returning in the afternoon to camp, he was very much surprised and disgusted not to find the tusks of his elephant. He became still more surprised when the men told him that they had been at the spot where the elephant fell, but had failed to find any trace of him. Of course, Mr. Selous, therefore, at once started for the place and found, to his utter amazement, that the huge beast, which he had believed dead, and on which he had rested the evening before, had not been killed after all, but was still roaming around somewhere in the vicinity, now minus his tail."

This and another incident which I will relate in the chapter on Antelopes, go to show how necessary it is to put an extra shot into the head of any big and dangerous beast that has been apparently killed, for there have been a good many instances where ferocious animals have only been stunned for the moment by the bullet just grazing the spine, and then been able to get up again and kill their assailants unawares, when suddenly awakened to consciousness.

It is most interesting to watch a herd of elephants feed, play, or rest when they are undisturbed. The larger ones often help the " babies " by breaking down branches or whole trees to make it more easy for them to feed. On Kenia I once found that a perfectly sound tree, measuring *thirty-three and a half inches* in circumference, had been broken off by an elephant, about seven feet from the ground! This shows that a man has to climb a good-sized tree if he wants to be safe from elephants, whose destructiveness is appalling. Very often a few of these beasts may, for instance, in a single night spoil a whole plantation of sugar cane, of a dozen or more acres, trampling down what they do not devour. Elephants have often even broken down native huts and killed their inhabitants in an effort to get at sugar cane and other coveted " delicacies," when they had suspected the presence of such in the huts.

The wild Wandorobbo and other native hunters kill elephants in different ways. Sometimes they make big pits with or without sharp poles, stuck into the bottom, while the hole is carefully covered over with branches and grass. The pit is generally dug right in a regular elephant path, so that when the huge beast strolls along in his old track, suspecting no danger, he suddenly steps on the frail " roof " and falls headlong into the pit, where he is then killed by the natives with their long, sharp spears. Another and more " sporty " way is this: The hunter, armed only with a short, sharp steel spear, stuck into a very heavy, wooden shaft, climbs up a big tree, overhanging the elephant path, where he expects the animal to come along. When the unsuspecting elephant reaches the tree, the bushman throws his heavy, double spear with all his strength down into its back, the spear often penetrating to the heart. The iron or steel point of the spear, sometimes also poisoned, remains in the body of the elephant, while the heavy wooden shaft falls off and can be used again. The elephant, thus wounded by the poisoned spear or arrow, will, if not hit through heart or lungs, go on for several hours before he falls, closely followed by his slayers. These, then, do not only take out the tusks, but feast on the flesh with relatives and friends, until there is not enough left of the carcass to attract even hyenas or jackals!

Some natives are courageous enough to track the forest giant in an entirely different way. Armed with a heavy, sharp sword, they follow their intended victim carefully, until he is within touching distance, which, for naked, light-footed savages, is not a difficult task if the wind is " right." Then with a couple of terrific cuts they sever the sinews of the elephant's hind legs above the feet, which make it impossible for the animal to take another step. The powerless beast is then killed, either by being hit through its heart by a spear, or by being shot with poisoned arrows.

The Wandorobbo, who once acted as my guide in the Kenia Province, told me of how the rhinos feared the elephants, and how he had once been an eyewitness to a fight between a large rhino and a full-grown, young elephant bull. The rhino was a female, which was lying down together with her small calf. Suddenly hearing the noise of the elephant near its "baby," the rhino rushed up to defend its offspring, apparently not knowing what it did. The next moment the elephant had its trunk round the rhino's neck, threw it to the ground and gored it to death in an instant with its powerful tusks. Then he walked off, trumpeting as if triumphing over his victory. Needless to say, the Wandorobbo feasted upon the dead rhino, and even killed the young one, as it returned the next day to look for its mother.

Most people, including even a good many African hunters, affirm that the elephant never lies down to sleep or rest. Although I had repeatedly heard natives say that they had seen elephants lie down, both on their sides and on their belly, I would not believe it, until so eminent a naturalist and explorer as Dr. Carl Peters himself told me that he *had actually twice seen* elephants, that were not wounded, lying down resting. Another German, the elephant hunter Mr. G. Ringler, tells how his own brother was crushed to death by an elephant, which he thought was already dead, when he found it lying motionless on its side, as he had just a moment before shot at a large bull. Mr. Ringler went up to the sleeping monster without hesitation, but as he touched the elephant it started up with lightninglike rapidity, caught hold of the unsuspecting hunter, and before his brother, who was only a few yards away, could kill the brute, the unfortunate sportsman was dashed against a rock and instantly killed. Mr. Ringler also confirmed the curious story of native hunters that the elephants in a certain district in German East Africa like to eat a kind of root, which makes them so intoxicated that they lie down and sleep hard enough for the natives to be able to kill them easily with swords or spears.

Among hunting trophies none can be compared with a well mounted head of a big tusker. The writer was fortunate enough to get home a perfect head skin of one of his big elephants, with tusks over seven feet in length. The whole head, mounted, weighs over one thousand seven hundred pounds. The tip of the trunk projects almost fourteen feet from the wall, and the head measures over ten feet from tip to tip of the mighty ears! This magnificent and especially well-mounted trophy is at present on exhibition in the New York Zoölogical Park, Bronx, among the National Collection of Heads and Horns.

CHAPTER V

THE tallest of all living creatures is without doubt the giraffe. When seen in the open or even in thin bush country, he reminds one very much of the curious creatures of prehistoric times, exhibited in the museums of natural history, so queer does he seem. Giraffes exist now only in Africa, although a good many discoveries of fossils show that they, like a good many other huge tropical animals of ages past, were formerly found also among the hills and valleys of southern Europe, Persia, and India. The giraffe is a kind of link between the deer family and the bovine animals, such as oxen and buffaloes, being, like the latter two, a cud-chewer.

The hairy horns of the giraffe are in young calfs easily separable from the bone of the skull, but the inside core grows in time together with the head bones, like the horns of oxen or buffaloes. The giraffe's eyes are of a deep brown color, with large pupils and long bushy lashes, and they are wonderfully soft and beautiful. The tongue is extremely rough, a very necessary quality, as the animal feeds chiefly from the thorny desert trees, and it is unusually long, measuring from fifteen to eighteen inches. The upper, prehensile lip is also very long, tough, and covered with thick, short hair, so as to enable the giraffe

75

to feed more easily upon the mimosa tree without getting stung by the sharp thorns.

One of the most curious-looking sights in Africa is a herd of giraffes trotting off with a sort of rocking-horse, single-foot motion, with their enormous necks carried a trifle lower than the line of their backs. The animals stand much higher over the shoulders than over the pelvis. Although absolutely harmless and mild-tempered, the giraffe is, on account of its unusual height, sometimes a " menace " to civilization in British East Africa, for it has repeatedly happened that a big bull-giraffe has forgotten to " duck " when crossing the telegraph line along the Uganda Railroad, broken the wire with his lofty head, and thus disturbed communication.

The great height of the giraffe enables him to eat the young shoots and leaves off the topmost branches of the mimosa and other trees, which constitute his chief " menu "; but it makes it, on the other hand, very awkward for him to partake of the " salt licks " on the ground, or drink from a shallow water hole or stream, for he has then to spread out his front legs so far, to be able to reach the water, or the ground, that it takes him a considerable time to get up and away again if disturbed.

Fortunately for the giraffe, he seems to need but little water, and in this respect he is very much like the camel, which animal reminds one more of the giraffe than any other living creature. The natives of different districts in British East Africa have assured me that the giraffe can go for many weeks and even months without drinking, and this partly explains the fact that he is mostly found in dry and practically waterless countries. Such favorite feeding grounds are, for instance, the Seringetti Plains, between Kilima-Njaro and Voi on the Uganda Railroad, and in the thorn and fiber plant deserts around the latter place. He is also found in the central parts of the Protectorate, to the northeast of the Athi Plains, which he occasionally crosses over to the big Southern Game Reserve. In the northern part of the Protectorate he is abundant both north of Mt. Kenia and the Guasco Narok river, in the partly waterless Samburu country, and on the Guas Ngishu Plateau, southeast of Mt. Elgon. As the dew is generally very heavy in these districts, he may get almost all the water he needs from the dew-covered leaves that he eats in the early morning.

Almost every animal makes some kind of a sound when angry, wounded, or when wanting to " communicate " with other members of its family, but the giraffe seems to be absolutely mute. I have asked several hunters, who have had opportunity to observe a great many giraffes at close quarters, about the muteness of this animal, and they have all assured me that they never heard the giraffe utter a sound of any kind, neither when pursued, scattered, cornered, wounded, or dying. This native trackers and hunters all over East Africa have also repeatedly corroborated.

In 1906, not far from the Maungu station on the Uganda Railroad, I shot my largest giraffe, which measured over seventeen feet in height. We had started from our camp at Maungu long before daybreak in search of a big giraffe, which was reported as having been seen the previous day from the railroad. After having marched for over an hour, feeling our way in the dark, I suddenly stopped in the twilight, seeing a small object falling down from the branches of a mimosa tree. In the twinkling of an eye I saw an animal run up in the tree, only to drop down again the next second like a ball into the high grass. My first thought was to take the shotgun and bring the animal down, but fearing that the giraffe might be in the vicinity and take alarm from the crack of the gun, I whispered to some of the natives to rush forward the next time the animal fell to the ground and throw themselves over it. They did so, far quicker than I could imagine, for the next moment one of the men rose from the grass holding between his hands a beautiful Civet cat, which had injured him considerably with its sharp claws and teeth.

I was right in my supposition about the giraffe, for we had only gone forward some fifteen minutes more, when I saw a large giraffe head towering above a good-sized mimosa tree some five hundred yards away. By this time it was light enough both to shoot and to take photographs, and, as I was very anxious to have this magnificent animal " kodaked " before it should fall, I ordered my men to throw themselves flat on the ground, and with only Mr. Lang, the expedition's taxidermist and photographer, and one gun bearer, I approached the giraffe as carefully as possible. When within about one hundred and fifty yards, the giraffe had caught a glimpse of us from his exalted viewpoint and started to walk away with long strides before it was possible for Mr. Lang to snap him with his camera. I then raised my .405 Winchester and fired, aiming at his heart, but the giraffe continued his walk as if nothing had happened. I fired a second and a

LARGE BULL GIRAFFE; SHOT THROUGH THE HEART NEAR MAUNGU
R. R. STATION.

BULL GIRAFFE IN THE MIMOSA JUNGLE ON LAIKIPIA.
Note how his bright coloring blends perfectly with the sunlight and shadow
in the landscape.

third time, but with the same result. I knew that I must have hit the animal, and said to the gun bearer: "He must have a charmed life; give me the big gun." This was the powerful .577 Express rifle, by the natives called "msinga" (cannon).

We had in the meantime kept pace with the giraffe, as he was still simply walking away, and at about the same distance I fired with the big gun, aiming again for his heart. Now the big bull instantly stopped and allowed us to come right up to him. This splendid opportunity was used by us to make some good pictures of the old giraffe, which tried in vain to walk away from the spot. He could evidently only lift one of his front legs a little. There he stood, without uttering a single sound, looking straight at us for a few minutes. Then his hind legs gave away, and suddenly he toppled over backwards and fell dead.

The fact was disclosed, when we were skinning the animal, that all the three "soft-nose" bullets fired from the Winchester had only penetrated his skin, which is about an inch thick, and lodged in the ribs right over the heart, not more than a few inches apart from each other, whereas the one steel-capped bullet from the .577 Express had crashed through the side of the giraffe, penetrated its heart, broken two ribs on the opposite side and almost protruded through the skin! As the wounded giraffe looked up at me with his beautiful eyes, I felt that, had it not been for the sake of the American Museum of Natural History in New York, for which I was collecting specimens of big game at the time, I would never have forgiven myself for killing this magnificent animal. I thought, however, that he was more worthy of being admired by thousands of intelligent Americans in one of the finest museums of the world, than to continue to roam around, hidden in the jungles of Africa, and one day to die of old age, or fall an easy prey to a bloodthirsty lion!

It probably very seldom happens that a full-grown, healthy giraffe is attacked, or killed by a single lion, unless suddenly overtaken, when, for instance, in a drinking position, when old and feeble, or sick. For with his powerful front feet he could well beat back and even kill a lion. A cow giraffe was once seen attacking a lion which tried to kill its calf. The furious mother drove off the lion with its forefeet, but also unfortunately hit its own "baby" with one of the blows, instantly breaking its back and killing it on the spot. A German settler from the country southwest of Kilimanjaro told me that he had succeeded in capturing a number of wild animals, which he subsequently had sold to the well-known wild animal merchant, Mr. Hagenbeck, of Hamburg, who near that city has one of the finest private zoölogical gardens in the world, which is well worth a visit. The German settler also wanted to capture young giraffes, but had, according to his own almost incredible story, repeatedly been "driven off" by their desperate mothers, as he was not allowed to shoot them, according to the game laws of German East Africa. One day, however, he succeeded in separating a young giraffe from the herd, and with his black helpers he got hold of the "baby," which, although probably but a few months old, stood fully nine feet high. After a hard struggle, during which two of the negroes had been rather badly hurt by kicks, but during which ordeal, to use my spokesman's own expression, the "youngster never said a word," the young giraffe was finally overpowered and driven into the "shamba," or farm, where it, in a very few days, became so tame that it followed its capturers around like a dog, freely mingling with the cattle.

But, alas! a couple of days before it was to be shipped down to the coast, it quite suddenly developed some malignant disease, growing thinner and weaker every day. One evening it did not return home with the cattle, and when the people went out to look for the giraffe, it was found dead under a mimosa tree, with two leopards feasting upon its body. Whether slain by these cunning and powerful bush animals, before it had died from its disease, or whether it was found already dead by the leopards, could not be ascertained, as the big felines had already devoured too much of it. Later on I shall tell the circumstances under which these two leopards were subsequently killed.

A British sportsman and settler who keeps a regular "shooting box" in the lower Kedong valley, only a day's march from the Kijabe Railroad station, a Mr. Barker, a great animal lover, succeeded also recently in capturing a young giraffe, which soon became very tame. Sometimes, when "just playing," this beautiful animal hurt several of the men by "friendly kicks" from its powerful hoofs. Even this young giraffe developed some disease and soon died, in spite of the best of care. These cases show that, although it may be comparatively easy to capture and tame a "baby" giraffe, it is very difficult to bring it up on ordinary cow's milk or artificial food until it is old enough to make its own "living" from trees and shrubs.

There is little or no real sport or excitement in giraffe hunting, for, as already remarked, the animals are absolutely harmless and will never, even when wounded or cornered, really attack a man. On the other hand, as the giraffe is exceedingly wary and has doubtlessly good scenting qualities, like almost all wild animals, and very good eyesight, he is most interesting to stalk with a view of obtaining an insight into his habits and of " taking his pictures."

Tales about charging giraffes should not be taken very seriously, for no really authentic case can be found of giraffes actually charging a hunter. On my first trip to Africa I had shot a large bull giraffe near the little Koma Rock, on the northwestern part of the Athi Plains. As soon as the bullet hit the animal it went down, and when Mr. Lang and I ran up to the bull and had got up to within fifteen yards of him, he gathered all his last strength, got up and staggered toward us before he, hit by another bullet, went down, never to move again. We were both absolutely sure that the wounded giraffe never intended anything in the way of a charge, but that he was so bewildered from pain and excitement that he simply did not know what he did. Mr. Lang remarked to me that probably a good many " nervous " hunters, with vivid enough imagination, would be able to construct out of this occurrence a " terrific charge."

When a fresh giraffe track is found, it is generally not so difficult to follow, for the great weight of the animal impresses his large hoofs in the soil deep enough to be readily seen by any man, even with a limited experience in tracking. The imprints of the giraffe's hoofs are very much like those made by the oxen, although considerably larger and more oval. Some of the giraffe countries are very "thick"—i. e., overgrown with thorn and mimosa trees and the strange-looking euphorbia, a cactus-like plant which grows up into large, often queer-shaped, trees, while the sharp-pointed seesal, or fiber plant—from which a superior kind of rope is made—mercilessly stings right through trousers, leggings, and even the thickest boots. If the track is quite fresh and the wind "right," one may soon catch up with a giraffe, if he thinks himself undisturbed, and it is very interesting indeed to observe the huge animal feasting among the top branches of his favorite trees. He may stroll from tree to tree of apparently not only the same kind, but also in the very same condition, and yet some of them he will just only sniff at, while of the others he seems greatly to enjoy the leaves and young shoots. Great care has to be taken in the stalking of the giraffe, for from his exalted position he will very quickly notice anything that moves anywhere within a radius of several hundred yards or more, if the stalker is not well hidden behind some thick cover.

The last giraffe I stalked I found on the beautiful Laikipia Plateau, not far from the upper part of the Gardomurtu River, and southwest of that stream. When I first noticed his track across our path, it ran down in the very direction from which we had come. Concluding, therefore, that we already must have been noticed by the wary animal—for I was at the time trekking along with over sixty men—I did not intend to follow this track. I then told my men to wait a few seconds and then follow at some distance, as quietly as possible, in case there would be any other giraffes in the vicinity. Hardly had I given this order before I saw something queer-looking moving in the top of a mimosa tree, some one hundred and fifty yards away and right in front of us. At first we thought it was a marabout stork or some other big bird, but soon we discovered the two front horns and the ears of a giraffe. The caravan was now ordered to sit down on the ground behind trees and bushes and not to talk or move before I signaled to them to come on.

With only one of the gun bearers to carry my Winchester, I took my camera and began carefully to stalk the giraffe. It has often been remarked that if the coloring of animals is supposed to hide them from their enemies, or to make it easier for certain animals to catch their prey, the giraffe in that respect would be very unfortunate, with his bright and strangely checkered coat. I myself had thought so several times before, when seeing giraffes on the open prairies, where they are only found when trekking between their regular feeding grounds. This time, however, I had to change my mind. It was just about eleven o'clock on a cloudless day when, in spite of the altitude of over 7,000 feet, the sun was very powerful, for this part of the country lies exactly on the equator. Now, as the strong, bright sunlight and the deep shadows of the branches and leaves interweaved into one wonderful " carpet," the big bull giraffe was, even at fifty yards, hard to make out, except when moving, so perfectly did his big dark and bright spots blend with the whole sun-flooded landscape! A passing look at the picture facing page 78 will prove how protective the giraffe's coat is under the above circumstances even at twenty-five yards, from which distance it was taken.

The tall bull now saw me, stopped eating, and looked carefully around; but as my gun bearer lay prostrated on the ground behind a tree, and I remained perfectly immovable in a kneeling position, from which I had taken the above picture, the giraffe seemed to think that he had made a mistake, and soon began to feed again from the top of the mimosa tree, every second or so looking in my direction to be on his guard. By being exceedingly careful to watch all his movements, I succeeded in creeping unnoticed still more forward, until I had taken two more photos, one at twenty and the other at fifteen yards, both of which pictures unfortunately became sunstruck in some inexplicable way, but which show how near it is possible to creep up even to a wary giraffe, if one uses but a little patience and cunning. As my roll of films was exhausted, and it being entirely out of the question to recharge the camera unnoticed then and there, I quietly rose and walked with empty hands up toward the giraffe. Still he did not notice me—a good wind blowing steadily from the animal to me—before I had got up to within six or seven yards of the magnificent old bull! Then he made off at a heavy gallop, increasing his speed as I shouted my thanks for his " posing."

There are in East Africa at least two distinctly different species of giraffe, which, however, in reality differ very little from each other. The only marked difference between these two species is the shape of their heads, or rather, the number of horns. The ordinary giraffe found in the central and southeastern part of the Protectorate has two horns with a rather pronounced bump in front below the horns. The other variety, the so-called five-horned giraffe, which is generally found on the Guaso Ngishu Plateau, has, behind the ordinary two horns, two smaller hornlike projections—hardly worth the name of horns—and the bump on the forehead grown out into a more hornlike projection than that of the ordinary giraffe.

The height and color of the giraffes vary greatly. The younger the giraffe is, the lighter is his skin, and it is only the old bulls that have very dark, brown spots. The height of giraffes varies a good deal. Full-grown males have been shot in Africa measuring from sixteen to seventeen feet six inches. Record bulls of South Africa have been as tall as nineteen feet and over, but in that part of the country the Boers have now almost exterminated the stately animal. The reason for this was that the white settlers coveted both the giraffe's meat and the skin, which they use for harness, traces, and whips. The natives also kill the giraffe whenever they have a chance to, partly because they are very fond of its meat and the great amount of marrow in its big leg bones, and partly because they use the strong sinews of the animal for their bow-strings, instead of twine, and for the strings of a kind of rude musical instrument, on which they play their weary monotonous tunes.

CHAPTER VI

THE HIPPOPOTAMUS, OR RIVER HORSE

BUT two species of hippopotamus exist, and both are now confined to Africa. The little Liberian, or pygmy hippo, lives, as his name indicates, in West Africa, where he rarely attains a height over the shoulders of more than some two feet six inches, while the whole length of his body does not exceed six feet. The so-called common hippopotamus is now only found in the central parts of Africa —i. e., not farther north than the upper Nile, south of Khartum, and not below the Orange River, although only a few decades ago he was very common all over South Africa.

Van Riebeck, the Dutchman, reports having seen hippos in 1652 in a swamp, now occupied by Church Square, in the very center of the present Cape Town, and the last hippo in that district was killed in 1874. In prehistoric times even these big pachyderms were distributed over a much larger area, well-preserved fossils giving evidence of their existence in lower Egypt and southern Europe, where exactly the same species roamed around as far north as England, the river Thames being one of their favorite haunts.

The hippopotamus, or "river horse," as the name is to be interpreted, forms a family all of his own. The early Dutch settlers called him "lake cow," the Arabs sometimes "lake buffalo." The ancient Egyptians, however, used the name "river hog" for the huge mammal, which from a zoölogical point of view is the most befitting name of all, for in his habits and general appearance he is more like the pig than any other existing animal. The meat of the hippo, and the great amount of fat, which he generally carries under his thick skin, are also very much like that of the pig.

The hippopotamus is next to the elephant the "bulkiest" land animal in existence. It is not unusual for a full-grown hippo to measure anywhere from twelve to thirteen feet in length, the line taken from the tip of the nose to the root of the short, stiff, and flattened tail. Sir Samuel Baker once killed an old bull which measured fourteen feet three inches, including a tail of nine inches in length. A large hippo, which died a few years ago in the London Zoölogical Garden, was over twelve feet in length, and weighed somewhat more than four tons. The color of the skin varies between almost black to dark brown, dark slate, pinkish brown on the belly, and sometimes almost light gray, which latter color has occasioned some naturalists to give him the name of "white hippo."

Of all animals none is perhaps more hideous-looking than the clumsy hippo, with his enormous mouth, mammoth lips, big tusks, disproportionately small eyes and ears, ponderous piglike body, and short legs! His heavy, wobbling gait, when on land, he can suddenly change into a similar trot when frightened, and I have heard hunters say, although it seems almost incredible, that a hippo is even able to gallop, when hotly pursued and is trying to rush into some nearby water. Once there, he feels safe again, and if the water is that of a good-sized lake or large river, he is soon practically out of harm's way, for although the hippo has to put his nose up over the surface of the water to breathe, at least every two or three minutes, he usually does this with such rapidity, when alarmed, that it is exceedingly difficult to get a shot at him.

The only method of instantly killing a hippo is to shoot him through the brain and, as under ordinary circumstances, the whole head of the hippo is exposed over the water; this is very easy indeed, unless the wary river horse knows that he is in danger. Then he is so cunning that an accurate shot is almost impossible, for the hippo is able to place his body at such an angle to the surface that, when he is exhaling the foul air, or inhaling the fresh, he only shows the mere nostrils above the water, and the upper vulnerable part of the head is held sufficiently low so as to make a shot of no effect at all. Another trick that the wary monster plays is this: Instead of exhaling and inhaling in quick succession as he usually does, giving the hunter thus two or three seconds in which to turn in the right direction and shoot, he just barely brings the nostrils to the surface of the water and " puffs " out the foul air, only to disappear instantly. Then he moves a few yards away in another direction, before he raises his nostrils again, this time a trifle higher, to take a deep breath of fresh air, before he again sinks out of sight.

It certainly is most remarkable how well the hippo is able to deceive his pursuers when in his favorable element, the water. After he has breathed in a place as above described, he will often swim a good distance in the water, until he suddenly " bobs up " where the hunter least expects him. Sometimes when the river or lake shores are overgrown with trees and bushes, overlapping the water's edge, the big pachyderm will try to hide under such cover, or in the deep shadow of overhanging rocks, where he lies absolutely motionless, with eyes, ears, and nostrils just above water, and is thus seldom detected.

Once I came upon a hippo—in fact, the first I ever saw outside of a zoölogical garden—in the Athi River, which, at that particular place, is only about one hundred and fifty feet across, and where the length of the still flowing " hippo pool " could not have extended more than eight hundred to one thousand yards. The wary " river horse " saw me at the same moment that I discovered him. Our eyes met for a second, but as soon as I moved to lift the gun up to my shoulder, he instantly sank out of sight. With eager curiosity I waited with the gun ready to fire, expecting the hippo to come up somewhere near the place where he had disappeared. Instead of that, I suddenly heard his peculiar " snorting " and " puffing " at least some three hundred yards farther upstream, while I was looking in the opposite direction.

I had sent some of my men to a place above the " hippo pool," where the river was very shallow, to watch so that the hippo should not be able to get up and disappear that way, and I also dispatched some men to go to a similar place below the pool, while a dozen or so of the rest of the porters were strung along on both sides of the pool, a few yards away from the water. There they could not be seen by the hippo, while they could watch him, so that he would not be able to disappear in the bush on either side.

After almost an hour of impatient waiting, the big head suddenly appeared right in the middle of the pool. As I had been ready for an emergency of this kind, I fired instantly, but it seemed both to me and the gun bearer, who stood close behind, as if the hippo had sunk at the very moment I fired, so that the bullet had hit the water right over the head instead of the head itself. Still, we were not certain whether I had hit the hippo's head or not, so the only thing to do was to wait for another hour or two. If a hippo has only been wounded, he may swim a great distance away and then put up his nostrils under some kind of cover, where he lies immovable for hours, breathing as silently as he can. But when he has been instantly killed, he immediately sinks to the bottom, where the body remains for from half an hour to two or three hours or even more, according to the temperature of the water. The warmer the water is, the sooner the gases form in the intestines of the dead hippo, and these cause the body to rise to the surface, when it can be easily dragged ashore. In this case, however, we waited in vain for over four hours, from the moment I had shot. Although we scanned the pool and all the men watched as carefully as they could, none of us ever saw a sign of the hippo, nor heard any "snorting," after he had once disappeared. Finally, we had to give up our coveted trophy, for it certainly looked as if it had sunk out of existence. The cunning beast had probably found some safe cover, behind which he lay immovable, until he was sure his enemies had vanished.

Colonel Roosevelt, whom I had the pleasure of meeting several times in East Africa during 1909, and who most kindly invited me to join his shooting expedition, when near Lake Naivasha, told me of a most interesting experience he had had with a big hippo in that lake. As soon as the beast had been wounded, he charged down on Colonel Roosevelt, who, with his son Kermit and a few negro hunters, had gone out hippo shooting in a good-sized rowboat. With open jaws and terrible snorts, the big monster made for Colonel Roosevelt's boat as quickly as he could, only to receive two deadly shots from the colonel's heavy Express rifle right in his very mouth, while Kermit was lucky enough to secure a couple of fairly good photographs from the charging beast. This incident has since then been published at length.

A German official, a Mr. C. E. Schmidt, was nearly killed by a hippo in the Rufiji River in German East Africa under most curious circumstances. With another white man and eight natives he was out hippo shooting in the above-named big stream, at a place where the river widens out considerably, and where the waters were literally alive with the big pachyderms.

The whole party had embarked in a good-sized rowboat to tow ashore the bodies of two large hippos that had been killed only about half an hour before, but which had already appeared on the surface. Mr. Schmidt had taken with him a very long and strong rope, to which they fastened both bodies. Hardly had the men begun to row the boat toward the nearby shore, having only about twenty to thirty yards more to cover, and before they reached a good landing place, an immense hippo suddenly rushed for the boat so quickly that before the sportsman had a chance to fire he had upset the little craft with his big head. Fortunately, both the white men and the natives knew how to swim, so they all made for the shore as quickly as they could. Immediately one of the men gave a tremendous scream, and Mr. Schmidt, turning to see what was the trouble, was horrified to behold the big hippo just closing his enormous mouth over one of the unfortunate natives, whom he almost cut in two. All the shooting paraphernalia of the two friends—their guns, cartridge bags, and hunting knives—were lost when the boat was upset, and as the river at that place was very deep and had a muddy bottom, they were never able to recover even the guns. The natives were so frightened that the two sportsmen could not induce them to go out in another boat of larger size to righten the upset craft and tow ashore the two dead hippos.

In Uganda these monsters are so ferocious and so dangerous both to native crops and " shipping " that they had been declared a "vermin," the government encouraging the killing of them as widely as possible. It has repeatedly happened in the waters of Uganda, particularly in the Nile and in the Albert Nyanza, that native canoes of good size, and even small steam launches, have been upset by these powerful beasts. They seem to have found out that sugar canes and other "hippo delicacies" are often shipped in these crafts. Even if the natives, when their boats were thus capsized, have escaped from the hippos, they have often been killed and eaten by crocodiles, which are very numerous in these waters. In British East Africa, however, the hippopotamus is not so numerous; there is no lake or river shipping to be imperiled by them, and the ordinary sportsman is, therefore, restricted to only two on his license.

Colonel Roosevelt was probably the last man who had a chance of shooting hippos in any of the beautiful lakes of Nakuru, Elmenteita, or Naivasha, in which latter water he shot several hippos during August of 1909, after which time, upon the issuance of the new game license, the three above-mentioned lakes were declared game preserves for hippos.

In districts where the " river hog " is seldom or not at all disturbed, he is often seen resting or sleeping on the sand banks in the middle of the rivers, or even on the sandy shores of lakes and streams. He generally lies with his body half submerged in the water, so that if he scents danger, he may be able instantly to disappear under the surface. Sometimes, however, he gets up entirely out of the water, even in broad daylight, to bask in the sun close to the water's edge. I once saw three big hippos, sleeping on the northern banks of the Sondo River, in the Kisii country. They were huddled up very close to one another, as they so often are seen when resting on dry land. The one nearest to the water was perhaps only three yards away from the edge, and all were lying parallel to the river, facing upstream, although, strangely enough, a strong wind was blowing the opposite way, much to my delight. Alone, with an eleven-millimeter Mauser rifle in a sling over the shoulder, and with camera in hand, I began to stalk the three sleeping hippos, with a view of doing my utmost to get a snapshot of them at close quarters before they should roll into the stream.

When I first detected any hippos in this place we were

HIPPO HEADS SHOWING ABOVE THE SURFACE OF THE WATER IN THE
SONDO RIVER.

SLEEPING HIPPOS IN THE TANA RIVER NOT FAR FROM FORT HALL.

all on the march and had stopped on the hills above the river, from which elevation I scanned the waters with my strong Zeiss No. 12 field glasses at a distance of about half a mile. I could plainly make out the big heads of about a dozen or more hippos, floating along in the mighty stream. Between where I stood and the river the country was dotted with bushes and trees, but within one hundred yards or so of the water it was entirely open and only covered with coarse grass, not high enough to afford any cover. Strung along the edge of the river were a good many trees, and upstream in front of the three sleeping hippos was a little hill, only about ten yards away from the animals, on the crest of which elevation were two or three good-sized bushes, which afforded excellent cover for anyone walking close to the river's edge.

As the wind was " right " I made a large semicircle from where I stood down to the river in front of the trio. I found that only by going through water and soft mud, sometimes over my knees, could I proceed in a line behind the little hill, if I wanted to approach the hippos unseen. As silently as possible I waded forward, being careful to keep camera and gun above water all the time. This was often not so easy, having once slid down almost to my hips in a muddy hole, only some twenty-five yards away from the hippos. I must then have made somewhat of a splash, which was instantly answered by a much louder splash, as, to my dismay, one of the hippos rolled into the river.

With the utmost effort I succeeded in a few seconds in getting up on dry ground again, this time on the slope of the little hill, just in time to hear another big splash, as hippo No. 2 took to the water. With fast beating heart, I finally ventured to peep over the top of the hill between the bushes, with the camera ready for a " snap," when, to my great delight, I found hippo No. 3 lying exactly where I first had seen him. In an instant I had focused and, just as I snapped, the wary monster awoke, so that in this picture he is seen with half-open eyes. As quickly as possible I changed my film, but before I had a chance of using either camera or gun, the hippo had discovered me and quickly dived into the stream.

All along the shore of this river we found well-trodden hippo tracks of their peculiar characteristic shape; the hippo is so thick and his legs so short in comparison that between the imprints of the fore and hind legs on one side and those of the other side there is a regular track, formed sometimes by the belly of the big pachyderm, as he waddles along. We were surprised to find that the hippo in these regions sometimes goes as far as a mile or more away from the river at night to feed on his favorite grass and leaves.

After I had succeeded in photographing the sleeping monster, I signaled to the men to come on. I then sent one party half a mile upstream, while another went down about one thousand yards, to where the still flowing stream tumbled down in a long succession of rapids. Both parties were instructed to frighten the hippos away toward me. With a few men I remained in the shadow of a tree that overhung the little hill, from which I had taken the successful photograph. From this place we had an excellent view over the whole hippo pool. We quickly constructed a good cover of branches and high grass, behind which we

SLEEPING HIPPO, PHOTOGRAPHED CLOSE TO THE SONDO RIVER, 1909.

HUNTING LEOPARD, KILLED BY A SHOTGUN WITH No. B. B.

sat down to await developments. Head after head popped
up all over in front of us, just long enough to exhale and
inhale, only to disappear again in the next moment. As we
kept perfectly still behind our screen, more and more of the
hippos began to show their whole foreheads above water,
and did not dive as quickly as before.

Presently my gun bearer, Mwalimu, gave me a slight
nudge, and pointing to a big black hippo head on my left,
whispered: " Huyu mmume mkubwa sana! " (" This one
is a very big male "). Up went my gun, a flash, a sharp
report, followed by a tremendous commotion in the river,
and then the stillness of the grave seemed to reign for
a while, until some distant snortings announced that all
the hippos had scattered up and down stream. Both the
gun bearer and I thought that we heard the bullet hit the
hippo's head, but it was impossible to tell this with any
certainty, for, as already remarked, if hippos are instantly
killed, they sink at once to the bottom of the river to reappear in about an hour. As the waters of the Sondo in this
still flowing pool were rather warm, I expected that the
body would reappear in less than an hour. Looking at
my watch, I saw that it was exactly 11 A.M., and so getting the camera ready for any snapshots, if in the meantime any head would appear in the vicinity, I dispatched
some men to the bulk of the caravan to bring them down
to a level place, within some five hundred yards of the river.
There we made our camp for the night, as I knew it would
take considerable time to skin the hippo, even if we got hold
of him by twelve o'clock.

To the surprise of us all, the body appeared above the
surface of the water like a dark, shiny hulk, at exactly

11.27—or not quite half an hour from the moment the hippo had been killed. The stream formed in this place a fine, oblong pool, but only a very few hundred yards farther down the foaming rapids began. Halfway to the rapids there was a sharp bend in the river, and we thought that the body, which now floated just about in midstream, would surely land at our side of the bend. Much to our dismay, however, the body seemed to float over nearer and nearer to the opposite shore; we had no boat available, and there was no bridge or ford for many miles to either side. Unless the hippo should be lost to us in a few more minutes, by being dashed down the rapids, someone would have to swim out to the carcass to fasten it to the end of a long rope, which I always carried on safari, and by which it could then be easily hauled ashore.

No promise of reward, nor anything else, could induce any of my men to make this venture. I was very much disturbed, thinking that, after all, this beautiful trophy should be lost, and so, for a moment forgetting my dear ones at home, I flung off my clothes, took the end of the rope between my teeth, and jumped into the river, having tied my big hunting knife to a string around my waist. I must say that this was one of the most foolhardy things I have ever done, for not only was the river filled with hippos, but was also said to contain crocodiles, although as yet we had not seen any. When within a few yards of the hippo I felt a sudden stinging pain in my left leg; I certainly thought I was done for then, imagining that a crocodile or a hippo was trying to chew me up! However, I safely reached the carcass and, after having climbed up on his side, I found myself bleeding from a wound some three inches long, but not very deep, just above the knee. I then realized that I must have knocked my leg against some pole or other sharp object, which had stuck in. the bottom of the river.

Having cut two holes in the skin of the hippo's neck, I tied the end of the rope through the loop, and called to the men to pull us ashore. Just as the line began to straighten I lost my balance for a moment, and rolled completely over with the hippo, a rather unpleasant experience that I repeated twice before we were landed on the opposite shore. But my trophy was saved, and no one in the world could have been more delighted than I when we began to cut up the big monster.

Another hippo shot in the same river a few days later floated up in exactly thirty-two minutes, taking five minutes longer than the one just referred to. The second one was a very much larger bull hippo, and was shot in a smaller pool, above which was a rather deep ford, and below which there was another succession of foaming rapids. As soon as the body floated up, it was unfortunately carried by the current in among the bushes on the opposite shore, where it began to go slowly downstream. As the rapids were only about one hundred yards farther down, and as the swiftness of the current increased with every yard, I rushed some men across the stream to fasten a rope to the hippo, while we held on to the other end. They succeeded in reaching the carcass only after it had moved along another fifty yards and had come into rather swift-flowing water, but close to the opposite shore. As the two men had finished tying the rope to the big body, they swam ashore —a distance of only some four or five yards—and at the same time my men began to pull in the line. Just imagine our surprise when, in the middle of the stream, the line suddenly parted, and the big hippo shot downstream at a tremendous speed. It had not gone far, however, until it struck a rock, standing out just at the beginning of the rapids. Here the body was almost doubled from the force of the stream, which held it fast against the rock.

Now, there was only one way of reaching our trophy and that was for some one with a rope to throw himself in the pool and let the stream take him down to the hippo. This was not quite so dangerous in a certain way, because there was no other hippo in the pool, and there were no crocodiles in this place; but the men, fearing the force of the water, again refused. Again I had to seize the rope myself and jump into the water, the next moment being hurled with great force against the side of the hippo, which was fortunately soft enough not to injure me, the carcass lying with the back down and the feet in the air.

I realized now that it was impossible to save the whole hippo, for the current was too strong; so I fastened the rope around his under jaw, behind the big tusks, shouting to the men to tightly fasten the other end around a tree which stood at the water's edge. My gun bearer and two of the natives now volunteered to slide down the rope with an ax to help me cut off the head, so that we could, at least, save that for a trophy. One by one they shot down along the rope and reached me in safety. Mwalimu carried the big American ax. When everything was ready and only the vertebræ of the neck needed to be severed to separate the head from the body, I again went into the water and, with great efforts, succeeded in hauling myself up against the stream to the shore; I shouted to Mwalimu to cut off the head, which he did with a couple of mighty strokes, and the men began to pull in the magnificent head. The reader cannot imagine how badly I felt, when, by the increased force of the water, the new, more than half-inch-thick line again parted, and the big head was swept down the rapids, never again to be seen by us: and thus ended my hippo hunting in East Africa.

The hippo is a very destructive animal. On his long nightly wanderings, when he sometimes goes as far as one to two miles from the water, he seems to develop an enormous appetite. Very often he goes right into the gardens of the white settlers or natives, where in one night a single hippo is able to devour more vegetables than a settler and his whole family could eat in a month! This is nothing to wonder at, when the fact is known that the mighty pachyderm carries a monstrous stomach, unproportionately large, which by actual measurement has been found to exceed even eleven feet in length, and capable of containing four to five bushels of food!

The hippos vary in size quite a little, those of the streams being considerably smaller, as a general rule, than the ones found in larger lakes. From three to four thousand pounds is a heavy weight for a river hippo, whereas animals have been shot in the lakes both of Uganda and German East Africa weighing more than twice as much. In the same proportion do their tusks vary from twelve to eighteen inches in length on the outside curve of a good-sized river hippo, while I recently saw a pair of tusks from a monstrous old bull, killed in a Nyassa Land lake, whose tusks measured twenty-eight and a half inches. The largest hippo tusks on record reached the enormous size of thirty-one and a half inches in length, with a girth of nine inches at the base. The hide of an old bull hippo is exceedingly thick and weighs, just after having been taken off the animal, from four hundred to five hundred pounds.

In spite of all the persecutions to which the hippo is nowadays exposed, he will probably be the last of the big African game animals to become extinct, being still very numerous in most of the large lakes, streams, and swamps of the greater part of Africa.

CHAPTER VII

THE AFRICAN OR CAPE BUFFALO

THE family of hollow-horned ruminants, including the ox, the bison, the buffalo, and the musk ox, is to mankind perhaps the most important of all animal groups. For what would the civilized American or European, or the naked savages of Africa, or the hundreds of millions of Hindoos, Chinese and Japanese do without the work of the ox and the milk of the cow? Of the existing wild animals of this family, the American bison, now practically extinct as a wild animal, the Indian, and the African, or Cape buffalo are the most important. Of these species again the Cape buffalo is the largest and by far the " gamiest."

The buffaloes are so far distinct from other wild cattle that they will not interbreed with them. Among the buffaloes themselves, even in the one continent of Africa, quite a difference exists both in size and color. The Congo buffalo with shorter and more upturned horns is much smaller than the Cape buffalo, and of an almost yellow tint. The Abyssinian buffalo is brown and also somewhat smaller than the Cape buffalo, as are also the Senegambian and the " gray buffalo," supposed to exist in the regions around Lake Tchad.

The Cape buffalo inhabits to-day all the central and eastern parts of Africa, from the Cape in the south to

Abyssinia in the north, although he is now rare in South Africa, having been practically exterminated there in modern times, as the country became more and more settled with white people. In Portuguese, German, and British East Africa the once countless herds of buffalo were very materially reduced some eighteen years ago by the terrible "Rinderpest," which threatened them with total destruction. But they have in the last years fortunately increased there again in great numbers.

These buffaloes are most powerfully built animals. The body of a full-grown bull measures from tip of the nose to base of the tail from eight to nine feet in length, and he stands fully four and one half feet high at the shoulder. The buffaloes live in great herds, feeding together like cattle, but old bulls often separate from the main body and live by themselves, as do the old males of elephants, rhinos, and giraffes. The color of the Cape buffalo is black, with very little hair on the body, which on old bulls seems entirely to disappear except upon the head, where it then generally turns gray. The shape and size of the horns of buffaloes vary a great deal. The horns of the female are much thinner and flatter than those of the bull. They never meet at their base and are also much smoother on the surface than the horns of the male buffalo. Even among the bulls there is a great difference in the horns, which of even some very old ones never touch each other at the base, while those of others seem to be almost grown together. I have seen a pair of horns that were actually so close together at the base that it almost appeared as if they formed one solid mass; but this, I believe, is very unusual. There is generally enough space between the horns, even of the bulls, to allow a little tuft of hair to grow. This hair, as well as the hair on most parts of the head, turns often, as already remarked, gray on very old animals.

The appearance of the surface and also the shape of the horns vary greatly. On some, the horns are rather flat and smooth, while other bulls carry enormously thick and rugged horns, with such miniature cañons and ridges at the base, that they appear, as someone has said, like " sides of a volcano, with its lava streams and rugged ridges." Then, again, on some old bulls the tips of the horns are rather close together—from twenty-four to thirty inches apart—turning inward and downward toward the base, much like fish hooks, while others have their horns less curved and with points turned more forward and upward and with as much spread as thirty-six to forty-five inches from tip to tip.

The African buffalo is without question one of the finest-looking beasts imaginable. With his massive but not clumsy body, his powerful neck, and magnificent horns, he is the very picture of beauty and strength. Indeed, a great many hunters class him as No. 1 in the list of dangerous game. Even the lion is then often placed as No. 2, and the elephant, rhino, and leopard are generally considered the three next most dangerous beasts. It is, however, very difficult to say with any accuracy which of these animals is really the one most to be feared, for the same kind of animal will not only behave differently in varying circumstances, but the same individual beast will also act entirely differently one day from what it will another, although under exactly the same conditions.

The Cape buffalo will hardly ever attack a human being, unless hunted, wounded, or molested in some way, or perhaps suddenly surprised in his own haunts. But all African hunters agree in this, that once wounded or cornered, the buffalo is one of the most dangerous beasts to approach. If he has been wounded but not instantly killed, he will either charge straight down on his assailant, if the latter is in plain view, or else he will make for some thick cover, which generally is not far away, as the buffalo is seldom found on the open plains in the daytime. His favorite haunts are in the dense jungles of both the hot lowlands along the coast of the Indian Ocean, and of the higher inland plateaus, preferably in the vicinity of rivers, swamps, and lakes, where he sometimes stands for hours up to his belly in the water or resting in the thick papyrus or under overhanging trees. On the mountain ranges he is almost invariably found in large numbers on the foothills even up to an altitude of some seven to eight thousand feet. These forests offer the buffalo occasional larger and smaller open spaces, overgrown with luxuriant grass, which seems very attractive to the beautiful beast.

The buffalo is one of the most wary animals. He has so fine a sense of smell, that only the elephant and the rhino can be compared with him in this respect, the elephant alone being his superior in being able to scent his enemies at long distance. This fact makes it very difficult to get a shot at the buffalo at close range, particularly in localities where he has been much disturbed. Here he hides in the daytime in the thickest jungle, often sleeping for hours in the shadow of big trees. He is even then,

A Magnificent Bull Buffalo, Killed in the Kedong Valley.

Large Head of the Ordinary Water Buck (*Cobus defassa*).

however, very difficult to approach, for he sleeps very lightly and hears exceedingly well, so that the slightest noise, the breaking of a twig or the rubbing of the branches against the hunter's hat, clothes, or shoes is enough to wake him up and arouse his suspicions. Instantly he is on his feet, and usually manages to get away so quickly and so cautiously that the hunter in most cases only hears him darting through the dense bush, without having a chance to photograph or shoot him.

This has been my own experience time and again. Native trackers have told me repeatedly that they were sure they could lead me up to buffaloes, which they had seen at close quarters, for these naked savages can creep through the most dense bush apparently without the slightest noise; and yet again and again I myself failed to find them, when we started out together.

One day a Wandorobo came running into camp at about two o'clock in the afternoon, just as I was returning from a long and successful hunt for water bucks to get my lunch and rest a little. He told very excitedly that he had been tracking a small herd of buffaloes all day, until they finally had lain down to sleep under some big trees in a very dense forest, only about three miles to the south of our camp. He further said that there was one " very, very large old bull " with magnificent horns among the herd, and that he could easily take me up to within ten yards of the creature.

After such a tale, of course, I could not take the time to sit down and eat, and so, picking up a piece of bread and half a roasted guinea fowl, I started off at once for the buffaloes, taking the gun bearers and about a dozen fresh men with me. After a little over thirty minutes of half-walking, half-running, the Wandorobo stopped and asked me to let the bulk of the men wait there, while he and I with only one gun bearer should sneak up to the buffaloes, which were now only some six to seven hundred yards away. An order to sit down and wait was always obeyed with much satisfaction, and as a fairly strong wind was blowing in our faces from the direction of the herd, we soon caught their wind, noticing more and more their peculiar strong odor.

With the utmost caution, we followed the naked Wandorobo, who penetrated the dense bush like an eel through the water, without making the slightest noise, while my gun bearer and I were not quite so successful in avoiding dry twigs on the ground, and the noise of the scraping of branches against our clothes. To make it easier for me to move on quietly I had already left my big sun helmet behind with the men, and had donned a small, soft, green cap. I could do this with safety, for the jungle here was so dense that hardly a ray of equatorial sun could penetrate to our heads.

After a while my guide stopped again and, pointing forward, whispered in my ear: "Huko nyati mkubwa, chini ya miti mkubwa." (The big buffalo is there, under the big tree.) The tree to which he pointed with his spear was only about fifty yards away, and right in front of us. I took up some dry, fine sand, which I always used to carry in my pocket, lifted it up and let it fall to the ground to see if the wind was still right. To my dismay, the sand fell down as straight as it could, showing that at the time there was no wind at all. Here I left even the gun bearer behind, exchanging with him the .405 Winchester, which I had been carrying up to that time, for the big .577 Express. This evidently much pleased my Wando-robo, as the size and weight of this weapon, by the natives generally called " msinga " (cannon), had greatly impressed him.

On we went, nearer and nearer to the big tree. Suddenly there was a loud snort, followed by angry grunts, only some twelve to fifteen yards away! In another instant the whole buffalo herd rushed up and crashed through the bush in a mad rush for safety! So dense was the jungle, that although the nearest animal could not have been more than twelve yards away from us, and we could even see the tops of the bushes and trees move as the beasts pressed by—it was absolutely impossible to get a glimpse of a single animal, notwithstanding the fact that I flung myself after them as fast as I knew how, receiving cuts and bruises from thorns and larger branches in my path, as I ran blindly through the thickets in a vain attempt to be able to sight one of the fleeing beasts. The wind must have changed to another direction at the last moment, or we made some noise, unnoticed by ourselves, which frightened the herd. However this may be, the buffaloes had vanished, and we, sad and weary, had to give up the chase, reaching camp just as the sun went down.

On another occasion I was more fortunate. We had found fresh buffalo tracks on one of the foothills of Mt. Kenia, at an altitude of somewhat over eight thousand feet. Magnificent cedars, with their straight trunks, intermingling with enormous deciduous trees of different kinds, composed this forest, the undergrowth of which contained a great many dense bushes, and here and there an occasional rubber vine of the Landolphia family. After more than two hours of difficult tracking we finally sighted some buffaloes about one hundred yards distant, standing across a small open grass patch in the midst of the forest. From where we stood we singled out the one that seemed the largest bull, as it was impossible to get any nearer to the herd, there being not the slightest cover to stalk behind, and the grass too short to conceal a man, even if creeping.

I fired with the big Express gun, aiming for the buffalo's heart. At the crack of the gun the herd made off in a wild stampede, disappearing in the thicket. My gun bearer said in a sad tone in his pidgin swahili: "Hapana piga bwana." (You did not hit, sir.) Indeed, I thought the same, for the big buffalo, at which I had aimed, bounded off with the rest of the herd with mighty leaps, as he vanished in the bush. I decided to cross the open grass patch to see if there would not at least be some blood marks that we could follow, feeling certain that the buffalo must have been hit somewhere, even if not in a deadly spot. It now became evident how much the natives themselves fear the buffalo, for they followed me most unwillingly, saying that if a buffalo is wounded and followed in the dense jungle, he is much more ferocious and cunning than even the lion; that he often doubles in his tracks and hides in the dense bush close by, until his pursuer is almost upon him. Then he makes a wild dash at him, and either tosses him to death, or gores him with his powerful horns.

With the greatest caution, therefore, we crossed the

open space and entered the dense forest, where the buffaloes had been standing only a few seconds before. With the safety catch of the big gun pushed forward, and straining my eyes and ears to the utmost to be fully on my guard, and ready for any emergency, we went into the bush. We had gone but a few paces, when we suddenly heard a loud groan and, expecting a charge at any moment, we held our breath and stopped to listen and look around. Another drawn-out, bellowing-like groan followed close to our right, and turning in that direction, I had only gone a few steps, when I saw that the magnificent buffalo had breathed his last! After skinning the beast I wanted to see where he had been hit, and discovered now that the large, steel-jacketed bullet had gone clean through the very center of the heart and penetrated to the other side until it had almost protruded through the skin. And yet with such a wound the buffalo had been able to run for over fifty yards!

In Uganda, where buffaloes are more plentiful than in British East Africa, they often become so daring that they run at night into the plantations of the natives, which they destroy in a most thorough manner, often killing the savages who try to chase them away. The government, therefore, has recently taken the buffalo off the list of protected animals and declared it, together with hippos and crocodiles, to be " vermin." In Uganda anyone can now shoot as many buffaloes as he wishes and has a chance to, if he thinks that this is " sport." In British East Africa, however, where the buffalo is not quite so plentiful—one of the results of the terrible rinderpest—he was altogether protected until two years ago; up to that time the sportsman could only kill one male buffalo on *a special license,* for which he had to pay twenty-five dollars. Then for two years the hunter was allowed to kill *one bull buffalo* on his ordinary sportsman's license. Since the middle of December, 1909, when the present new game laws went into effect, a sportsman is allowed *two bull buffaloes* on his license, the animals having greatly increased during the last few years.

Mr. F. C. Selous, who has probably killed more buffaloes than any man living, and who has had a great many narrow escapes from wounded and charging beasts, classes these as the most dangerous of African game. This opinion is undoubtedly shared by many other hunters. On one of my trips to East Africa I met a certain Mr. Morrison, an American, who told me how he, a few years ago, had lost his left arm in a buffalo hunt. With another white man, a Portuguese lawyer, he was out buffalo hunting some sixty miles to the northwest of Mozambique, in Portuguese East Africa. Each of them had already succeeded in felling one fine, old bull, when toward evening one day, as they were returning to camp, a small buffalo herd suddenly appeared within shooting distance. They could plainly see that there was one very large bull among them.

Both sportsmen fired at this animal, but the wounded buffalo disappeared with the rest of the herd into the jungle. Morrison and his friend followed in hot pursuit, and a moment later they saw a pair of fine horns behind a bush. Morrison fired at once, mistaking it for the bull that he had already hit, as the beast rolled over dead at the crack of the gun. The two delighted friends now ran forward toward the fallen buffalo, when suddenly, without a moment's warning, the first bull they had wounded charged down on them with such ferocity that, before they knew what had happened, Morrison was caught up by the mighty horns of the enraged beast and tossed high up in the air. He landed unconscious on his back in a thick bush, with his left arm broken in three places, and almost severed from his body. During this time the Portuguese had just had time to fire before the beast turned on him. He succeeded in killing the buffalo instantly with a shot in the brain, from a distance of only about five yards.

Although, as before mentioned, the buffalo is taken off the list of protected game animals in Uganda, and each sportsman is allowed at present to kill two bulls a year in British East Africa, yet with the present excellent and rigid game laws, and vast, suitable game preserves in many parts of East, Central, and South Africa, the Cape buffalo is apt to survive and even increase still more in numbers for centuries to come, unless another and more serious rinderpest should threaten the magnificent and courageous beast with total extermination.

CHAPTER VIII

NONE of the big cats is so widely distributed as the leopard. From the sun-scorched African and Indian plains and damp tropical forests, as far as Manchuria and Japan in the north, and up on the lofty Tibetan plateaus, the leopard inhabits to-day the whole of Africa and the greater part of Asia.

Of the leopard proper there is evidently only one species. The commonly made distinction between the leopard and the so-called panther is, from a zoölogical standpoint, untenable, although a good many sportsmen and hunters affirm that there is a great difference in size and markings between the two animals. The panther in such case is supposed to be the larger and more ferocious of the two, but from the zoölogical point of view no real difference exists, the panther being simply an ordinary, although perhaps somewhat larger, leopard. Both the ordinary leopard and the hunting leopard, existing also in India, are there by the natives called " chita," by most Europeans often spelled " cheetah," the Hindu word simply designating a spotted cat.

Then there is an almost raven-black variety, which was often described as being a different species of leopard. This black variety, commonly called the " black leopard,"

114

was formerly believed to exist only in the Malay peninsula and on the Island of Java, and is, like the snow leopard of the Himalayan Mountains and other high regions, more seldom met with than the ordinary black and yellowish white spotted varieties. Even the black leopard shows, if examined closely, that his coat is spotted much in the same way as the ordinary leopard, but the rings of the spots are more intensely black in color. Of all these different varieties of leopards, the snow leopard is without a question the least common and the most beautiful.

In many prominent zoölogical works it is said that the black leopard exists only in Asia, and this is generally believed even in sporting circles to-day. The fact, however, is that although much rarer, the black leopard also exists in Africa. In 1906 I was told that Mr. W. McMillan, the well-known American, on whose vast estate, " Juja Farm," Colonel Roosevelt had some excellent shooting in the summer of 1909, had killed a black leopard in British East Africa. I could hardly believe this tale, until I, upon the invitation of Mr. McMillan, visited his beautiful home in London. There in the vestibule of his house stood a large, well-mounted, and absolutely black leopard, which this great Nimrod had actually slain in Africa. That the black leopard does not form a distinct species, but is a mere " freak," or but a different variety of the ordinary leopard, is evident from the two facts that there is, in the first place, absolutely no difference in its general build or habits, and, secondly, that we have authentic records of ordinary female leopards, which have born both spotted and absolutely black cubs in the same litter.

The ordinary spotted leopard is very much feared by

the natives, more so than even the lion, for he often plays great havoc with their cattle. Not only does the daring, bloodthirsty feline kill the cattle or sheep that he wants to devour, but he also goes in for wholesale and wanton destruction of the animals. Not infrequently has a single leopard killed a dozen or more sheep and goats in one night, without completely devouring a single one; he may have drunk the blood from all of them, or eaten a few pounds of meat from some of the victims, while there may be still others, which he does not seem to have touched, after they had been killed.

The leopard often springs upon the back of his prey, killing it with a single bite in the neck, or by catching hold of the animal's neck with his paws and biting through the throat, or by strangling the victim. Then he invariably tears his prey open with his mighty paws and generally devours first the heart, lungs, and liver, licking out the blood in the cavity of the chest, before he begins to devour the other parts of the body. Leopards often climb up in trees with chunks of meat in their mouths, which afterwards they can devour at their leisure, undisturbed by their mightier rival, the lion, for which they invariably leave their prey, if on the ground, and instantly disappear, when the king of beasts approaches. As lions cannot climb trees, these are the leopards' only safe retreats. When the leopard is unable to devour the whole animal killed, he often drags the remainder up in a tree, so as not to have it eaten by the hyenas.

There have been recorded a good many instances where leopards have turned man-eaters and killed and devoured natives, mostly women and children. I once met a Kikuju

man who had lost not less than two children in this way:
One of them, a little girl of perhaps four to five years of
age, had been taken away by the leopard in broad daylight
and but a few yards from the hut, in which the little one's
mother had gone the moment before to prepare some food.
As she heard the screams of her baby, she rushed out, only
to see the leopard dart into the bush with her little girl
between his jaws, disappearing so quickly that no trace
was ever found of the unfortunate baby. One cannot wonder very much at this audacity of the leopard, when the
fact is known that the Kikuju people never bury their
dead, but throw them out in the nearest bush, to be devoured by leopards, lions, and hyenas. But worse than
that, not only do these cruel savages throw out their dead
in this way, but they also do the same with old, sick people,
who they think will not recover. In such cases the old
men or women are led or carried out into the thorn bush,
and there often tied and left to be killed and devoured by
these bloodthirsty, nocturnal animals. Several authentic
cases of this cruel treatment came to my knowledge during
my stay in East Africa.

Being so often bothered and harassed by leopards, both
settlers and natives try all sorts of schemes to get rid of
them; by shooting, by poisoning, and by trapping them in
various ways. The leopard is very rarely seen in the daytime, and he is therefore seldom shot by any man, white or
black, for it is a rare chance if the sportsman, in his wanderings, comes across one of these graceful and cunning
animals. It is sometimes possible, however, to put up a
leopard in a " donga "—a river bed, on the sides of which
there are thick patches of trees and bushes—in which both

leopards and lions like to hide during the daytime. Most of the leopards killed have been either shot on moonlight nights or at the morning dusk, as they were found lying on some dead animal upon which they were feeding, or else they have been caught in traps by settlers and natives, and then shot or speared.

The savages make good leopard traps by driving strong poles deep into the ground, and so close to one another that the beast is unable to squeeze even a paw through. These poles are then tied together with bark to other poles, horizontally placed, so as to form a strong roof for the trap, which generally contains two compartments, a smaller and a larger one, separated by a strong partition, also made of poles. In the smaller compartment a live kid or lamb is placed to attract the leopard with its bleating. The entrance to the trap and the whole trap itself is so narrow that there is not room enough for the leopard to turn around, and a heavy plank, serving as the door of the trap, is suspended by a pole over the entrance. The other end of this pole is held down by a twig so placed that when the leopard enters the trap and wants to get at the little kid or lamb he has to push this twig aside. Instantly the rear end of the pole above is released, and the plank falls down behind the leopard, thus preventing his backing out of the trap. As he is also unable to turn around, so as to be able to lift up the door with his paws, he cannot escape, and is subsequently killed by spears, which the delighted natives thrust into him, between the side poles. After the same pattern I once made a leopard trap and put in a little kid for bait, but as I had made the larger compartment a little too wide, the cunning beast first took out the kid, then turned around, lifted up the door with his paw, and disappeared with his prey.

Many white people trap leopards, and even lions, by making a strong and high circle of thorn branches, in the center of which a kid or some other small live animal is tied. The only opening to this little circle is a narrow "alley" between the thorn branches, about six or eight feet long. In this narrow passageway one or two steel traps are placed with a small ridge of thorn twigs on either side of them. In attempting to avoid the thorns, the big cat steps right into the trap and is caught. The best way is to have the trap fastened to a strong chain, the other end of which should be tied to a good-sized log or big branch, so that the leopard is able to move away a little, otherwise he may tear himself free or even bite off his own leg in his attempts to escape.

Great care should be taken in approaching a trapped leopard or lion, for, seeing their pursuer approach, they may free themselves at the last moment by a supreme effort, and woe to the man who is not then ready for such an emergency! An El-Moran, or warrior, to whom I had given a steel trap in 1906, and who had caught a number of leopards in it, selling the skins for his living, once approached a trapped leopard rather carelessly. In an instant the big feline, which had been caught by one of the hind paws, made a wild dash for him, freed himself from the trap at the cost of half the paw, and badly mauled the young warrior before he finally succeeded in killing the brute with his "panga," a long, swordlike, double-edged knife.

Leopards are sometimes caught by placing a piece of

meat on the large limb of a tree not too far from the ground. The trap is placed between the trunk of the tree and the meat, concealed as much as possible under leaves, and fastened to a chain long enough to reach the ground with the other end, where it should be fastened to a log, but it must be well hidden, for otherwise the cunning cat would be suspicious and not go into the trap at all.

At one time on the Naivasha plateau, when marching with my caravan from the western slopes of the Aberdare Mountains toward the Kijabe Railroad station, I saw a leopard at a distance of some seven hundred yards. The beautiful beast was walking slowly, almost parallel to us. On account of the high grass I could only see his back, and occasionally caught a glimpse of his head and the tip of his long tail. As there was no cover behind which I could stalk, I quickly screwed the Maxim gun silencer on to the 6-millimeter Mannlicher, which was my farthest shooting weapon. In the meantime the caravan had thrown themselves flat on the ground, so as not to attract the slightest attention from the leopard, which up to this time had not noticed us at all. As I had underestimated the distance in the beginning, I set the telescope sight of the rifle up to four hundred yards, and fired.

The leopard, not hearing the crack of the gun, stopped and looked suspiciously down into the grass as the bullet hit the ground in front of him. It was then clear to me that the bullet must have hit the soil right under the animal's neck, and that I had been aiming too low. Just as the leopard resumed his slow walk, the second bullet cut one of his front legs near the paw. Still hearing no noise, but feeling the sudden pain of the wound, the leopard evi-

WOUNDED LEOPARD ON THE SOTIK PLAINS.

YOUNG MALE LEOPARD.

dently thought that some enemy from underneath had gotten hold of his leg, so he began to dance around the spot in the most curious manner, scratching up the grass and ground with his powerful front paws. It was all we could do to refrain from laughing aloud at this strange performance.

Suddenly the leopard stopped and looked carefully around in all directions before he began to resume his walk. Just then I fired for the third time. Now we plainly heard a sharp click a fraction of a second later, but as the leopard had disappeared, my talkative gun bearer remarked that he had run away, and had not been hit. But from that little click that we heard, I was rather certain that the bullet must have struck his head. We ran forward in a straight line to where we had last seen the leopard, and there, to our delight, we found the beautiful animal dead, with a bullet through its brain.

We then found that the second bullet, which had caused the leopard to dance around and dig up the ground in a vain effort to find his enemy, had only made a small flesh wound on his left front leg, some three inches above the paw. I measured the distance between the leopard and the spot where I stood when I fired, and found it to be exactly six hundred and seventy-five yards, which shows the superiority of the Mannlicher for long-distance shooting. Of course, such a shot would have been impossible, if I had not had the gun fitted with a very superior telescopic sight, for with the bare eye the little front bead of the gun would have entirely covered the animal, and thus prevented an accurate shot.

To show the cunning of leopards I will here relate the

killing of two of these dangerous beasts by a German settler, previously referred to in the chapter on the giraffe. One evening a couple of natives reported that the young giraffe, captured and tamed by the settler, was being devoured by two leopards, not far from the farmhouse. The fearless young German instantly made for the place, armed only with a double-barreled shotgun and an automatic pistol. As soon as the leopards heard his footsteps they both stopped eating. When the hunter appeared from behind the last bush that afforded any cover, and only some forty yards away, both animals, a male and a female, snarled at him for a second. The next moment they made a desperate attempt to escape by jumping right and left into the jungle, each receiving a load of buckshot in their sides as they ran. The male bounded off into the bush, but the female fell to the ground like dead. While two of the natives kept watching this apparently dead leopard, the settler ran after the fleeing male, which he dispatched with another shot at close quarters.

Just as he was bending over his trophy, desperate screams rang out from the place where his men were left to watch the other fallen leopard. The big female had only feigned that she was dead, for when she heard the third shot she flung herself upon the two negroes, who had ventured right up to the supposed " carcass." Both were badly scratched and bitten, and would doubtlessly have been killed had not a well-directed bullet from the splendid Mauser pistol, aimed at the brute's head, and at only three yards' distance, put a quick end to the fight.

The hunting leopard, or cheetah, as he is often called, differs a great deal from the ordinary leopard. The cheetah is much taller, and his whole form is much more like a dog's than that of a cat, with the exception of his round head and extremely long tail. Then, the spots of the two animals are entirely different, those of the cheetah being simply solid black or dark brown, while those of the leopard are like irregular, sometimes open, rings of mostly black color, with the center of an almost pure white, making the markings of the ordinary leopard much more beautiful than those of the plain-spotted cheetah. Another distinct difference between the two is that the cheetah is not able to draw in the claws of its paws as the other cats do. One can, therefore, at once see the difference between a track made by a leopard or by a cheetah, the claw marks in the latter's track showing plainly, like those made by hyenas or dogs.

The hunting leopard is found almost all over Africa and India, but does not seem to go east of the Bay of Bengal. In India he is captured, tamed, and often used by the native princes for sport instead of hounds. This has doubtlessly given the cheetah the name of "hunting leopard." He is one of the swiftest mammals, being capable of remarkable speed for a couple of hundred yards, but after that distance he soon gets out of wind, and may easily be outdistanced by a good horse.

The natives have practically no reason to fear the hunting leopard, which usually preys on the smaller antelopes, and very seldom tackles a kid or a lamb. I have heard from "reliable" natives that the cheetah often kills and eats the larger game birds, such as the goose, the partridge, the guinea fowl, and even the giant bustard, measuring sometimes as much as ten feet between the wings. I have

never heard or read of any authentic case where human beings have been attacked or killed by the cheetah, although
when wounded and cornered, this animal puts up a determined fight, and may then be a very dangerous antagonist.
I have twice had the pleasure of facing wounded hunting
leopards, who were certainly bent on mischief, and both
of which showed great courage.

After a couple of days' very successful hunting in the
country southwest of Lake Baringo my taxidermist asked
me one day not to bring home any more skins of big game
for a day or two, as he and his men had all they could
do to take care of the animals shot the two previous days.
But as there were in the vicinity a great many beautiful
birds, which I coveted for our New York museum, and
as some of the men, specially trained to skin birds, had
nothing particular to do, I went out one morning with my
double-barreled shotgun to collect birds, taking some ten
or twelve men with me. The gun bearer was ordered to
walk close behind me with one of my powerful rifles, for
the great charm of hunting in Africa lies partly in the
fact that while the sportsman may start out with the intention of shooting small antelopes or birds, he may suddenly
and entirely unexpectedly be confronted by a lion, a rhino,
a buffalo, a leopard, or even an elephant, of whose proximity he had no idea.

After having shot a number of birds, which from time
to time I sent back to camp, I suddenly saw, through a little
opening in the bush, a strange-looking heron, staring in a
certain direction, and moving its head most curiously up
and down, as it intently gazed into the bush. From this
attitude of the bird, I presumed that some other animal

must be stalking in from that direction, and, making a semicircle around the bird, I discovered a big cheetah carefully approaching him, crouching down on bent legs, in much the same way as the ordinary house cat stalks a mouse just before it is ready to spring on its prey. The leopard, which had not yet observed me, was only some forty yards away. Looking around for the gun bearer to get hold of the rifle, I found, to my amazement, not a man in sight!

Not wishing to lose the cheetah at any price, I made up my mind that it would be a case of either " his skin or mine." So, emerging from my cover, I fired with the right barrel of the gun, containing shot No. 5, meant for small birds. The charge hit the leopard squarely over the heart, but had not power to penetrate more than skin deep. Just as I had anticipated, the leopard instantly charged down on me in big leaps. Deciding to reserve the left barrel, loaded with only No. 2 shot, I waited until the very last moment, and just as I thought the leopard was about to make his last leap for me, I " let go," hitting the base of his neck.

At such close range, the muzzle of the gun being certainly not more than, at the most, three yards away from the leopard's neck, the charge had a tremendous effect, the shot tearing a big hole in the neck and turning him in an instant. The moment the leopard received the second shot, he swayed around sideways, made two more leaps, and rolled over dead. This was the only time, I am happy to say, that I lost my patience with my gun bearer, for when he came forward first after the second shot, I " touched him " rather unceremoniously, so that he tumbled into one of the nearby bushes. Had I not been so fortunate with my last shot, I might have, through his negligence, in not keeping close to me, either lost the beautiful trophy or else been scratched and possibly badly mauled by the big cat.

The cheetah is a very wary animal and seems to possess most excellent eyesight. There are probably no other animals that can see as well both by day and by night as the members of the cat family, and so far as my experience goes, none of the felines is able to detect a sportsman at a greater distance than the cheetah. I have been seen repeatedly by hunting leopards, on the plains at distances of fully eight hundred or one thousand yards, when they have made good their escape into the high grass before I had any chance of stalking them. In 1909, however, when hunting on the Sotik plains, only a few weeks before Colonel Roosevelt made his shooting expedition to these famous regions, very early one morning we espied two cheetahs lying on the grass close to each other. The sun had not yet risen, and there was just light enough to shoot, when we detected these two animals at a distance of some six hundred yards. As I was whispering to Asgar, our brave lion chaser, and pointing out the leopards to him, the big cats saw us, and made off in long bounds. In an instant Asgar flung himself on the hunting pony; and then followed a most interesting chase. For the first few moments the two leopards, probably male and female, ran close together and seemed to outdistance Asgar and the pony, but after having run for a few hundred yards they separated, Asgar chasing the big male, now gaining on him more and more. We followed behind as fast as we could, but to our dismay Asgar soon disappeared behind a small hill, over which the leopards had sped.

Running along as rapidly as possible, we came upon a herd of topi, which had been startled by the sound of the galloping horse, and, in their bewilderment, ran almost right into us in their mad effort to escape. Believing that a shot would not interfere with the pursuit of the leopard, I fired at the finest bull in the herd, which, while galloping at top speed, was instantly killed with a shot in his neck, and rolled over in a heap, turning a complete somersault as he fell. Leaving a few men to take care of the topi, we ran on as hard as we could.

Soon we reached the crest of the little hill, when, to our amazement, we saw Asgar in the saddle facing us, and brandishing his whip in the air. We fortunately took this to mean that he had the leopard already at bay somewhere nearby, so we ran down the slope of the hill as fast as possible. When we came within speaking distance, Asgar shouted to us that the cheetah was hiding in a hole, made by a wart hog, only some twenty yards away from the horse; although we looked in the direction to which he pointed, it was impossible for us to detect any animal there at all. With camera and gun in either hand, I approached within thirty yards of the place, where the leopard hid, and yet it was impossible to see anything but a little mound of earth dug out by the pig.

I then looked through my field glasses and discovered the two eyes of the leopard, just glaring at us from the top of the hole. As it was impossible to take any photograph of this, I aimed for the top of his head, which I missed by the fraction of an inch. The next moment the leopard bounded out from his hiding place, only to receive shot No. 2 in his right shoulder. The shock of the bullet stopped him for a moment, and, turning in our direction, he snarled fearfully, with half-open mouth. Taking advantage of this opportunity, I advanced to within fifteen yards of the furious cheetah. Here I succeeded in getting two good photographs of him. Just as I had snapped him the second time, he decided that he had had enough of "posing," and made a leap toward us, certainly intending to charge, when the third bullet, plowing through the heart, finished him in an instant. In the stomach of this cheetah we found evidence enough that its last meal had consisted of a little "tommy," seeing pieces of the peculiarly marked black and white skin, which showed that the meat must have been either that of a Thomson's or possibly a Grant's gazelle.

The habits of the cheetah do not vary much from those of the other leopards, but he is not often found on such high altitudes as the latter, and seems to prefer the open country and bare plains. The ordinary leopard likes the densest bush country the best. In such places one will hardly ever meet a cheetah. Although the latter is considerably taller than the ordinary leopard, he does not weigh so much, being much less solid than his cousin. The length of the cheetah is also greater than that of the spotted leopard, particularly if the measurement includes that of the tail, which is in proportion longer than the tail of the leopard. My first cheetah measured seven feet four and a half inches from the tip of the nose to the end of the tail before it was skinned; the second one, measured in the same way, was seven feet seven inches long. Much larger specimens than these have been recorded. One, recently shot in German East Africa, was almost nine feet long, measured in the same manner.

As the hunting leopards cannot be classed among the animals which are very destructive or dangerous to natives and settlers, they are put on the " protected list," and the hunter is allowed to kill only two cheetahs on the ordinary sportsman's license, which is now in force in British East Africa.

CHAPTER IX

THE AFRICAN RHINOCEROS

THERE are not less than five species of rhinoceros in existence. Of these, Asia claims three. The great, or Indian, rhinoceros, and the Javan variety, carry but one horn, whereas the Sumatran, the smallest of all living species, has two horns, like his African relative. The Sumatran seems to be more closely related to the African rhino than the other two Asiatic species, for he has not only two horns, but his skin has not the large armor-plated patches as clearly defined as the Indian and Javan rhino.

Of the two African species, the white or square-lipped rhinoceros is the larger of the two. This rhino is also much the rarer, existing only in a few small districts in South Africa and in the Lado Enclave, to the north of Uganda, where recently Colonel Roosevelt was lucky enough to secure several fine specimens. The skin of the " white rhino " is in reality not white at all, but dark gray, and only very little lighter than the ordinary " black rhino." His front horn attains a height of some thirty to sixty inches, a good deal larger than any horn of the common black rhino, while he stands about six feet high over the shoulders.

The black rhinoceros, usually met with all over East and Central Africa, is somewhat smaller, averaging five feet to five feet six inches in height, while one of the largest horns on record measured only forty-two inches in length. This species is prehensile-lipped and almost black in color, except that, from wallowing in different colored mud and clay, the animals appear sometimes red, sometimes dark gray.

The African rhino feeds exclusively from twigs and leaves of trees and bushes. He is not as fond of swamps as his Asiatic cousin, and is often found even in practically waterless country, where he goes considerable distances from the nearest stream or water hole. As a rule, he will return to drink at night, and sometimes he also drinks in the early morning. It has been said that the black rhino does not like cool weather, and that he seldom goes higher than 5,000 feet on plateaus and mountain ranges. This, however, is a mistake, for he is very abundant on the Laikipia Plateau, lying at an altitude of over 6,000 feet, and in 1906 I shot a charging female rhino, accompanied by a half-grown calf, which I met on one of the foothills of Kenia, at fully 8,000 feet altitude. It was evident from the many rhino paths on this side of the mountain that it was a favorite feeding place for the big pachyderms.

I have noticed that there are two somewhat different species even of the black rhinoceros, for I have always found certain differences between those living on the plains and the rhinos inhabiting bush and forest country. The rhino of the plains has, as a rule, a much thicker and shorter fore horn than the bush rhino, whose horn is more curved backward, much more slender, and very sharply pointed. I have also noticed that the feet of the rhino inhabiting the plains are, in comparison, larger than those of the bush rhino. As to viciousness, I believe that the rhino of the bush is much more bad tempered than the one inhabiting the open plains, which is said to be true also of lions.

One of the most curious of pachyderms is without a doubt the African rhinoceros. He distinguishes himself from his Indian, one-horned cousin by having two horns, one straight behind the other. Both horns vary a great deal in size. Usually the front horn is the larger of the the two, curving slowly backward, much in the shape of a Turkish saber, and being in most cases round, very thick at its base, and tapering to a sharp point at the end. The other horn is generally much smaller and somewhat like a short Roman sword, being much flatter than the front horn and almost straight.

The front horn of the male rhinoceros is a great deal thicker than that of the female, but a good many rhinos have been seen and killed on which the second horn was larger than the first. I myself have seen on the Sotik plains a huge female rhinoceros which had the second horn very much larger than the first, and curving forward over the first horn, which was a small, swordlike one, just exactly as the second horn generally is. The curved, second horn of this rhinoceros protruded at least six inches in front of the nose and appeared to be almost resting on the top of the small front horn.

I had told Colonel Roosevelt that I was only going to stay on the Sotik plains for about a week or ten days, as he himself had planned to go there right after me, and, hoping that the colonel might be able to secure this strangely shaped head for the Natural Museum at Wash-

TWO RHINOS ASLEEP ON THE PLAINS TO THE NORTHWEST OF GUASO NAROK,
DISTANCE ABOUT FORTY YARDS.

THE SAME ANIMALS.
Note the tick birds on the backs of the beasts.

ington, I did not shoot the beast, which I could very easily have done, as the rhino, followed by an almost full-grown calf, passed in front of me at a distance of not more than fifty to sixty yards; I was fortunate enough, however, to secure a couple of good photographs of this curious-looking animal.

In 1906, when hunting northwest of Mt. Kenia, I saw at a distance of some two or three hundred yards an unusually large rhino with a long and abnormal-looking horn. In this case it was the front horn, which had grown up to a length of probably some forty inches or more, while almost at its middle it had a sort of extension which, at that distance, looked as if the rhino had put its horn through a pumpkin. For hours and hours I tried to get within shooting range of this queer-looking beast, but before I could find any cover, the wind being unfavorable, he scented us and made off at a very quick gait, never to be seen by us again. In 1909 I saw some trophies that were sent down from German East Africa by way of Victoria Nyanza and the Uganda Railroad, and which belonged to a German settler. He had shot, among other animals, a most curious-looking rhino, having both horns of about the same size and length, but both curving toward each other until they met, thus forming a perfect arch over the nose.

While the skin of the Indian one-horned rhinoceros is thicker than that of the two-horned African, and divided in large, armorlike patches, the latter has a more uniform and much smoother skin, varying in thickness from one third of an inch under the belly and inside of the hind legs to fully one inch and more on the sides and back. The skin is always thickest on the sides, over the shoulders, and on the back of the powerful neck. It is rather remarkable that, in spite of the great thickness of the rhino's skin, it should be possible for parasites to live and feed on these great pachyderms, some of which are literally covered with these giant ticks. They seem to be able to find cracks and soft places in the heavy skin, through which they are able to suck the animal's blood, and in such places they congregate in great masses, sometimes causing bad ulcerations and sores.

In such circumstances it is a blessing to the rhinos that the so-called " tick bird " exists. This is a brownish-looking little bird with a strong, straight bill, which always seems to follow the rhino both in the bush and in the open country. These wary little friends not only serve the rhinoceros as " tick-eaters," but also warn him of any approaching danger. Many a time I have stalked a rhino with my camera under the most favorable conditions, and I would have been able to come within a few feet of the powerful beast without attracting his attention, had it not been for the little tick bird, which with its shrill " pt-jaeh, pt-jaeh," warned the rhino of the approaching hunter, and, to my disgust, the coveted trophy would either run away or make a vicious charge.

It must be said, however, to the credit of the tick bird, that it is sometimes useful also to the hunter. For in dense bush the sportsman would often not be able to see the rhino, until almost right upon him, if the tick bird with its " pt-jaeh " did not warn the hunter of the proximity of this dangerous beast. One morning when I was encamped with a large caravan not far from the junction of the

THE SAME ANIMALS.
The one facing the camera is about to charge at full speed.

AT ABOUT TEN YARDS HE FELL, KILLED INSTANTLY BY A BULLET FROM THE
BIG .577 EXPRESS RIFLE.

Guaso-Narok and the Guaso-Nyiro, I started very early for the jungle with some twenty-five men. Before it was quite light enough to shoot accurately or to photograph, we had to go through a stretch of very dense bush. As we had not seen any rhinoceros tracks or other marks of their presence in that particular place, we did not imagine that there were any of these beasts around, when suddenly a little tick bird flew up out of the thicket right in front of us, and with his shrill " pt-jaeh, pt-jaeh " warned us to be on our guard.

No sooner had I heard the bird before the angry sniffing of a rhino announced that we were in dangerous company. The moment the tick bird gave the signal, my gun bearer, of his own accord, reached forward the big .577 Express with the words, " Kifaru karibu, bwana, kamata msinga " (" A rhinoceros is near, sir, take the ' cannon '!") The next minute two rhinos rushed forward and faced us, right across a small opening in the bush, and for several seconds we eyed each other at a distance of only some ten yards or less. It was a big mother rhinoceros with her half-grown calf, snorting at us from across a low, red ant-hill. Unfortunately it was still too dark for a snapshot.

With the big gun at my shoulder, with safety-catch pushed forward, and finger on the trigger, I was ready for a " brain-shot," if the rhino had moved forward an inch, but there she stood for a good many seconds motionless, except for a few tossings of the head. Then the animal turned around just as suddenly as she had appeared, and rushed off into the dense bush, crashing down everything in her wild attempt to escape. I was glad that the " interview " ended thus, as I did not want to kill another rhinoceros unless absolutely obliged to do so to protect my life.

The strength of the African rhino is almost incredible. With ease he roots up trees and bushes, and is able to break down the jungle and go through the thickets so thorny and dense that one would think it absolutely impossible for any beast to penetrate. During the construction of the Uganda Railroad it more than once happened that rhinos took exception to the invading of their country, routed the workmen off the track, and upset and destroyed wheelbarrows and tools. On one occasion a huge rhinoceros rushed forward toward a gang of workmen, who were fastening a rail to its sleepers, scattered the men, and then made for the construction car, which stood on the completed track a few hundred feet farther away. It put its mighty horn under the car and literally lifted it off the track, after which performance the beast, sniffing and puffing, departed. It took the workmen several hours to recover from their fright and to jack the car onto the track again. Horses and mules, and even cattle, have often been attacked by these vicious brutes and tossed many feet up in the air, horribly gored and mutilated by the powerful horns of the rhinos.

Much has been said about the poor sight of the rhinoceros, and I have even heard prominent lecturers on African topics, and also sportsmen, speak about it as the " blind rhino." Although I know it is a generally accepted fact that the rhino is " almost blind," this theory is, in my opinion, not altogether warranted. I do not believe that he is nearly as badly off in this respect as he is supposed to be. On my first visit to Africa in 1906 I started out rhi-noceros hunting with the belief that the beast was extraor-dinarily nearsighted and stupid, but a good many of my experiences, some of which I will relate in the following paragraphs, have made me change my mind considerably on this subject.

It is generally said that the rhino cannot recognize an object at any farther distance than seventy-five to one hun-dred feet, and it is contended that if a rhino has observed a person at a longer distance than this, it is probably not through the sight, but through his wonderful scent that he has detected the hunter. In a good many instances it may be hard to say whether this is so or not, but as I had heard from one man, who had a great deal of experience in big game hunting in Africa, that he, for one, did not believe in the bad sight of the rhinoceros, I made up my mind that I should make as many thorough "tests" in this respect as possible.

While I have seen that the rhino, like a great many other wild animals, both in Africa and in other continents, cannot very well distinguish between a man and a tree stump, if the former stands perfectly motionless, particu-larly if he is well or partly hidden by bushes, trees, or long grass, this may often be the case even with human ob-servers, if only the distance is increased. As to the rhi-noceros, I have found that in bush country, when the wind was such that it was absolutely impossible for the beast to scent me, he would not detect me, even ten to fifteen yards off, if I stood motionless among the bush. On the other hand, I have seen how the rhino clearly discovered my pres-ence when I was moving along in the bush, or even standing still in open places, at a distance of from two to three hundred feet.

Both on the Sotik plains and on the plateau to the northwest of the Guaso-Narok River I have repeatedly had experiences with rhinos which prove that their eyesight is really not as bad as it is generally believed. On the former plains I saw two rhinos lying down in the open, just about the noon hour, taking a sleep and exposed to the burning rays of the equatorial sun. I advanced unnoticed to within one hundred and fifty yards for the purpose of taking photographs, when the noise made by one of the gun bearers, as his hob-nailed shoes crashed against a stone, awakened both animals. They sprang to their feet, and, although the wind was very strong and blowing from them to us, so that it was absolutely impossible for the animals to get our scent, they both saw us. They whirled around instantly and faced us, sniffing and puffing and wobbling their heads sideways and up and down, evidently attempting also to get a " whiff " of the disturbers of their siesta. We all three stood as motionless as we could, except that I tried to focus my lens on them, but just as I snapped the first picture both animals turned and ran away at high speed.

One morning on the Laikipia Plateau I had the opportunity of seeing no less than eleven rhinos in three hours, during which time I repeatedly tried to stalk right up to the beasts. A strong southwest breeze was blowing, and as I approached the animals from the northeast there was no possible chance for them to get a whiff of our wind. Time and again, I noticed, to my dismay, that the big pachyderms had an eyesight good enough to detect us at distances of from one hundred to two hundred yards and over, when all of them would run away, with the exception of one old bull, which was lying down when I approached him. This rhino remained motionless, with his eyes evidently fixed on me, as I advanced with camera in one hand and the big Express in the other. Finally, when within less than fifty yards of the beast, as I was trying to make a semicircle around him to the southward, so as to be able to get a better light for the picture, he followed me with his head, and then suddenly rushed up, made a couple of angry sniffs, and charged right down on us, snorting like a steam engine.

In spite of very careful work, great patience, and strong, favorable wind, I have never been able to approach a rhino that was awake nearer than about seventy yards on the open plains before he noticed me. I have several times actually paced the distance between me and the rhinos, which ran away, when they saw me even as far off as from one hundred and twenty-five to one hundred and seventy-five yards. The distance at which the beasts would either run away or charge us depended doubtlessly also on the different districts where they were found—i. e., whether they had been much hunted or not. If much disturbed, even the vicious rhino learns that man with his firearms is too dangerous an enemy to encounter. On the other hand, one of the most sudden and dangerous charges I experienced was made by an old bull, which had evidently been wounded a good many times before, as I found in his skin two Wandorobo arrowheads and several other wounds from bullets.

Accompanied by a few men and taking only a rifle and

a shotgun, I had gone up into the dense bush near the Kijabe Railroad station to shoot a small antelope for my table. We had walked fifteen to twenty minutes, when we suddenly came across fresh rhinoceros tracks, but, as we had only gone out for the antelope, we left the track and went in the direction of an open place, overgrown with grass, where the natives had told me that they had seen the antelopes feeding about an hour before. Just before we reached this place, the vicious old rhino dashed out at us from the thick bush. My men disappeared as if swallowed up by the ground, and, although I turned around as quickly as possible, the rhino's head was not more than two yards and a half from the muzzle of the gun when I pulled the trigger of the little Mannlicher. The beast fell instantly, but the momentum of his charge hurled his body to my very feet. I assure the reader that it is no exaggeration to say that it was actually less than six inches between the rhino's nose and my left foot! Had the bullet not found the brain, nothing in the world could have saved me from being killed by the ugly brute. This rhino must have been very old, for his horn, so powerful at its base, was worn down until probably only one third of its original length remained.

The scent of the rhinoceros is very sharp indeed, and in this respect he is exceeded only by the elephant. I have tried on the open plains to see how far a rhinoceros would be able to scent a couple of men if the wind was not too light. Rhinos that were feeding with their noses to the ground and evidently not suspecting any danger at all, scented us often at a distance of from two hundred and fifty to three hundred yards. When the big pachyderm scents a human being, he generally runs forward in the direction of the place from which the scent comes, to locate his enemy, and to "investigate," not always meaning to charge in any vicious way. Eight out of the twelve rhinoceros that I have shot, I have had to kill, as they charged down on me, evidently meaning mischief, although in several instances I waited with the fatal shot and gave the rhinos a chance to change their minds, until they were within a few yards of me, when I did not care to have them "investigate" any closer.

It is impossible to say what a rhino will do in certain circumstances, for one time he will run away from and another time he will charge down on his pursuer in exactly the same situations. I remember once, when our caravan was marching from the Laikipia Plateau toward Mt. Kenia, how a large rhinoceros was feeding right in the little native path, which we were following at the time. Not wanting to kill the animal, but at the same time not willing to risk the lives of any of the porters of the caravan, I consulted with the gun bearers and nearest men as to what we had better do. They proposed that we should make as much noise as possible, shouting and beating with sticks on empty water pails, to frighten away the rhino. As we began this terrible "kelele" the rhino, which was only some seventy-five yards away, threw up his head and tail and rushed away as quickly as he could.

A few months later, however, when we were marching toward Sotik through the Southern Kedong Valley, we had an experience of an entirely different character. We were following along an old Masai cattle trail, close to the foothills of the Mau escarpment, when, reaching the top of a little ridge, we discovered two large rhinos calmly feeding close to each other on either side of the little path, only a few hundred yards away from us. The animals were walking slowly in the same direction as we, and as we would have caught up with them in a very little while, we decided to try our old method of scaring them away with great noise. On a certain signal, some fifty of us shouted at the top of our lungs, while others beat empty water cans and pails. This had the unexpected effect that both animals instantly whirled around and charged down on us like a team of horses, running along close to each other, one on each side of the little path.

I had several times heard that if a large animal is hit on one side, it invariably turns out toward the other side to find his pursuer, and not wanting to kill any of the beasts, I fired, when they had come within some fifty yards, hitting each of them on the side facing the other. It was just as if a mighty wedge had been driven in between the animals, for they suddenly separated and ran away in different directions. The female disappeared on our right into a clump of bushes, whereas the larger one, an old male with a fine horn, rushed off to our left into the open. After making a run for a few seconds, he suddenly changed his mind, possibly annoyed by the noise and laughter of the men, and turning around, he charged us again with uplifted tail and lowered horn, coming on as fast as he could!

In the meanwhile I had had time to reload the big rifle and was ready to give him a " warm reception." Between us and the charging brute was a low, circular anthill, only some fifteen yards away, and I said to Mr. Lang and the gun bearers, who begged me to shoot, that I would wait until the rhino had reached the anthill, to see if he would not change his mind before that. It seemed almost as if the rhino had been a mind-reader, for, having reached the outer edge of the hill, he suddenly stopped, snorted and puffed, and threw up the red clay with his front feet. With the gun to the shoulder, I shouted, much to the amusement of my men, " Njoo, Mzee, mimi tayari " (" Come on, old fellow, I am ready "). He showed his anger in this way for a few seconds, and then turned around and ran off to our left, exposing a long flesh wound of about eighteen inches, from which the blood was trickling, proving that the big bullet had only plowed through his thick skin for that distance, causing him no serious injury whatever.

Of the ferocity and courage of the African rhinoceros many contrary things have been said. While some people hold that the rhino is an exceedingly clumsy and stupid beast, which very seldom attacks the hunter, and in most instances runs away when molested, others consider him one of the most dangerous animals in existence. I myself side with the latter, having had, as already mentioned, a good many narrow escapes from these vicious brutes. Before I had ever met a rhino, I believed that they were not to be classed among the more dangerous game animals, but my first experience with these beasts soon gave me a different opinion about them. One day when encamped not far from the Kijabe railway station I had remained in my tent, as the rain was pouring down, and as I also had some writing to do. Suddenly a Wandorobo hunter came running into the camp, shouting that he had located a rhino, and that he knew from the tracks that it must be a very large one. As I had never seen a rhinoceros yet in his wild state, and was most anxious to secure a fine specimen for the museum, besides having the excitement of a rhinoceros hunt, I flung away my writing paraphernalia, took a couple of guns, the gun bearer and a few men, and followed the tracker.

We soon had to go through an almost impenetrable jungle, where we in places had to crawl on hands and feet to be able to advance at all. After two hours of such hard marching in the pouring rain, we finally found the fresh rhinoceros track. Having followed it for another hour through similar circumstances, the men suddenly stopped and consulted with one another. They then all tried to make me understand that it was no use to go any farther, because the " rhino had gone too far away." But I gathered enough, from what they had said, to understand that they were afraid to follow the beast any longer in this terrible jungle. I was sure that they wanted to deceive me, and that they were simply tired of the pursuit and afraid to go any farther, as we could plainly see that not only one, but two rhinos had passed over the same path, one after the other. I upbraided them for their cowardice, and told them to go ahead, and that under no circumstances would I return to camp before we had at least seen the rhinos.

Now they came straight out and told me that it was a most dangerous undertaking to follow two of these big brutes in such dense jungle. They said that if I persisted in going any farther I would have to take the lead myself and they would follow close behind me. This I did without hesitation, fortunately exchanging the .405

Winchester for the heavy .577 Express, which the gun bearer had been carrying behind me up to that time.

In perfect silence and as quietly as possible we followed in the tracks of the big beasts, being particularly careful not to step on any dead branches, nor to make any other noise, which might disturb the animals. We had not gone on thus more than perhaps ten or fifteen minutes before the men stopped again. They now tried even harder than before to make me give up the pursuit. Again they said that it was useless to follow the rhinos, as they were much " too far away " from us to be overtaken. Before I had even a chance to reply, the rhinos themselves answered with their peculiar angry sniff, only a couple of dozen yards or so away from us!

Where we stood, the jungle was so dense that it was almost impossible to move the arms freely, or to raise a gun, but I saw a little to my left, and in the direction from where the noise of the rhinos came, a small opening, for which I quickly made, thinking myself followed by the gun bearer and the rest of the men. Louder and louder sounded the crashing of the trees, as the big beasts came charging down upon us, and, turning around to see if the gun bearer was ready with the reserve gun, there was not a man in sight. It was as if the earth had swallowed them all!

As I reached one end of the little opening, out shot the head of a big rhino on the opposite side, only about twenty feet away. A flash and a tremendous roar from the powerful gun, and the huge rhino rolled over only a few feet away from me, his brain pierced by the powerful steel-jacketed bullet! Just as I was gasping for breath, and

145

before I had time even to lower the gun, Mabruki's, the gun bearer's, voice rang out from the top of a nearby tree, " Bwana, ingine anakuja " (" Master, another one is coming ").

Hardly had he finished his sentence than I saw Rhino No. 2 charging down upon me from another side, and, turning toward him, I gave him the second barrel, with which I was fortunate enough to hit the head again just back of the second horn, and down he went, stone dead. Within less than a minute's time and with only two successive shots of the big Express gun, I had succeeded in felling the first two rhinos which I had ever seen at large.

It is impossible to describe the joy I felt when I was resting on the side of one of my fallen " enemies," for if I had not understood any of the language of the men, or had I hesitated and returned to camp at their suggestion, I probably would never have had this wonderful experience. It is in a case like this that the hunter cannot depend upon anybody else for protection, and in such dense jungle he has to rely upon his own nerve, swiftness of decision and good aim, more than upon any fellow huntsman, be he ever so near at hand. To show how uncertain it is to count on the stupidity of the rhino, or to believe, as a prominent English sportsman and author affirms, that perhaps only once out of two hundred and fifty times the rhino means mischief when charging, as he is coming on only to " investigate," I will here relate a few facts that certainly speak for themselves.

Dr. Kolb, a German scientist and hunter, was one day bird-shooting a few years ago in German East Africa,

TWO DIFFERENT TYPES OF RHINOS.

The upper one represents the bush rhino, the lower one the rhino of the plains. Note the difference in the shape of the lips and relative position of the eyes. The little "extra horn" between the two horns of the upper rhino is, of course, unusual.

ANOTHER SPLENDID TROPHY.

when he was suddenly charged by a large female rhinoceros. Although not accompanied by any calf, a circumstance which often makes these "mothers" vicious, this rhino, without any provocation whatever, charged down on the doctor, who at the time was only armed with a shotgun. Hearing the angry sniffings of the rhino, and the breaking down of the bush as she came on, the doctor tried to run for cover, and for a few seconds raced around a small but dense clump of bushes, closely followed by the vicious brute. Having discovered a large tree with a big cavity near the ground, the doctor unfortunately made for the same. No sooner had he entered the cavity than the rhino was upon him, and with its powerful horn killed him in a few seconds, mutilating him in a most horrible way, while the cowardly native followers looked on from nearby trees, without doing anything to distract the attention of the rhino from the doctor.

Mr. C. Schillings, in his wonderful experiences as a pioneer wild-animal photographer, relates also in his interesting book, "With Flashlight and Rifle," a good many instances of having been charged by a number of rhinos, which he had not provoked in the least. In fact, he had several times made regular detours, so as not to come too near the vicious brutes, which, in spite of all precautions, had scented him and charged him and his caravan. Once, Mr. Schillings relates, one of his porters was badly gored and tossed by a rhino, which suddenly "ran amuck" of the caravan. Wonderful enough, this particular native, who had actually had his intestines thrown out of his body by the rhino, subsequently recovered, without seeming to be any the worse for his experience.

An Austrian nobleman, whom I met in British East Africa in 1906, told me of three very narrow escapes from charging rhinos. Once he himself had had his left shoulder bruised by a rhino which charged madly down upon him. In spite of having been twice badly wounded, the beast rushed so close past the Austrian, who with a side step tried to save himself, that the rhino's shoulder hit him, hurling him several feet out of the animal's way, while the brute fortunately continued straight ahead. On another occasion a female rhinoceros, accompanied by a young calf, was encountered in the dense bush country on the Mau escarpment, as the caravan was moving along in the early morning. Suddenly there was an outcry among the porters, who threw down their loads right and left, while an angry rhino mother made straight for the cook, whom it unfortunately succeeded in tearing to pieces with its sharp-pointed horn before the hunter killed it with a well-aimed bullet from his Mannlicher rifle.

Not even at night is the caravan perfectly safe from rhino attacks, and a good many times I have myself had nightly visits from the dangerous pachyderm. Once when in camp on the western slopes of Mt. Kenia I was awakened during a moonlight night by shoutings and great commotion in camp. Taking the big Express, I ran out in front of the tent and came just in time to see the hindquarters of a big rhino, evidently a male, which had run right through the camp between some of the porters' tents, and had passed within three yards of my own tent, although at the time a strong fire was blazing.

Mr. Percival, the assistant game ranger in Nairobi, told me of a similar, although much worse experience, which he had had a couple of years ago. One night he was awakened by a feeling of unrest, as if something had gone wrong in his camp. His inclination was to get up immediately to investigate, but being very tired from a long march the previous day, and seeing that the big camp fire was blazing, and the Askari awake, he again lay down, wishing he might be able to go to sleep again. For some reason it was not possible for him to feel comfortable, having again the strong feeling that he should get up and look around the camp. Finally he decided to do so, took his big gun, and went out among the porters' tents to see if everything was all right. Hardly had he left his tent, when a big rhino rushed, full speed on, through his camp. Passing right over the fire itself, he ran down Mr. Percival's own tent, and, putting one of his heavy feet right on the very couch, which a few minutes before had been occupied by the sleeping game ranger, broke it in pieces.

In 1909 I was told of a similar experience in German East Africa by a Mr. Herman Gelder, of Berlin, who had made an extended shooting trip through the southern and western part of the German Protectorate. With over one hundred porters, Mr. Gelder was encamped at the edge of a large forest not very far from the eastern shore of Lake Tanganyika. Having seen a good many rhinoceros's tracks in the vicinity, before camp was pitched, the precaution was taken of making a small " boma " around the camp. This was done by heaping cut-off branches of thorn bushes and trees in a circle around the camp. Having accomplished this, he ordered a big camp fire to be kept burning during the night. Suddenly, about 2 o'clock in the morning, Mr. Gelder was awakened by a tremendous outcry, and, when he had rushed out to investigate, he found that a rhino had broken through the boma, which was too low and thin, and had killed one of his Askaris, who had been sitting at the fire.

In camping in countries infested with rhinos and lions, the only safe device is to make a strong boma of thorn bushes all around the camp, or else in a horseshoe form, leaving a large camp fire to protect the small opening in the " wall." If this hedge is made eight to nine feet high and ten to twelve feet wide, it gives a perfect protection from rhinos and lions, although instances have occurred, as before related, where both rhinos and lions did not heed the camp fire. However, it very seldom happens that any wild beast ventures too near a blazing fire, particularly if it is of good size.

According to my own experiences with rhinos, I believe them to be the most dangerous of African game, as one never knows exactly what a rhino will do. As one is most often attacked by these vicious brutes in very dense jungle, it is impossible to see them before they are within a few yards. At such close quarters it is rather unsafe to let the rhino " investigate " any further, and the best thing to do then is to place a bullet in his forehead, for a heart shot will very seldom kill a rhino instantly. I have known of a case where an Englishman shot no less than twelve bullets from a .500 Express rifle into the body of a rhino, two of which bullets had touched the heart, and two or three penetrated the lungs. Yet the hunter was killed by this rhino, which, after goring his antagonist, walked over a hundred yards away before he fell.

THE AFRICAN RHINOCEROS

As the rhino, in spite of his dangerous character, is partially protected both in German and British East Africa, and as he not only exists on the open plains, where he is not nearly so dangerous, and much more easy to kill, but also inhabits the densest jungles, he will probably be one of the last big animals to be exterminated.

CHAPTER X

THE antelopes belong with right to the bovine family, and seem to be animals which are a good deal like both oxen and sheep, either of which species some antelopes resemble so much that they are not easily distinguished from the same. How little radical difference, for instance, between an eland and an ox, or between a chamois, generally classed among the goats, and a springbok, a puku, or even a reed buck!

The large antelope family is characterized from other animals of their size by their graceful build and their beautiful heads and horns, carried a great deal higher than the level of the back. In some species of antelopes both males and females have horns, but in a good many others of the finest of those animals only the males carry horns. The horns of the antelopes may be characterized by their long, slender, and more or less cylindrical form, and always by the fact that they are never grown out into different branches as those of the elk or moose. A great many of the antelopes carry most beautifully shaped horns, some of them, like the young impala, having horns forming a perfect lyre, while others, like the greater kudu, have them grown up in graceful spirals in the shape of enormous corkscrews. Some of the antelopes' horns show prominent year rings, running up to within a few inches of the tip, and all of the horns of the antelopes, with a few exceptions, grow almost straight upward and then forward or backward.

The bony internal core of the horns of almost all antelopes is not honeycombed and full of holes, like that of oxen, sheep, and goats, but hard and entirely solid. Another characteristic of the antelope, with very few exceptions, is an easily distinguished gland beneath the eye, which is entirely lacking in oxen and goats. Then again while certain antelopes' teeth very much resemble those of oxen, others are more like the teeth of sheep and goats.

The antelopes have in ages past exclusively inhabited Southern and Western Asia, from whence centuries ago they migrated into Africa, through Arabia. With few and less important species as exceptions, the antelopes proper now inhabit only the Dark Continent, having almost completely disappeared from their former home, a fact that still puzzles zoölogians. The whole of South Africa was once literally alive with antelopes of all kinds, and I have myself heard tales from a good many old Boers, telling of how, only a few decades ago, antelopes, such as the eland, gnu, the oryx, different kinds of hartebeests and others, existed there in uncountable herds. But, alas! most of these antelopes are now very rare, and some of them entirely exterminated in South Africa.

It is in the countries to the north of the Zambesi River, in Nyassaland, parts of Portuguese, German, and British East Africa, that the hunter now meets the largest antelope herds in existence. In these countries the vast plains attract the antelopes, and they can still be seen there in great numbers. I am sorry, however, to say that in the few years between 1906 and 1910 these herds have noticeably diminished. Where I in 1906 saw literally thousands of hartebeests, wildebeests, and zebra, I found in 1910 only hundreds. In spite of game laws and large game preserves, it is probably only a question of time when most of these graceful animals will be rare, and some of them possibly exterminated also in the aforenamed countries.

The eland is the largest of all antelopes. Years ago great herds of this magnificent beast roamed around all over South Africa, but they are now practically extinct in the country south of the Orange River. They are at present most plentiful in Nyassaland, German and British East Africa. In this latter country they are fairly common, and with the present strict game laws and big, suitable game preserves, the eland will probably survive in British East Africa for a good many decades to come. The best place to secure a fine eland in the last-named protectorate is, without doubt, the Kenia-Laikipia region. The eland seems to develop larger and more powerful horns in this part of the country than in the southern part of the protectorate, where he is easily found on and around the Sotik and Loita plains. Even not far from Nairobi, to the northeast of the Athi Plains, and down along both the Athi and Tana Rivers, the eland is still quite plentiful, although lately he has been hunted there considerably.

The eland is particularly fond of bush and open forest country, but in places where they are not much hunted they are quite often found even on the plains; still they never go very far away from some kind of cover. In districts where the eland has been a good deal disturbed he

ORDINARY BUSH BUCK, SHOT ON ABERDARE MOUNTAINS.

HEAD OF A NEW VARIETY OF BUSH BUCK CALLED "*Tragelaphus tjaderi.*"
Compare this with the photograph above and note the difference in the
markings and shape of head.

shuns the plains during the day, visiting them only at night for the purpose of drinking and feeding, returning at dawn of day to his favorite haunts, where he loves to stand, or lie down to rest and sleep during the heat of the day, preferably in the shadow of big trees. Native hunters have repeatedly assured me that the eland is one of those animals which are able to go for a long time without drinking any water, and this has been corroborated by the experiences of a good many hunters. It is possible that the eland for days, and perhaps for weeks, at a time may be satisfied with the water he gets, when he feeds on the dew-drenched grass in the early morning. Mr. Selous thinks that in Southern Africa the eland used to feed on melons, which temporarily satisfied his need of moisture.

As the eland is also one of the many African animals which is bothered with a great many ticks, he is very often accompanied by the " rhinoceros bird," which, as in the case of the rhino, not only helps the eland to get rid of most of the parasites, but also warns him of any approaching danger. Being, besides this, an exceedingly wary animal, with evidently very good eyesight, he is most difficult to stalk, and I have spent hours and hours trying to get close enough to the eland to secure a good snapshot, but failed to do so without first wounding the animal.

When a herd of eland is disturbed, the animals are able to run off at great speed, and it is amusing indeed to see how these heavy creatures are able to make such high leaps as they do when they stampede. When an eland observes the hunter at a distance, he generally stands still for a moment, squarely facing him and switching his tail to and fro, just a few minutes before he is ready to gallop off. A good horse is, as a rule, able to keep pace with, and even overtake, an average eland, if the ground is not too rough, the cows being better runners than the bulls.

A full-grown bull eland stands as high as five feet eight inches and more over the shoulders, while the mighty horns, spherically twisted, and with a sharp ridge running along almost to the tip, sometimes measure thirty inches. This animal is one of the few large antelopes among which the females also carry horns, although these are generally a great deal thinner than those of the bulls and have the ridges much less marked, but in length the horns of a cow may far exceed those of any male.

The color of the skin of the young eland is a reddish chestnut, and is often marked with well-defined, white stripes, which run down along the sides from a dark brown band on the back. Old bulls very often turn to a dark slate-color, sometimes appearing grayish blue. Both males and females carry large dewlaps, and particularly the males develop a large quantity of dark brown, bushy hair on the forehead, below the horns. The eland feeds, as a rule, in small bands of from ten to twenty, but after the close of the dry season much larger herds may be seen, often coming down to water holes on the plains. Single bulls, roaming around alone far from the herd, as in the case of elephants, rhinos, and giraffes, are rarely encountered.

As already stated, it is exceedingly hard to get up close to a herd of eland, for if a single animal detects the hunter, it seems to be able quickly and intelligently to communicate " the news " to the rest of the band. I found several times, when stalking small herds of eland, that if only a single animal could for a moment see me, the whole herd would gallop off in another second, with their strange, heavy leaps, and then sometimes go a long distance before settling down to feed again. On the Sotik plains I once put up a couple of fine eland bulls, which I succeeded in separating from a small herd and then stalked for hours, with a view of getting a good snap shot of them, but all in vain. The animals had evidently not been much hunted, for they would let me come up to within some two hundred yards of them each time. Then they galloped off for another few hundred yards, when they would stop again, until I had managed to steal up to about the same distance as before.

My experience this time proved the great vitality of the eland. At about four o'clock in the afternoon I had come up again within some two hundred yards of the animals, and determined that if I could not get a snap shot of them, I should shoot the largest of the two, both because we needed the meat and because some of my Kikuju men had begged me to let them have the tough skin to cut into straps, with which to carry their loads. This tribe generally does this in such a way that they let the load rest on the back, with the sling supporting it from the forehead, just as the hunting guides in northeastern United States and Canada. It was impossible to photograph the bulls, and so I fired with the .405 Winchester with a steel-capped bullet, aiming for the heart of the largest eland. At the crack of the gun both bounded off in big leaps, and my gun bearer expressed his disappointment again in the words: " Hapana piga, bwana," or " You did not hit, sir." I felt quite surprised myself, as I thought I had taken a very careful aim, but being sure that I must have hit the animal at least somewhere near the heart, I started toward the clump of big trees, in the shade of which the two eland had stood when I shot.

There was not a sign of any blood marks on this spot, but as we followed the spoor of the two, one of the native trackers observed a few drops of blood on twigs, which evidently had rubbed against the side of the wounded eland. From the height of the marks, I understood that the shot must have hit somewhere in the vicinity of the heart. After having gone exactly two hundred and twenty-five paces from the place, where the eland had been when I fired, I found the big bull dead on the ground. The steel-capped Winchester bullet had gone in through his right side, clean through the lower, pointed part of the heart, broken a rib on the opposite side, and was buried in the fat under the skin on the left-hand side of the animal, from where I cut it out. Had I not been sure that I must have hit the eland in a good place, I might have given up the chase when we saw the two animals dart away. This shows how very careful one must be in following up any game shot at, that the trophies may not be lost, or that the animals be not put to unnecessary suffering through the carelessness of the hunter.

In spite of the great size and comparative strength of the eland, which would make him a terrible antagonist to either a man or a horse, if he were bent on mischief, it must be remarked that the eland is of a wonderfully mild temperament. Although it has been said that eland cows, when accompanied by very young calves, sometimes have courage enough to attack hunting dogs, and even men, in the attempt to defend their offspring, I have had several opportunities to see how perfectly gentle a big, strong eland bull is, even if cornered and wounded.

Once while marching along the Guaso Narok River on the Laikipia Plateau, I was suddenly confronted by a large eland bull, which was accompanied by two or three cows. I had been expecting leopards from fresh tracks, seen only a few minutes before, so that when I saw the bush move some fifty yards in front of me, I had the gun already up to the shoulder. When the big eland bull suddenly emerged, I half involuntarily pulled the trigger, with the result that the stately beast instantly sank down on his knees, while the cows galloped away. Feeling very bad over my mistake, I handed the rifle to the gun bearer, and took the camera to get a snap shot or two before the magnificent old bull should expire. As I came around the nearest bush in front of the eland, I faced him not more than eight or ten yards away. Instantly he got up on his legs again. I snapped the camera and was just trying to change the film, when the big bull whirled around and took a few leaps away from me, after which he fell dead. I am perfectly convinced that had he wanted to do so, he could easily have gored me, unarmed as I was, if he had attacked me at the moment I was trying to take his picture.

The meat of the eland is perfectly delicious, and during the season when the animal has plenty of fresh grass to feed on, it would favorably compare with the best of beef. The eland is one of the few African antelopes which is blessed with a considerable amount of fat. His mighty leg bones contain a great deal of marrow, which is delicious to eat on toasted bread, or else very useful for the purpose of greasing guns and knives, in which respect eland marrow fat is without a superior.

The eland is quite easily tamed and could, I believe, with great advantage, be domesticated, and also crossed with native cattle, which doubtlessly would procure a superior race, for the milk of the eland cow is very fine and rich. Some government officials have been of the opinion that the eland should be withdrawn from the list of animals allowed to be killed without a special license, as they believe that, if domesticated, it would materially improve the native stock of the country. Elands have been easily brought over to the different zoölogical parks of the civilized world, and thrive in the open, even in England, if only protected during the coldest part of the winter.

The Roan antelope is another of the large and beautiful animals of this group. A few decades ago this animal was found almost all over Africa, from the vicinity of Cape Town up to the southern part of the Sahara Desert, with the only exception of the damp Congo forest. To-day the roan is totally exterminated in all parts of Southern Africa, below the Limpopo River. From this region, however, as far north as to the Upper Nile, the lovely roan still exists, although never in abundance, nor in such vast herds as many other antelopes.

The roan selects his feeding grounds with a great deal of care and " taste," and being very fond of good water, he is never found very far from some stream or water hole. He seems to love a parklike, half-open bush country with undulating hills. One of his favorite feeding grounds in British East Africa is the beautiful wooded valley on either side of the Uganda Railroad, between the

HEAD OF A LARGE BULL ELAND.

WOUNDED ROAN ANTELOPE, JUST BEFORE THE LAST CHARGE.
Shot near Muhoroni R. R. Station.

station Muhuroni and Kibigori, not far from the Victoria Nyanza. Here, on the northern side of the railroad, I went out for the first time to hunt the roan in January, 1910.

I arrived at Muhuroni railroad station after a long and tedious march of a whole day, during which I had severely injured my right leg in a successful attempt to scare off a number of actually charging Masai bulls. At the station I met two Englishmen, who had both been out for several days in the vicinity, looking for roan antelopes, but who saw only fresh tracks of them. They were very much discouraged, and told me that I had no chance whatever to get a roan, particularly as I was not in any condition to make a very long tour on foot. This part of the country lies rather low, and is very much hotter than most other parts of British East Africa. It is also infested by the dangerous tsetse fly, so deadly to horses that the hunter cannot with safety use ponies. This news was rather discouraging, but as I had come all the way to this place to hunt for a roan, I did not feel it fair to myself to give up before I had at least tried my luck for one day.

The Hindu station master at Muhuroni told me that in the country to the north of the station, some three miles away from the track, was a place near a little stream where I was most likely to find roan antelopes at this time of the year. With my right leg black and blue, and swelled to almost twice its size, I started out before four o'clock the following morning. Guided by the half-moon, shining down from a clear sky, we started off toward the region mentioned by the station master, with one of his private servants as an additional guide.

Every step hurt me so that it seemed as if it would have been a relief to scream, and the progress we made was rather slow. We had just descended a small ridge of hills, and were making for the stream of which the station master had spoken, when the sun rose. First, then, it became possible for me to scan the lovely parklike country all around with the powerful field glasses. After having searched for a few minutes, I soon discovered, to my indescribable joy, a big roan antelope all by himself, proudly walking along with slow strides and erect head, making for the source of the stream up among the mountains, some three miles farther away to our right. The roan was about eight hundred to nine hundred yards away from where we stood, and as there was absolutely no cover in a straight line between the antelope and us, we remained motionless, until a few minutes later the beautiful animal became partly hidden by trees and bushes. I saw that it was impossible for me in my condition to run down toward the river in time to get a shot at the animal before he would be too far away. I, therefore, sent two of my swiftest Kikuju men to run as carefully and fast as they could up along our side of the stream, crouching down in the high grass in open places, so that the roan should not be able to see them before they had reached the place where the river emerges from the mountains.

From there I told them to cross the stream and walk slowly down along the little river, one at fifty yards distance and the other about two hundred yards from the water, so that they would head the animal off and possibly make it return the same way it had come. In an instant the two light-footed savages ran off and soon disappeared among the bush and high grass. The rest of us made a bee-line for the river, so as to be ready on the other side, should the antelope return, as I had calculated. As quickly as I could with my wounded leg, we went down to the stream, which we immediately crossed. After having arrived on the other side, I left a string of men from the river up to a thick clump of bushes, some two hundred yards away from the water, where I sat down to watch developments.

Everything worked to perfection and exactly as I had calculated. The two runners had arrived just in time to turn the roan antelope back again, and as they, strangely enough, strictly obeyed instructions, and only walked slowly down without making any noise, the antelope simply strolled back in the same direction in which he had come up. I had only watched from behind the bushes for some four to five minutes, when my gun bearer first spied the antelope, and whispering " Anakuja " (" He comes "), pointed out the beautiful roan coming leisurely along at some seventy-five to eighty yards distance.

First taking a couple of snap shots, which unfortunately afterwards turned out to be too " thin," the light not being strong enough for so rapid exposures, I brought the animal down to his knees with a bullet from the 11 millimeter Mauser. Thinking that the roan now was too badly wounded to be able to escape, I exchanged the gun for the camera and cautiously walked toward the wounded antelope, the gun bearer, of his own accord, following very closely with the rifle. I had only gone a few yards, when the antelope suddenly jumped up and ran away, but after a few seconds stopped again and sank to his knees. Ad-

163

vancing as quickly as I could, so as to be able to secure another snap shot at closer quarters, and when within some fifteen yards of the animal, I took two successful pictures of the stately antelope. Once more he tried to get up, but this time, to my amazement, not with the intention of escaping, but with revenge in his mind. With lowered horns and uttering some strange-sounding bellowlike grunts, he rushed at me. Once more he went down on his knees, only a few yards away, when I had time to "snap him" again. Quickly I exchanged the camera for the rifle. This was hardly done, before the courageous roan made a last attempt to attack, but as he struggled to his feet, another shot put an end to his agony.

A large bull roan will reach five feet in height over the shoulders. He carries a pair of beautiful, sharp-pointed horns, curving backwards like a Turkish saber, and showing very marked, round year rings. The color of the grown-up animals varies from light brown to dark gray. The face is almost black, with lovely white patches of hair on the forehead, below the eyes, running down in a wedge-shape toward the nose. The roan is one of the few antelopes that carries a well-developed mane, which consists of very straight, coarse hair, about three to four inches in height. The under side of his neck and lower jaw, as well as part of his belly, is almost snow-white, which makes the skin of this animal very beautiful indeed.

The roan antelope goes, as a rule, in small herds of twelve to eighteen. They are very shy and wary, and belong to the most courageous of animals. It has often happened in South Africa, where this antelope was often hunted on horseback with a pack of dogs, that a wounded bull roan finished two or three hunting dogs before the sportsman got a chance to kill it with a shot at close range.

According to many hunters' opinion, the sable is the most beautiful of the large antelope family. He is somewhat smaller in the body than his cousin, the roan, but his horns are considerably larger and more beautiful, not seldom attaining a length of forty to forty-five inches, measured along the curve. At the base of the same there is a kind of bump over the eyes, from which the horns gracefully sweep backward in the same shape as those of the roan, and ending also in very sharp points. The year rings are well developed and beautifully marked, reaching almost to within three inches of the tips. The sable antelope has even more of a mane than the roan, and the patches of white below the eyes run out into a point near the nostrils, where they join the white streaks of the under jaw. The color of the upper part of the sable antelope's body is of a rich glossy black, strangely contrasted with the almost snow-white tint of his belly.

The sable is now rarely ever found south of the Orange River, and does not go farther north than to the southern part of British East Africa. In this protectorate he is only found in the hot and damp coast belt south and southwest of Mombasa. The richly wooded Shimba Hills, a day and a half's march from Mombasa, seem to be one of the favorite feeding grounds of this beautiful antelope. These hills can be reached either by marching overland most of the way, or else by hiring a dhow, which may take the hunting party for a good many miles southwest over the Kilindini Bay, from where it is only a short day's march to the shooting grounds. As the Shimba Hills and

165

their surroundings are practically the only places where the sable antelope can be hunted in British East Africa, it has been shot over a good deal of late, so that the horns of the remaining animals are not nearly as large and beautiful as those from German East Africa and Nyassaland. It was around these hills that Mr. Kermit Roosevelt, in the fall of 1909, succeeded in getting a couple of fairly good heads.

The sable antelope is one of the most wary animals and seems to be possessed of splendid eyesight, which makes him very difficult to stalk. He is nowhere very plentiful, and seldom seen in herds of more than twenty to forty animals, but more frequently met with in small bands of from ten to fifteen, males and females. If pursued, the sable antelope is capable of great speed, and as he also seems to possess a good deal of staying qualities, he is very hard, indeed, to overtake on horseback. However, if the country is not too rough or dense, a good horse will, as a rule, be able to catch up with this antelope, unless he has had too much of a start.

The sable, together with his cousin, the roan, are probably the two most courageous of the antelope family. If a bull sable is wounded and sees his pursuer at close quarters, he will invariably charge down on him with great speed and determination, and with his mighty horns he might be a very dangerous antagonist. In South Africa, where in former days he was also hunted with dogs, he often used to play great havoc with the pack, when they approached him too closely. The natives are very fond of making flutes of the horns of the sable antelope by cutting a couple of holes in the upper part of the hollow horn.

WOUNDED SABLE ANTELOPE.

SMALL HERD OF WILDEBEESTS, THE WHITE BEARDED GNU, SOTIK, 1909.

On this improvised flute they sometimes play for hours two or three notes, which, with the dull sound of the native drum for an accompaniment, constitutes the only " music " to the much-liked " ngoma," or native dance.

Of all antelopes, none is more curious looking and strangely behaving than the wildebeest, or gnu, as it is often called. There are a number of very closely allied species of the wildebeest, distributed from the northern parts of the Cape Colony up to Uganda and British East Africa. In the southern part of the latter protectorate the white-bearded gnu is one of the commonest game animals, sometimes seen even from the Uganda Railroad in herds of hundreds at a time. Mr. Selous describes the beast very characteristically in a few words when he says: " It appears to have the head of a buffalo, the tail of a horse, and the limbs and hoofs of an antelope."

The gnu has a short and broad head, and a very wide muzzle, fringed with coarse bristles of considerable length. The nostrils are large and very far apart, and the neck carries a stiff, erect mane, and is also covered with hair on the under side. The wildebeest's tail is unusually long and bushy, and is, both by settlers and natives, used as a fly switch and duster. The head looks in the distance just like that of a buffalo, the horns having nearly the same shape as those of the latter. They first curve somewhat downward and outward, afterwards bending the tips inward in a graceful sweep. The inner bony core of the gnu's horn is not solid, like those of most antelopes, but porous and honeycombed, like the horns of oxen and sheep. Both sexes carry horns, those of the males being much thicker and more rugged than the horns of the female. In very old bulls the base of the horns grow together as on the buffalo, forming a strong armor, which protects that part of the skull.

The gnu is as inquisitive as he is curious-looking. In places where he has not been much hunted, whole herds will gallop up to within two to three hundred yards to view the hunter and his party. There they will stand motionless for a few seconds, until one of the more wary and restless cows suddenly whirls around and gallops off in a semicircle, generally followed by the whole herd. Their bounds and leaps and " sham fights " are most amusing to observe. Sometimes the bulls will go down on their knees, fight and lock horns for a while, and then dash away again with the rest of the herd, switching their long tails and kicking high up in the air. All of a sudden the whole company swings around, like a well-drilled cavalry troup, and again faces the hunter.

By a little strategy and patience it is quite easy to come up close enough to a herd of wildebeest to be able to single out the largest bulls, although this antelope never frequents forest or bush country, where the sportsman can stalk behind some kind of cover. The gnu does not go very far away from water holes or rivers, where he often drinks, not only in the early morning and also at night, but sometimes even in the middle of the day. Whether this is unusual or not I am unable to say, for I have myself only once witnessed wildebeests drink in the daytime. It was on the southern Loita plains, not very far from the border of German East Africa, where I was resting one day to take lunch in the shadow of some mimosa trees, which grew along a good-sized water course. This was rather wide near our place, and still contained a good deal of water, although there had been no rains in this part of the country for many weeks. Suddenly my attention was called to a herd of about forty wildebeests, which were coming along almost in single file toward the widest stretch of the water course, and hardly more than eighty to ninety yards away from us. As they were crossing the water, a great many of them drank, while two bulls fought fiercely in mid-stream. As we were hoping to get some more lions in this vicinity, I did not molest the herd which, totally unaware of our presence, marched leisurely up on the other side of the river bed and began to feed again as they were moving along over the plains.

From the many bleached skulls of wildebeest, which we saw strewn about on these and other plains, I believe that the lions are very fond of " gnu steak," and that perhaps next to the zebra they prefer this kind of meat. I often noticed that old, stray bulls used to feed among little groups of zebra, and they always seemed to be on the best terms with each other. The gnu is a very cunning animal. When, for instance, he is hunted near the game preserves, he seems to know, almost to the foot, where the border of the preserves begins. As soon as he notices the hunter he gallops off at a great speed until he is within the protected zone. Then he whirls around and looks at him in defiance, switching his sides with his beautiful tail, evidently knowing that he is safe there.

The wildebeest also shows a great deal of vitality. I had once been trying for several hours to stalk an old bull gnu on the Athi Plains. When I finally succeeded in getting up to within two hundred yards of this fine-looking beast I shot at him with my little Mannlicher, " long distance " rifle. When I fired, the gnu stood on the slopes of a little hill, and about one hundred and fifty yards from the top of the same. As soon as he was hit, for I plainly heard the bullet strike the animal, he galloped off over the crest of the hill and disappeared. We ran as quickly as possible up to the top of the hill, as I thought the bull might stop on the other side, as soon as he was unable to see us any more, but coming up over the ridge we found him standing on the plains over four hundred yards farther away, with outspread legs and lowered head, his tail hanging straight down. Here he stood motionless for several seconds. Understanding that he must have been very severely wounded, I took the camera and ran down as fast as I could to photograph the animal before it should fall. I was really fortunate enough to get a couple of good pictures of the grand old bull before he fell. When dissecting the animal we found that I had by mistake used a steel-capped bullet in the 6 millimeter Mannlicher which, although it had gone through the heart and one of the lungs, had only made such a small hole that the animal was able to go as far as it did before it died.

One of the most curious experiences which I have ever had with any kind of an animal happened with an old gnu on the Sotik plains in 1909. Finding a splendid-looking bull standing alone, I ventured a shot with the small Mannlicher at the great distance of over three hundred and fifty yards. As soon as the gun cracked the animal went down in a heap and we all rushed forward to claim our trophy. As the horns were rather fine, I wanted to photograph the animal before we should begin to skin it, so I laid down the gun and went up with my camera to take a good photograph of the apparently dead gnu's head at only three yards' distance. Just as I had done this and was changing my film, I asked the men to turn the wildebeest over on the other side, which they at once proceeded to do. Some of the men got hold of the legs, others of the head and horns, and thus turned the antelope over.

Imagine our surprise when, just as he had been turned over, the gnu suddenly got up and ran away! The men and I were so amazed that we did not know what to do for a while, the old bull galloping off as fast as he could over the plains! As my gun was several yards away, the gnu succeeded in getting two or three hundred yards' start before I could shoot. The third shot broke the animal's back and he went down never more to move again. When we came up to the gnu we found that the first bullet had barely grazed his spine and so only stunned the animal for a moment. Had it been a rhino or a lion it might easily have been able to kill me before I could have gotten hold of the gun. Mr. Selous told me of having had several similar things happen to him, some of which I have related in previous chapters, and he argues from his great experience as a big-game hunter that it is the safest thing to put an extra bullet into any animal's head at a few yards' distance, even if the beast is apparently dead.

A great many " stories " have been told of gnus having attacked hunters, but I myself am unable to believe this antelope capable of any such ferocity. I have had opportunity to go up to several wounded gnus which, if they had been bent on mischief, certainly would have had the chance of charging, but they never showed the slightest intention of so doing, contrary to the courageous sable and roan antelopes.

In spite of the good game laws and other circumstances favorable for the survival and even the increase of the gnu, it seems to me that he has either diminished in some degree in British East Africa during the last four years, or else been cunning enough to take to the big-game preserves for the greater part of the year, for the number of wildebeest which I saw in 1906 was far greater than those I encountered four years later on practically the same ground.

CHAPTER XI

THE greater kudu is one of the most coveted prizes for the East African big-game hunter, not only because he is such a magnificent looking animal, but also because he is very hard to bag. The wide range of this beautiful antelope, so common years ago all the way from Cape Colony up through Central and Eastern Africa as far as to the Abyssinian Highlands, has of late years been materially shortened. Mr. Selous told me that the animal has now entirely disappeared from Cape Colony and is fast becoming very rare in all the countries south of the Limpopo River.

The kudu is fond of undulating and hilly country, but is often seen on level ground along rivers and lakes, if he only finds plenty of trees and dense bush to feed among. This stately antelope may dispense with the hills, but he will never be found on the plains or anywhere else where there is not an abundance of cover, such as wooded and bush country can afford. In the latter part of the dry season the kudu feeds chiefly on young and tender shoots and twigs of trees and bushes, particularly before the young grass has grown up after the regular grass fires kindled by the natives.

The kudu is not easily obtained, for he is nowhere very

numerous. He is generally found in pairs or in very small herds of six to ten, although I have heard that in certain parts of German East Africa it is not an uncommon thing to find as many as fifteen to twenty-five of these beautiful antelopes in one herd. They are also said to be fairly numerous in a few districts of Somaliland, where they are ruthlessly killed by the natives for the sake of the horns, which are brought over to Djibuti or Aden, and sold to the tourists, as the big steamers coal in these ports.

The kudu is next to the eland in size, attaining a height over the shoulders of from four feet four inches to four feet seven inches. The magnificent horns sometimes measure more than three and a half feet in a straight line. They have very sharp and well-defined ridges, running almost up to the very tips of the spiral-shaped horns. The female kudus carry no horns. The color of these antelopes varies from grayish and reddish brown in young males and females to a kind of bluish gray in old males, in which respect they are much akin to the eland. Like the latter, the kudu's skin is also marked with narrow, white stripes running down from the back. Its beautifully marked head carries several white spots, and a white V-shaped chevron between the eyes.

In British East Africa the kudu is rather scarce. In the Baringo district he was formerly very abundant, but was so much shot at there by British officers, garrisoned at Fort Baringo, and also by " safariing " sportsmen, that he was finally threatened with total extermination in that part of the country. The government has, therefore, now forbidden all kudu-hunting in the whole of the Baringo district. Another place where the kudu may be found, and where he is allowed to be shot at present, each sportsman being licensed one bull kudu, is the vicinity of the Kiu and Sultan Hamud stations on the Uganda Railroad. There he is sometimes found among the undulating, parklike, wooded hills and the dense jungle of mimosa and thorn trees. He is, however, very seldom obtained in this part of the country, for he is exceedingly shy and difficult to stalk, and seems to have learned, like the gnu, that if he returns into the nearby southern game preserve, he is safe from the hunters' persecution.

After many hours of tracking two kudus in these regions I once finally succeeded in getting up to the animals late in the afternoon. The day had been very hot and the wind rather uncertain, but after the noon hours a steady southeast breeze sprang up, which made it more easy to gain on the animals. It had rained quite hard in the morning, so that the clearly visible imprints of the hoofs made tracking comparatively easy, although for hours it seemed impossible to catch a glimpse of either of them. Finally, when we were almost completely exhausted, I, all of a sudden, obtained a perfect view of the pair, as I emerged from behind a clump of thick mimosa trees. There they stood, not one hundred yards away, both evidently listening intently, and standing on a small open space between dense bushes on either side. Unfortunately they were too much in the shade to be " snap shot " from where I stood. To my utter disappointment the pair consisted of a young bull with only half-grown horns, and a fawn. Although I had never shot a kudu before, I felt that I did not want to disturb the peace of this pair. After having admired the

175

beautiful antelopes for a few seconds longer, we retraced our steps without even having frightened the animals.

The water buck is an entirely different species of antelope. Although not much smaller than the kudu, standing sometimes fully four feet at the withers, and having powerful, sometimes almost lyre-shaped, horns of considerable size, yet the water buck cannot be compared with the kudu as to beauty. The skin of the water buck has an abundance of long, coarse hair, and his tail is short and bushy. The color of his skin varies considerably from light brown and almost dark red to bluish gray, with white stripes over the eyes. He has also patches of white on the throat and muzzle, while on the buttocks there is a large half-moon-like field of white which extends above the tail, the hair of which on the sides and the end is often white.

The water buck is, as his name implies, very fond of water. He is a great swimmer and often stands for hours belly-deep in the stream eating the tender leaves and shoots of water plants. Strangely enough, this aquatic antelope sometimes roams quite far away from his favorite element, and seems then to prefer steep and stony hills, up and down which he is capable of running with great precision and speed. If disturbed, the water buck will instantly make for the nearest river or lake, and there seek his safety in hiding among reeds and rushes. I have several times seen the animal more than a mile from the nearest water hole or stream; in fact, once a female water buck showed us a much-needed water hole, so completely surrounded with high grass and bush that we should probably not have found it, had not the frightened antelope made its way there.

Another time in trekking along the Guaso Nyiro we came upon an unusually large herd of water buck, containing at least thirty animals, among which I easily singled out a very fine old bull with magnificent horns. There were also a great many females in the herd and several very small "babies." The water bucks were all feeding a few hundred yards away from the river on the stony slopes of a hill, but as soon as they observed us they made a bee-line for the stream. I fired at the big buck, which brought up the rear of the fleeing herd. As he received the bullet he tumbled over, making a complete somersault, but regaining his equilibrium in the next instant, he got up and reached the water before I had a chance to fire at him again. When we came down to the river's edge we could see no trace of any of the animals until one of the men detected the mighty horns of the wounded bull among the reeds only some thirty yards away from us. The cunning animal, when it saw that it could not escape with the rest of the herd, had submerged its whole body in the river until only the head stuck up out of the water! I believe that if he had not moved his head he would not have been discovered, but now he was detected and dispatched with another shot through the brain. The water was rather deep; two of the men, however, volunteered to swim out and bring the buck ashore, for which they received an extra " bakshish."

There are several kinds of closely allied species of the water buck, the most common in British East Africa being the Cobus defassa. On one of my trips to East Africa I shot a water buck which seemed to be somewhat different from the ordinary Cobus defassa. The skin of this animal, which I shot on the Laikipia Plateau, I later presented to the Royal Swedish Academy of Science in Stockholm to be mounted for the Museum of Natural History. I mentioned at the time to the curator that I thought it might be a new species. I was more than delighted, therefore, when a few weeks later I received a letter from Prof. Einar Lönnberg, inquiring about when and where this animal had been shot, as he had found that it evidently represented a new subspecies, which he described in a pamphlet issued by the "K. Svenska Vetenskapsakademien in Stockholm, Band 4, No. 3."

As the reader may be interested in the characteristics of this new subspecies, I will here reprint the Professor's own description:

"*Cobus defassa tjaderi* (*new subsp.*)

"The typical Cobus defassa (Ruppell) is a well-known animal, distinguished from its nearest allies (those which are, like the defassa, provided with a white rump-patch), by its rather long and somewhat pointed ears, a white patch on the upper throat, the red color of the forehead and the general rufous brown coloration of the body.

"The specimen presented by Mr. Tjader, and named after him, undoubtedly belongs to the defassa group, but it differs so much from the typical form that I believe it must at least provisionally be regarded as representing a new geographic subspecies. This difference makes itself known especially in the much dark areas, which later may be seen on the accompanying figure of the skin.

"The black of the face extends above the white ring round the muzzle upward to above the middle of the white eye-stripe and on the sides to the corner of the mouth. It has thus a considerably greater extension than in the true

SMALL WATER BUCK, KILLED ON LAIKIPIA.
Found to be a new subspecies of the *defassa* family and subsequently called
"*Cobus defassa tjaderi.*"

SEMI-TAME FEMALE WATER BUCK NEAR THE SOTIK PLAINS.

defassa. The white eye-stripe is clear and well defined, but does not extend farther backward than over the anterior third of the eye. Above the black face the forehead is bright rufous, somewhat mixed with black. The sides of the face behind the lateral extension of the black have the same color as the forehead, except that the region from below the eye to the root of the ear is paler, buffish brown, shading into whitish at the ear. The sides and the under parts of the lower jaw behind the clear white chin are dark brown, somewhat mixed with hoary white from the basal parts of the hair. The back of the ears is rufous, but with broad white areas on either side; the tip is black and the inside white.

" The upper side of the neck is rufous with black tips to the hairs, but the sides and the lower parts of the neck behind the white throat patch is of a mixed grayish brown color, produced by the hairs having their distal parts blackish and their basal parts light gray and partly rufous. The color of the body is also mixed in a peculiar manner. It is dark brown, in some light, almost blackish brown, but to a certain degree mixed with red. This is effected by the hairs having long black tips and rufous bases, and besides some scattered hairs are (basally or wholly) whitish. Toward the root of the tail and at the borders of the white rump-patch the rufous color is more dominating, but otherwise the whole animal is much darker than the rufous brown typical Cobus defassa. The hairs are rather short, only measuring about 2 cm. on the back and sides.

" The under parts are dark brownish gray, the distal parts of the hairs being dark smoky brown, and the basal parts hoary gray. The posterior of the belly, from the inguinal tract to around the naval, is whitish with long hairs. At the prepuce a tuft of brown hairs is placed. The legs and feet are black with a brownish shade in front. A

179

narrow white line rounds the hoofs. The tail is proximally colored like the back; distally it is almost black, and so is the tuft; below it is white. Its length without the tuft is about 32 cm. The length of the ears is about 22 cm.

"The horns appear to be rather short and stout and less curved when compared with a typical defassa. Their length along the anterior curvature is about 48 cm. and their basal circumference about 18.5 cm. They are provided with 20 rings. This shortness of the horns is not due to youthfulness, as the animal, to judge from the well-worn molars, might be termed middle-aged.

"Basal length of skull......................... 374 mm.
Length of nasals............................. 165 "
Distance from gnathion to orbit............... 253 "
Length of upper molar series................. 99 "

"This water buck was shot by Mr. Tjader the 5th of September, 1906, to the west of the junction of the rivers Guaso Narok and Guaso Nyiro, that is in the northwestern part of the Laikipia Plateau."

I may mention in this connection that I was fortunate enough to bring home at least two other new species of East African mammals, one being a small dwarf antelope, or dik-dik, the other a different species of bush buck, which latter has gone to the American Museum of Natural History in New York and received the name "Tragelaphus tjaderi."

The impala, often also called "Pala" and "Impalla," is one of the most graceful of antelopes. A full-grown impala stands only from three feet to three feet three inches high, but appears to be much larger, as the animal carries its head a good deal higher than most antelopes do. The horns of young males form a perfect lyre, but as the animal grows older they spread out more, turning first forward, then in a bold sweep backward, and then forward again, so that the horns, seen from the side, almost form an " S." The year rings are few and very widely spread, and do not reach more than about one half the length of the horn, which ends in a slender and very sharp point. The horns of the impala vary from some twenty to twenty-four inches, measured in a straight line; the female of this species has no horns. The color of the impala is reddish, which in young animals sometimes turns to almost bright red, which merges at the flanks into a snow-white belly.

The impala is very common in Southern, Central, and East Africa. It often goes in large herds of from twenty to one hundred, and sometimes even more. The animal loves sandy plains dotted with low scrub and thorn bush, but is fond of water, and never goes far away from some supply of this kind. In fact, some hunters say that the very presence of an impala guarantees that there is water in the neighborhood. I have several times noticed large herds of impala without a single grown-up male among them, and I have also on several occasions found small bands of bucks by themselves, generally following some old, magnificent animal which, in spite of its beautiful horns, has escaped the sportsmen.

Every observer of big game in Africa will bear me out when I say that the impala is certainly one of the swiftest animals in existence. It is a wonderful sight, indeed, to see a herd of impala fall into the most graceful gallop, when frightened, making leaps over high bushes and broad streams, throwing, like the race horse, the front legs almost flat under the belly as they bound. I have myself actually measured some of the longest jumps I saw an impala take and found that one young buck, which I had slightly wounded, had leaped clear over a bush, the highest point of which was five feet from the ground, apparently without touching the leaves. I found that this one leap measured exactly twenty-four feet and three inches. The next bound of the same animal measured nineteen feet four inches. I have heard of instances where impalas have leaped as far as twenty-five and twenty-six feet, which seems almost incredible for an animal of its size.

When a herd is suddenly startled, they go off in most beautiful, gliding motions, and they can keep these up for a great distance, racing over the ground at high speed. When suddenly disturbed they often eject a certain sharp, barklike sound, not unlike the cry of a wooing bush buck. Impalas are hardly ever seen on the plains, and they also avoid thick forests, being fond of a parklike country with low scrub, as before mentioned. Once on the Laikipia Plateau I succeeded in chasing an impala out of cover into a large open space, when my " lion rider," Asgar, pursued it on a swift hunting pony in the wildest gallop. Yet it was utterly impossible for him to gain on the antelope which, after a few minutes' flight, disappeared among a little clump of bush.

Like most of the African antelopes the vitality of the impala is remarkable. On one of my marches to the government station at Rumuruti, where I wanted to visit a British official, I wounded a young impala, which bounded off like the wind in front of us. It was, indeed, as if he had been shot out of a gun, and we all thought that I

SPLENDID IMPALA FROM LAIKIPIA.

HEAD OF LARGE BULL ORYX.

must have missed him, from the speed he maintained before he disappeared from our sight. A few minutes after this, our whole caravan sat down for its lunch and " pumzika," or rest, which the porters always enjoy whenever they have a chance. After more than an hour's rest we took up our trail again, and when we had marched at least three miles farther we saw a great many vultures circling close over the ground some fifty yards away from the little path which we were following. Being curious to see what kind of animal the vultures were about to devour, I ordered a halt and started off to investigate. Imagine my surprise when I here found the beautiful impala, which we did not even think I had wounded, and which had run all this distance before it expired! When cutting the animal open we found that the bullet had gone right through the cavity of the chest, severing one of the large arteries, which resulted in the filling up of the whole cavity and intestines with blood before the animal succumbed.

The meat of the impala, as well as that of the water buck, is not very appetizing, and is, particularly if the animal is old, or has been killed at the end of the dry season, quite bitter. The impala seems to belong to the " exclusive set," for I have never found impalas feeding together with animals of any other kind as so many other antelopes do. Of course it is impossible for me to state positively that the impala never does mingle with other animals, but it has never come under my own notice, and none of the sportsmen and natives, whom I questioned on this topic, had observed the same.

The oryx is another beautiful antelope. It is somewhat larger than the impala, standing as high as four feet

183

one to two inches at the withers. There are five somewhat different species of the oryx family, all of which have nearly straight, long horns, slightly curving backward and growing out almost in line with their straight foreheads. The neck of some of the species has a small mane and also tufts of hair on the throat, while the tail is long and bushy. The oryx family is at present spread over the greater part of South and East Africa, Somaliland, Arabia, and even as far north as Syria.

The most common of the oryx family in East Africa is the lovely oryx beisa. This species is distinguished by not having any tufts of hair on the throat and by its white face being marked with a large patch of black which covers the greater part of the forehead under the horns with the exception of the nose. Then it has two smaller black patches which surround the eyes, and thence run down like a wide ribbon to where the slit of the lips begins. The color of the oryx beisa is a kind of dark bluish gray, separated from the almost snow-white belly by a wide, raven black stripe on either side.

The horns of this species are very nearly straight, only slightly curving backward, and they have well-defined year rings, reaching up about two thirds of the horn, which tapers up to a very slender and exceedingly sharp point. The average length of good oryx horns is from twenty-eight to thirty-two inches, but horns of a male have been recorded as large as thirty-six and a half inches, and thirty-eight inches of a female. The horns of the female are, as in most cases where female antelopes carry horns, much thinner. This beautiful oryx loves arid country of a parklike nature. Like the impala, it never frequents the plains, neither is it found in deep forests. The animal is said to be able to get along with very little water, which explains the fact that it frequents such dry countries as parts of East Africa, Somaliland, and Arabia.

The oryx beisa are very often seen in considerable numbers, herds of forty or more being not uncommonly encountered. Like the impala, they sometimes go in great herds of only females, while small batches of rams roam around by themselves. It is not an uncommon thing to find a lone old male feeding away off from the rest of his family. The oryx is one of the very few antelopes which, like the roan and sable, shows a great deal of courage and pluck if wounded and cornered.

My first experience with an oryx beisa was a very memorable one. It might, therefore, interest the reader if I quote the same from my diary: " One beautiful morning in July, 1906, we had left our camp near the southern end of Lake Hannington, where we had pitched our tents on the eastern banks of a small, hot stream of crystal-clear, good-tasting water, which came bubbling up from under some rocks a few hundred yards away from the place selected for our camp. After having walked a few hours without seeing anything worth shooting at, my gun bearer and two Wandorobo guides simultaneously noticed fresh oryx tracks. Instantly we took them up, walking along with a great deal of care and expectation.

" I had never as yet seen a ' choroa,' the native word for the oryx beisa, and was, therefore, most anxious to secure a good head or two. After having followed the track for a few minutes it merged into a whole network of evidently fresh oryx track, which led down to a large water hole a little farther to our left. As we approached it, we saw from the number of tracks that we could easily make out in and around the shallow water, that there must have been hundreds of oryx around the place during the last few days. As it was utterly impossible for us to find the freshest tracks which led away from the pool, we started off in a northwesterly direction, following a small valley, jammed in between two rather high and steep ridges of wooded hills. After having gone along for another twenty minutes, looking all the time for fresh tracks, we heard a noise as that of galloping zebras, and looking up we saw at a distance of some one hundred and fifty yards a herd of from fifty to sixty oryx, which swiftly galloped away at a right angle to our line of march. They were racing down from the escarpment to our right and evidently intending to run up on the opposite one.

"Being always ready for any emergency like this, I aimed quickly, although the gun bearer said it was useless to try to hit the animals at such a distance. I fired three shots at two large bulls before they disappeared behind some bush. We took up the chase 'on the run,' and soon found that both animals had been slightly wounded. As fast as we could we ran after the antelopes up to the top of the escarpment. As we carefully peered above the highest stones, we saw the herd slowly walking off at a distance, switching their long tails, while the wounded animals lingered behind. They were not more than about one hundred yards away from us, as we emerged from over the crest. Quicker than I can describe it I fired again with the .405 Winchester with the result that both animals went down. One of them was some thirty yards nearer to us than the other and was killed on the spot by the second bullet, which had broken his back.

" As soon as I had measured this beautiful specimen and given it over to the second gun bearer and a couple of other men to do the skinning, I went with the first gun bearer and a few other men to the other antelope, which had fallen a little farther away. This fellow, Mabruki, was always very anxious to cut the throat of any animal before it was ' stone dead,' as he otherwise, being a strict Mohammedan, would not eat the meat. Seeing that this oryx was not as large as the first one, I told Mabruki that he could put his knife in the throat of the antelope, near the chest, while I took up the tape measure and got the camera ready to take a ' picture study ' at close quarters. Just as I was examining the camera to see if everything was ready for a time exposure I heard Mabruki scream. As I looked up I saw the wounded oryx trying to spear him with his long and sharp horns. Dropping the camera, I quickly gave the furious animal another shot, which ended his life. As the oryx was trying to get at the gun bearer, he ejected some ugly-sounding, barking grunts, and I am sure that if I had not been so quick with the gun this time, Mabruki would have been gored by the courageous beast."

My largest oryx I obtained on the Laikipia Plateau a couple of months later. The horns of this big bull measured, the one twenty-eight and one half inches, and the other one quarter of an inch less, the very tip having been broken off some time previously. Once I noticed that an oryx which we secured near Mt. Kenia must in younger years have had a bad fall from some precipice, for the tips of both horns had been knocked over so that they formed almost perfect hooks. Big scratches on the skin of this oryx and an old wound on his right thigh showed that he had probably just escaped from a lion or a leopard, when he tumbled down the precipice in his mad attempt to escape from the bloodthirsty feline.

In the southeastern part of the protectorate the Oryx callotis, or " fringed-eared " oryx, is found. The face of this species is more of a fawn-color than that of the beisa, and has very sharply pointed ears with black tufts of long hair. The Oryx callotis is somewhat smaller than the beisa and is quite common in the Kilimanjaro district, and on either side of the Uganda Railroad between the stations, Voi and Simba, where he inhabits the sandy scrub and thorn country both in the game preserve and in the district to the northeast of the railroad.

The Grant's gazelle is without a question the finest-looking specimen of the smaller antelopes which are generally classed as gazelles. They are all of medium or small size and comprise a number of species found both in Asia and in most parts of Africa. These gazelles are animals of which both sexes carry horns, except in a few species, which are all confined to Asia. The gazelles frequent, as a rule, dry and sandy country. They prefer open plains, although some of them will occasionally be found in thin scrub or bush country. They will, however, never enter dense jungle or large forests.

The handsome Grant's gazelle was discovered some fifty years ago by the well-known explorers Speke and Grant, after which latter the species received its name. This gazelle is found in great numbers in East Africa any-

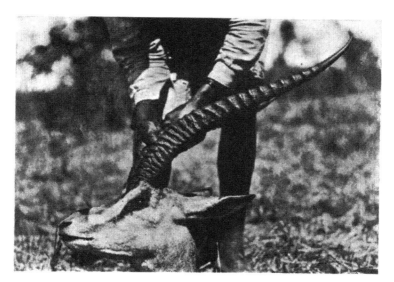

Fine Head of the Graceful Grant's Gazelle.

Wounded Grant's Gazelle, Fighting Mabruki, the Gun Bearer.

where south of Lake Rudolph, wherever the country suits his requirements. Like all true gazelles, he is mostly found on the vast plains, but is sometimes seen in very open bush country. They go in large herds, numbering any-where from a dozen to one hundred and fifty or more, and are not " exclusive " like the impala, but are often met browsing together with other animals, such as the zebra, hartebeest, oryx, and the little Thomson's gazelle, with which they seem to live on terms of great intimacy. This latter, a little fellow, generally called " Tommy," is so much like the Grant's in coloring and general build that he is often mistaken for the same at long distance. A careful observer, however, need not make this mistake, for the horns of the Grant's gazelle are much more developed than those of the " Tommy," and the latter is always switching his tail to and fro while he is feeding, which the former very seldom does.

The Grant's gazelle stands a little less than three feet above the shoulders. The color of his skin is dull fawn, separated from the snow-white belly by dark brown bands on the flanks. The beautiful head is marked with an almost black rufous band, which runs back from the upper part of the nose to the base of the horns. White stripes and other narrow black ribbons separate this band from the fawn-colored under part of the head and face. The very regularly ringed horns are most gracefully curved, bending first a little forward, then backward, and then again forward, while they also spread out consider-ably sideways. The local variety, obtained in the central and southern parts of British East Africa, has the horns much more spread out than the species the sportsman will find on the Laikipia Plateau and other places in the northern parts of the protectorate. There they are more often seen in open bush country than anywhere else in East Africa.

This beautiful antelope is an exceedingly keen-sighted little chap, and so wary that he is very hard to stalk, particularly in localities where he has been much disturbed. In most parts of East Africa he will now, as a rule, run away long before the hunter comes within two hundred to two hundred and fifty yards of the herd, but even this distance is not nowadays to be considered a very great one, when the sportsman uses such wonderful weapons as the 6.5 millimeter Mannlicher, with which he can shoot with accuracy from fifty to three hundred yards without having to change the sights.

The meat of the Grant's gazelle is most excellent and far superior to that of most other antelopes, with the possible exception of the eland, oryx, and little " Tommy." If caught when young, the graceful Grant's gazelle soon becomes very tame, and follows his captor around like a dog. The vitality of these comparatively small animals is nothing short of marvelous. They require, indeed, as some sportsman has said, " much lead " before they can be stopped. I have several times seen Grant's gazelles wounded in a way that would instantly knock down almost any kind of deer in Europe or America, and yet keep running for hundreds of yards before they fall from exhaustion.

When I first came out to Africa, I thought that a soft-nosed bullet would be unnecessarily powerful for these little antelopes, and that their skin would be too much cut up by the same, so that I used steel-capped bullets instead. These seemed, however, to have so little effect upon the animal that I soon came to the conclusion that it was too cruel and unprofitable to use anything but the regular, deadly " dum-dum " bullet. If wounded and cornered the Grant's gazelle sometimes gives vent to harsh barks, somewhat similar to those of an angry goat. Each sportsman is now allowed to kill but three of these lovely little antelopes, but as a good many settlers shoot numbers of them every year for food, and some of the best grazing lands are being rapidly taken up for cultivation or fenced in for cattle, the time may come when the Grant's gazelle will become very rare and perhaps exterminated, except in the game preserves.

CHAPTER XII

THE HARTEBEEST AND ZEBRA

THE hartebeests are certainly the ugliest looking of all antelopes. They are easily recognizable from all other game, even at long distance, by their peculiarly shaped heads, long, straight and narrow faces, and pointed noses. Another characteristic of the most common, or Cook's hartebeest, is the singular twist of the horns. When the animal looks straight at a person, it appears as if it had a double set of ears, the horns growing out from the forehead at almost right angles over the ears, leaving a space between of some three to four inches. Another thing which makes the hartebeest so different looking from all other antelopes is his contrast in build, standing a great deal higher at the withers than over the pelvis.

There are several species of hartebeest in British East Africa, of which the Jackson's and Cook's are the most common. These two differ from each other chiefly in their color and shape of horns. The Jackson's hartebeest has a more light reddish brown hue than the Cook's, and his horns differ very much from the latter's; they first turn upward a few inches, then curve slightly outward and again upward, after which they bend in almost a right angle backwards. I also believe, from specimens that I have shot, that if there is any difference in size, the Jackson's hartebeest is the larger of the two. He is also rarer than the other, and is only found in the northern and western parts of the protectorate, where his favorite haunts seem to be the upper Rift Valley, on the northwestern end of the Naivasha Plateau, and in the Nyando Valley, to the east of Victoria Nyanza.

The first specimen of Jackson's hartebeest that I was fortunate in securing, was shot near Lake Hannington, and had horns that were over twenty-four inches long. This bull was by far the largest hartebeest that I killed during my three expeditions to Africa. The animal showed a most remarkable vitality. I discovered it one day when we were returning to camp, after having had a successful oryx hunt. The big bull stood alone on a little opening on the sparsely wooded sides of a little hill. As we were all tired from a long day's tramp, having been continuously " on the go " from before five o'clock in the morning, I did not care to go far out of my way, but fired at the hartebeest at a distance of some two hundred and fifty yards. As the gun cracked, he bounded off in big leaps and soon disappeared among the trees. Sending one of our trackers to the spot, where we had seen the hartebeest, to examine whether there were any blood marks on the ground, we sat down to rest for a few minutes. Suddenly we heard the tracker shouting: " Damu mingi, Bwana! " (" Much blood, sir! ")

Instantly we made for the place as quickly as we could, thence following the blood tracks for over two hundred yards. There, under a good-sized mimosa tree, lay the big bull, dead. When we skinned him, we found that the soft-nosed bullet had not expanded, the distance being too great, but had gone clear through the upper part of the heart; yet the hartebeest had been able to gallop off as if nothing had happened. It was in very fine condition, was carefully measured and skinned, and afterwards given to the American Museum of Natural History in New York City.

The most common of hartebeests in British East Africa is the Cook's, or, as he is very often called, both by sportsmen and natives, the "Kongoni," which is certainly one of the most ungainly looking animals. The color of the kongoni is of a dark reddish brown, merging in the flanks and belly into an almost ash gray. He stands in proportion higher over the withers than the Jackson's hartebeest, and has a pronounced "hump" on the shoulders. This animal may still be seen in large herds in most parts of central and southern East Africa, and I have counted as many as three to four hundred feeding closely together. The kongoni loves the company of other game, and is often seen browsing among large herds of zebra and wildebeest.

Few animals are as inquisitive as the hartebeest. In localities where he has not been much hunted, he will run up to within one hundred and fifty yards or less of the hunter, then whirl around and face the two-legged intruder for a while, tossing his head quickly up and down. If the sportsman stands still, the kongoni might remain in the same position for several seconds, until he again swings around, makes a half circle, and returns to view the visitor in the same way. In localities where he has been much disturbed he will not show as much curiosity

BEAUTIFUL HEAD OF THE GRANT'S GAZELLE.

AN EXCEPTIONALLY FINE HEAD OF JACKSON'S HARTEBEEST, SHOT NEAR
LAKE HANNINGTON.

as cunning in getting away, often running up on ant-hills, or other elevations, to have a better view of the surrounding country.

Few animals are, I believe, as much hated by the hunters in general as the kongoni, for he is one of the most wary and keen-sighted beasts in existence. Innumerable times it has spoiled the day for the sportsman, because it startled the game, which, until then, he had been successfully stalking. I have myself repeatedly been thus disturbed by this animal, which will always try to play tricks on the hunter, warning and frightening the other game. Even if the hartebeest should be several hundred yards off, and the hunter stalk his game in a different direction, this bothersome animal will gallop off in a half circle to intercept the intended line of the attack, and thus scare off all the game in the vicinity.

This hartebeest also shows great vitality and is capable of a marvelous speed. Few antelopes are as hard to overtake, even when wounded. If not wounded, and not taken by surprise before he can get a start, there is hardly a hunting horse in existence that can outdistance a full-grown hartebeest; for they are not only exceedingly swift, but seem to be able to gallop with undiminished speed for almost any length of time. In British East Africa the hartebeest is also hated by the settlers for different reasons. In the first place, he is said to spread the dreaded cattle diseases; and then herds of hartebeest have often broken down and demolished miles of fencing, made to keep the cattle together. Previous to this year each sportsman was allowed ten hartebeests on his license, but on account of their destructiveness to the settlers, each hunter can now, if he chooses, kill twenty during the twelve months that his license is in force.

It is remarkable that the hartebeests are able to secure their feed on the sun-scorched plains, where to the human observer there is scarcely any grass to be had, and yet they always seem to be in good condition. And as for water, I believe the hartebeest can go for days without that precious liquid, getting perhaps enough moisture from the dew on the grass in the morning. The kongoni is one of the antelopes which constitute the principal menu of the lion and leopard. Several of the hartebeests that I killed showed unmistakable marks of having had narrow escapes from the big felines. If these should fail to get hold of the kongoni in their first leap, they would never be able to overtake him again. The hartebeest is a pronounced dweller of the plains. Neither the Jackson's nor the Cook's hartebeest are fond of real jungle, although both of them may sometimes feed in very open bush or parklike country. The meat of these antelopes is, as a rule, very good, although they have hardly any fat, in which respect they are like most all other African antelopes, with the exception of the eland and oryx.

The kongoni is hard to stalk in places where he has been much hunted. The best method seems to be to continue to walk straight for him, as quietly as possible. He will then run away at three or four hundred yards, but only gallop a short distance, and then turn around again to look at his pursuer. I have found that if I ran after the beast, as it turned and galloped off, but instantly stopped and began to walk slowly at the very moment the antelope turned around to face me, I could often, with a little patience and endurance, come up to within two hundred yards of it, which distance is not very great to a man armed with modern, long-distance guns. The young bull hartebeests often fight with each other in the most determined way, although perhaps not as frequently as the wildebeests do. I once shot a hartebeest which had evidently been in some kind of a desperate fight, for his left horn had been broken, but had not fallen off at the time; afterwards it had knit again in such a way that it pointed straight downward back of the ear, instead of upward and then backward.

As the traveler goes up country from Mombasa he may, if he has luck, see a good many animals from the track, such as giraffes, rhinos, wildebeests, zebras and even lions, but it is absolutely certain that he will see herds of hartebeests on both sides of the railroad before he reaches Nairobi. From my own observation, I believe it is correct to say that in the last three or four years the vast numbers of this antelope have greatly diminished. Whether this is a sign that the Cook's hartebeest is being threatened with extermination, or if it only shows his cunning in wandering over to the game preserve, as the wildebeests are so fond of doing, I cannot say; but the enormous herds, years ago always found on the Athi Plains, for instance, have certainly perceptibly decreased.

During one of the trips on the northeastern parts of these plains we very nearly lost our whole caravan. It happened in the following way:

We had marched that day somewhat over twenty miles, mostly over open plains, and exposed to the hot rays of the sun during the whole time. I had, as usual, gone ahead of the rest with our naturalist, Mr. Lang, two gun bearers, and two or three porters who carried our cameras. We knew that there was no water to be had except at a certain stream, which we hoped to reach before sunset. Suspecting that we might be able to find lions on these plains, we increased our lead more and more, so that the noise made by the bulk of the men should not frighten any beasts away from our line of march.

About two o'clock in the afternoon we went over a little hill, from where we had a good view over the country. We now saw the caravan a couple of miles behind us, but did not worry, being reasonably sure that the men would be able to trace our steps through the grass and reach us before the evening. A little after four o'clock we arrived at a small stream, where we decided to camp for the night, and made ourselves comfortable, while we were waiting for the men. We sat down, and I took my field glasses to see if any game animal was near. To my surprise I detected only a few hundred yards away from us five or six giraffes, which were slowly walking off toward the bush north of us.

Although very much tired out, I grasped my gun, asked Mabruki to come along, and started in pursuit of the giraffes. A few seconds later Mr. Lang and two of the other men followed us. After only a few minutes' walk, during which we had not been noticed by the giraffes, we had come close enough to shoot. I singled out the one that we thought was the largest bull, and fired. The animal fell to its knees, but rose again in a few seconds, when it received another bullet, which ended its life.

When Mr. Lang and the other two men arrived, we were very much puzzled what to do, as night was coming on, and the place we had selected for the camp being more than two miles distant. Having taken the correct measurements of the beautiful giraffe, I proposed that Mr. Lang, with the assistance of the gun bearer and the two porters, should skin the animal, while I was to return to the camping place, whence I should send back men with lanterns to bring the skin to camp.

When I came near to the place, where we had left the last of our men, I found, to my great surprise, that he was still alone, and that not another man of the caravan was in sight. This porter told me with the greatest excitement that he had seen some of the men of the caravan in the far distance, marching off in a different direction. He thought that the whole safari was lost, and that we would now have to sleep without tents, food, or anything. This was, indeed, not a very bright outlook, as that particular place was noted for its abundance of lions, leopards, and other dangerous game.

I took the expedition flag and, ordering the porter to follow me, ran up on a high ant-hill nearby. From this place I finally saw with the glasses some four or five men, with loads on their heads, march off in another direction about two miles away, soon disappearing among the bushes. I shouted at the top of my lungs and fired several shots with the big elephant gun, while I had the men wave the " Stars and Stripes." After a few anxious moments I noticed some men standing together in a little opening, as if consulting with each other. Again I fired the big gun several times. To my delight I now saw the men turn in our direction and move forward. As the sun by this time had already set and it began to darken, we quickly made a fire with grass and dry branches to further attract the attention of the lost safari.

About half an hour later our whole caravan was gathered together at the camping ground. Some men were then dispatched with lanterns to the place where the giraffe had fallen, whence they returned a couple of hours later with the beautiful trophy. I found that the reason why the men had gone astray was that they had seen a small native path going off in a different direction from where we were marching, and, not being able to see us, they believed that we had taken that way. I now learned that if we had thought of it at the time, and put a bunch of grass or some sticks across the path, the natives would not have followed it, but kept on straight ahead, looking for our tracks in the grass.

The zebra is one of the finest-looking wild animals in Africa. It is, indeed, very interesting to watch a large herd of them as they feed, play, or gallop off on the vast plains. Their black and white stripes make them appear, in the distance, as if the whole animal were either black or white, according as they appear in the sunlight or shadow. It is rather remarkable how the zebra is able to blend with its surroundings in grass country and among thin bush, so that, to the unaccustomed eye, it is hard to make it out at a distance, if it is standing still. The zebra is exclusively a native of Africa, where there are at present three distinct species—the Mountain, the Grevey's, and the Burchell's zebra.

Of these, the beautiful mountain zebra was formerly very common in the whole of South Africa, frequenting the rugged hills and big mountain forests all over Cape Colony. It has been so decimated during the last decades of the old century by the settlers of that country, that it is now almost extinct in the whole of South Africa, except in a few districts, where it is entirely protected by law. This species is the smallest of the three, standing hardly four feet at the withers. It has a comparatively short, erect, thick mane, long ears, and legs, which are striped all the way down to the hoofs.

In East Africa only the two last-named varieties are found. The Grevey's zebra the hunter meets mostly in the country to the south and east of Lake Rudolph, in a line toward Mt. Kenia. From here it ranges up to the central part of Somaliland. It is hardly ever seen to the west of Lake Rudolph, nor to the south of Mt. Kenia. The Grevey's zebra is the largest of the family, reaching a height of almost five feet over the shoulder. It differs from the more common Burchell's zebra, not only in size, but also in the color and number of its stripes. Those of the Grevey's are very much narrower, and, therefore, more numerous than the stripes of the Burchell's zebra, while the color of the former is of a much deeper black and snow-white color than that of the latter. Another difference between the two species is the stripes on the legs, which in the case of the Burchell's hardly run below the knees, whereas in the Grevey's zebra they extend right down to the hoofs, as in the true mountain zebra. Then, the belly and the insides of the upper part of the legs of the Grevey's zebra are almost pure white, and the ears are in proportion larger than those of the Burchell's zebra. The stripes of this latter animal are considerably wider, and the color of them is often dark brown instead of black, and yellowish cream instead of pure white. Very often a darker " shade line " runs down the center of the light stripes. The ears are, in comparison, smaller and more rounded, and the lower parts of the legs, above the hoofs, pure white.

In the northwestern part of Laikipia, not very far to the east of Lake Baringo, I once shot a zebra which seemed to be a kind of link between the aforenamed species. It had larger and more narrowly striped ears than those of the Burchell's zebra, while it was also larger in the body, and had the stripes on the legs running almost down to the hoofs. It may just have been a " freak," or possibly a cross-breed between the Grevey's and the Burchell's zebra, for it certainly had characteristics common to both of these animals.

The zebra is, perhaps, the most common of all African big game. It is simply met with everywhere, from the hot, sun-scorched plains in the southern and southwestern parts of the protectorate to the more temperate Laikipia Plateau, and even upon the chilly foothills of Mt. Kenia, where I have found this beautiful animal as high as between seven and eight thousand feet. From what I have heard from other big-game hunters, this is probably not very usual, but I have more than once met zebras at altitudes of over seven thousand feet, and once shot a Burchell's zebra on the southwestern slopes of Kenia, where we found a little herd of ten to twelve animals at an altitude of actually somewhat over eight thousand feet!

The only places which these two species of zebra seem to shun altogether are the damp forest regions around the Indian Ocean and the large forests and dense jungles of other parts of the Protectorate. The favorite feeding grounds of these zebras are, without a question, the plains, and possibly very sparsely wooded country, although on the Laikipia Plateau I have often discovered them in the outskirts of the big forests, where they seem to be attracted to the open grass patches among the cedars, which here grow, together with a great many deciduous trees. These often form islandlike patches or clumps of trees, between which are lovely glades with thick grass, which the animals seem to enjoy.

The zebra is certainly very fond of water, and is rarely, if ever, found farther than two to three miles from its nearest source. Sometimes when disturbed, or when wishing to communicate with other members of the herd, the zebra ejects a kind of sound, which is more like the barking of dogs than anything else. I often noticed that when a herd of zebras was scattered in different directions either by man or some carnivorous beast, they afterwards " called " to each other by means of their queer-sounding bark, and that sometimes even wounded zebras will make the same noise. A few years ago the Burchell's zebra was so exceedingly plentiful all over the central, southern, and southwestern parts of the Protectorate that it was not an uncommon thing to see several thousand of these beautifully marked animals feeding together in companies on the large plains.

In 1906 I saw an enormous herd of these animals in the upper part of the Rift Valley. We were encamped at a little stream coming down from the Aberdare Mountains, when my attention was called to the animals walking along in a northerly direction, and only a few hundred yards from our camp. Not wanting to shoot any of the animals, I watched them for fully half an hour with my field glasses, while they were feeding and playing, as they slowly moved along, until something must have startled the herd in the rear. As near as I could make it out, there must have been upward of four thousand together, and when they were disturbed they galloped off briskly, soon enveloping themselves in a thick cloud of dust, as they swept through the half-dry grass.

In localities where the zebras are not much molested they are not very shy, and are easily approached to within a hundred yards, and sometimes even less; but where they have been much hunted, they soon learn to look out for the sportsmen and are then, at least in the open, quite hard to stalk. A herd of zebras will act almost in the same way as the kongoni. They are very inquisitive, and will sometimes come up fairly close to a caravan, to " investigate," as it were, and then gallop off, only to make a half circle and come back again to look at the intruders. For this reason they are often very much of a nuisance to the hunter, just in the same way as the hateful kongoni; and they have often spoiled the day for me by disturbing the game with their cavorting and queer antics.

The zebras seem to be very fond of the company of other animals, such as the hartebeest, gnu, and the larger gazelles. Once I saw them freely and peacefully mingling

HERD OF ZEBRA, JUST ENTERING A FOREST ON KENIA.

WOUNDED ZEBRA.
Lake Ol-Bolossat and the Aberdare Mountains in the background.

with a herd of giraffes on the Loita Plains, not far from the border of German East Africa. The zebra is one of the few animals of East Africa that possesses a considerable quantity of fat, which often lies in thick, yellowish layers under the skin. As the natives are extremely fond of this " mafuta," or fat, they enjoy zebra meat very much; and if the animal is young and in good condition it is not at all an unpalatable dish even for the sportsman. The lion also seems to be extremely fond of eating zebra, and it is his chief menu in the greater part of East Africa, to which the vast number of bleached zebra skulls and skeletons on the plains bear witness. My first lion, as previously mentioned, was shot as it was devouring a zebra, which it had slain on the Athi Plains in broad daylight.

It seems almost incredible that the zebras should be as stupid as they are in regard to their protective instincts. In the dry season, when there are few drinking places, and the lions of the vicinity night after night have chased and killed zebras at the same place, they will return to the identical water pool as if nothing had ever disturbed them there. I once witnessed how, together with a few other animals, a small herd of zebras was leisurely walking along and feeding on the dew-drenched grass early one morning, when I detected, and subsequently succeeded in shooting, a big lion, which was lying down not more than perhaps fifty to sixty yards away from where the zebras fed. It could not be possible that the animals were unaware of the presence of the " King of Beasts," but rather must have known that it had had its "fill" so shortly before, that they were not in danger of being disturbed by " His Majesty." The stomach of this lion gave evidence of the fact that for its last meal it had had zebra meat, for we found in it a good many pieces of striped skin.

I have often seen zebras drink in broad daylight, coming down to the river, as if they felt sure that there was no lion around. Once I was having my lunch under some mimosa trees near a little water course on the plains, when I saw a whole herd of zebras of some seventy to eighty animals slowly coming down to drink, headed for the very same place where I was sitting. Making the camera ready for a snapshot, although the light was rather unfavorable, I waited for the animals to come nearer. Suddenly one of my stupid and careless porters stood up above the grass, where they all had been told to lie still, and thus scared the herd away before I was able to kodak it. If frightened, the zebra is able to bound off at great speed, and it takes a very good horse to catch up with, or overtake, a zebra, if on level ground; but if in stony and hilly country, the best horse in the world would have no chance at all to outdistance these sure-footed and swift animals, the deep-hollowed hoofs of which seem to be exceedingly hard and tough.

If suddenly frightened, a herd of zebras will dash away in the maddest flight, apparently without looking ahead in the least. Twice during one week, when encamped near the beautiful Lake Elmenteita, I had opportunities to observe this.

One afternoon, in fact just after we had arrived and begun to erect our camp on the eastern shores of this lake, I was told by some of the men that a small herd of zebras was feeding a few hundred yards away from our selected camping ground. As we had no meat in camp, and the porters were clamoring for "nyama," and zebra meat being a favorite dish with them, I promised to shoot one of the animals. With only the two gun bearers, I started carefully to approach the little herd, which was feeding on an open grass place, surrounded by small trees. After having stalked the animals for a few minutes, I found that it was impossible to come unobserved any nearer than about two hundred yards from our side, and as none of the animals appeared to be looking in our direction, I crept along on my knees a few yards beyond the nearest cover, having told both gun bearers to remain flat on the ground.

Suddenly one of the nearest stallions saw me. He must have given some kind of sign to his "comrades," for instantly the whole herd stopped feeding and looked around in different directions. I kept as still as I could and only raised my gun slowly to take a good aim. I then fired at the before-named stallion, but missed. I fired again, but with the same result. The open place, where the zebras stood, was surrounded on three sides by hills, so that the echo of the shots from the .405 Winchester rebounded from all directions. This made the herd stampede. It fortunately took the direction toward the place where I had remained on my knees. I did not move until the nearest zebra was within some forty yards, when I dispatched two of the animals in quick succession. I may remark here that during this expedition I had a special permit to kill a great many more zebras and other animals than was otherwise allowed on the ordinary sportsman's license, as I was collecting for a scientific institution.

The other experience, which showed me how imprudent these animals are, was made a few days later at the extreme south end of the same lake. We had been ascending and then descending a large, extinct volcano, from the top of which we had a most wonderful view of the surrounding country: to the north of us lay, glittering in the rays of the tropical sun, beautiful Elmenteita; to the northwest, the blue waters of Lake Nakuru, the Uganda Railroad winding its way between the two like a striped, shining ribbon; to the east and west we saw the high escarpments that limit the Rift Valley in those directions, and to the south of us we could look 'way down into the Rift Valley, where the mighty, extinct volcanoes, Longonot and Suswa, formed the background! We had just descended the volcano, and were lunching under a little tree in a narrow valley between two little ridges, when we were suddenly startled by the noise of clattering hoofs, and, looking up, we found a herd of several hundred zebras galloping right down upon us at top speed.

The tree under which we were sitting was too small to afford any protection from our being trampled down under the animals' hoofs, so we all ran forward, waving our arms and screaming at the top of our lungs, to head off the herd. Yet nearer and nearer they came, until at about forty yards' distance I dropped two of the animals in their tracks. The report of the gun, and the sudden fall of their two comrades, made the rest of the herd swing off right and left up the sides of the hills. The herd had probably been badly frightened, and in their mad attempt to escape had paid no attention whatever to our hunting party, before two of the animals had actually been killed! The skin of one of these was very beautiful. It almost appeared as if the skin had been doubly marked, the wide stripes having long, dark-yellow stripes in their center.

Many attempts have been made to tame and domesticate the zebra, both in German and British East Africa, but these attempts have not been successful from a commercial standpoint. It has not been found so very difficult to tame young zebras, but these liberty-loving animals do not seem to survive very long when they are put to work. The weak part seems to be their front legs, which do not enable the animals to pull loads of any size. Attempts have also been made to cross the zebra with donkeys and ponies, which has resulted in a somewhat hardier animal, but several deserted " zebra farms " in East Africa show that at present it does not seem to pay to domesticate the animal.

Not only is the zebra killed by the natives and settlers for the sake of its meat, but its hide is also often used by the white man for furniture covering and for mending harness and boots. By the natives of several tribes, belts and straps are made of zebra skin, with which the loads are generally carried by some tribes in a sling over the forehead. As the zebra is also said to spread cattle diseases, and is very destructive in breaking fences and trampling down the crops of the settlers, they are gradually being killed or driven away from the inhabited parts of the protectorate. The time will perhaps not be very remote when both the Grevys's and Burchell's zebras will be practically extinct in the protectorate, except in the game preserves, like the mountain zebra in South Africa. The government of British East Africa is fully recognizing the destructiveness of the animals and is allowing sportsmen and settlers to kill them off, permitting now on each license twenty zebras to be shot, instead of only two animals previous to the latest game regulations.

CHAPTER XIII

HYENAS, MONKEYS, AND PIGS

OF the Hyena family several species exist at present, both in India and Africa. Unmistakable signs, such as, for instance, a great many remains of the hyenas and bones they crushed, show that in earlier ages this carnivorous animal, which at present is confined to the tropics of the Old World, also inhabited southern and central Europe, where it went as far north as England. In East Africa there are two species: the striped and the spotted hyena. Of these two, the striped is a good deal smaller and less frequently met with than the spotted variety. It is more common in Abyssinia and Somaliland, where in many localities they are little or not at all disturbed by the natives, as they act as scavengers, and in that way are of some service to the population. They, therefore, become quite daring and often visit camps, where they grow so bold as to come close up to the tents to snatch away anything that they can find in the way of meat or bones. In fact it is told in one of the narratives of a shooting expedition in Somaliland, that the sportsmen sometimes amused themselves by throwing morsels of meat and bones from their evening meal just to hear them crunched up by the striped hyena but a few yards away from the table. This hyena hardly ever attacks people or cattle, confining its meals, as a rule, to putrefied meat.

The more common, and much larger spotted hyena is, indeed, a very uncanny-looking kind of creature. Although not quite as long, it stands somewhat higher than the lion, on account of its extremely long fore legs, which make the back of the animal slope down even more than that of the kongoni. The color of the spotted hyena is of a grayish brown, with irregular and very dark brown spots, which sometimes appear to be almost black. The head of this hyena is not very unlike that of a large dog; its upper part is very round and thick, and the ears are comparatively small and rounded; the tail is rather short and bushy. The jaw muscles and teeth of this beast are of the most extraordinary strength. I have heard from reliable sources that bones, which would defy even leopards and lions, were with ease crushed by the hyena. On visiting one of the places where I had the day before shot a giraffe, the leg bones of which had been left on the ground, we found to our amazement that these heavy bones had been crushed by the hyenas, and the greater part of them devoured for the sake of the marrow. From the disagreeable howls in the night, and from the tracks that we saw around the carcass of this giraffe, we had evidence enough that its bones had been devoured, not by lions, but by these scavengers, which would instantly have fled if the " King of Beasts " had appeared.

It has often been said that this spotted hyena feeds only upon animals that it finds already dead, and that it prefers putrefied meat to that which has been freshly killed. It is true that it does not abhor the most putrefied carcasses, but at the same time it has been proven in a great many instances that the hyena often kills its own prey, which it devours with the most ravenous appetite. Very often horses, mules, and donkeys have been killed by these hyenas, although they have been tied up close to the camp-fire of the hunting party. Settlers and natives also complain of the continuous attacks of hyenas upon their cattle and sheep. One gentleman from German East Africa told me of how three spotted hyenas in one single night had killed and partly devoured not less than eleven cows from his herd.

When this beast kills an animal, it generally does it in such a way that it rips open the belly with its sharp teeth, and then devours the soft intestines and licks out the blood from the cavity of the chest. One of the favorite meals of the hyena seems to be the udder of the cow, and I have heard of an instance in British East Africa, where a single hyena killed four cows in one night, devouring hardly anything else but their udders. That particular animal was probably not very hungry, for otherwise it would not have been satisfied with as scanty a meal as that of four cow udders, as a hyena has been known to devour almost a whole hartebeest in a single night.

A great many authentic instances are known where old and half-starved hyenas have grown bold enough to attack even white men who were sleeping at the time. I know the truth of the story, which tells of how an English sportsman, after a hard day's march, was taking an afternoon nap in his hammock. He had it suspended quite close to the ground, and had fallen asleep, with his right arm hanging down over the side of the hammock. He was awakened by a sudden pain, caused by a bite from a large hyena, which had taken hold of his hand, attempting to drag him into the bush. As the hunter awoke and shouted, the cowardly beast retreated quickly into the thicket, and, bent on revenge, the sportsman got his rifle and lay down again in the hammock in the same position as when the hyena caught his hand. He had only watched for a few minutes when the hungry beast came crouching out of the bush to attempt a second attack, only to fall dead the next moment, struck by a well-aimed bullet between the eyes.

The hyena is not as strictly nocturnal in its habits as it is often supposed. Once, when encamped on the eastern shores of Lake Elmenteita, I had shot two zebras, as related in the foregoing chapter. Most of the meat of the two stallions had been brought to camp, while certain parts of it still remained where the animals had fallen. There, in broad daylight, a large spotted male hyena came out of the bush to devour the remains of the zebras, when it was discovered by some of the porters. These fellows quietly notified their comrades and, without saying a word to me, as yet, they surrounded the hyena. With knob-sticks, spears and poles, they now made a concerted attack on the beast. Before the men could come near enough to strike, the hyena darted into a nearby thick bush, where it was safe from any blows from sticks or poles.

The bush had a circumference of some forty feet, and the delighted porters now closed in on it from all sides, yelling at the top of their lungs. This " war-cry " aroused my suspicion, and, just as I was going to start in that direction, one of the men came running into camp to tell me of what had happened. Unfortunately, the bush was too thick to allow any photographs to be taken of the live beast, which both Mr. Lang and I studied for several minutes before I dispatched it with a heart shot. As soon as we two white men arrived, the hyena seemed to turn all its attention toward us, and, displaying its big, snow-white teeth, it growled defiance. Yet it was not courageous enough to attempt an attack, which a leopard or lion, for instance, or even a smaller representative of the cat family, would have done under similar circumstances without a moment's hesitation.

That hyenas often attack and kill old and feeble natives, and drag little children away from the villages to devour them in the jungle, is not so much to wonder at, for the hyena is not the only carnivorous animal which, once having tasted human flesh, prefers it to any other meat. The natives themselves are to blame for the hyena's partiality to human flesh, for, as previously remarked, a good many of the tribes do not bury their dead, but throw their bodies, as well as, in many cases, old, sick people, whom they think may be dying, out into the bush for the very purpose of having them eaten by hyenas and other carnivorous animals.

The hyenas often go together in packs of from four to eight and possibly more, particularly in localities where there is plenty of game. It has been remarked by some old and experienced sportsmen that in certain districts the hyenas have greatly increased after the regions have been visited regularly by hunting parties. The reason for this is probably that a great many animals, which had been perhaps only slightly wounded, and not followed up by the hunter, have been more easily caught by the hyenas; and also that a great deal of meat is left on the plains from animals killed by sportsmen, who in many instances have only taken off the head and parts of the skin.

The hideous howl of a pack of hyenas can never be forgotten, if it has once been listened to in the wilderness. It begins with a low, growling tone, which generally works itself up to a high pitch, sounding not very much unlike the sirens which are used on certain lighthouses. During one of my visits to the Sotik we had been disturbed several nights by the incessant howls of hyenas close to the camp. My Kikuju headman, Mweri, who was very fond of catching all kinds of game alive, set a trap, in which one of these ugly-looking monsters was caught. As I wanted to secure some good photographs of the animal at close quarters, I let it stay in the trap until about seven o'clock the next morning. Then we surrounded the beast, and I succeeded in getting several very fine pictures of the hyena, which was a male in splendid condition. This specimen showed not the slightest sign of fight, only trying to frighten away its assailants with the most awful growling and constant snapping with the teeth. Mweri had tied the trap near to the carcass of a lion, which I had killed the day before, and from the howls we understood that the place had been visited by the hyena shortly after sunset. It had probably been caught very quickly, for its howls suddenly ceased, and it remained perfectly mute until we surrounded it the next morning.

If the sportsman wants to kill a hyena just for the sake of having shot one—for hyena killing can certainly not be classed among real " sport," unless one should come across

HYENA AT BAY.

LARGE WART HOG, SHOT IN THE KEDONG VALLEY.

a wandering hyena during the daytime, which very seldom happens—he might do so by leaving a freshly killed animal where it fell, without letting any human hand touch the carcass, and then go back to the place the following morning, an hour or two before sunrise. He will then very often find the hyenas still at work, crunching up the bones after they have devoured the meat of the carcass. When one of these animals is killed, the hunter will sometimes have hard work to persuade the natives to touch it, as most of them will have nothing to do with a hyena. This does not much matter, however, for the hyena skin is hardly worth while preserving for the trophy room.

The monkey is another animal which can scarcely be classed among "game," and yet almost every sportsman who goes to Africa likes to take home a few skins of these creatures for souvenirs and remembrances of happy hunting days in the big forests. It seems to the reader, perhaps, cruel that monkeys are killed at all, as some of them certainly are very "human" in their behavior and habits; but it must, on the other hand, not be forgotten that a good many species of monkeys are exceedingly destructive, both to the crops of white men and natives. I once visited a settler not far from Nairobi, who told me that although he, night after night, had been shooting at baboons to make them leave his garden alone, yet he found that the cunning creatures would sneak in when he least expected it, and so almost make him despair of the result of his labors. In certain districts of East Africa one of the smaller fur monkeys, with beautiful olive-green skin, by the natives called "engimma," is so destructive to their plantations that the government has taken this monkey off the list of protected animals for that locality, and allows the natives to kill as many as they are able to for the sake of getting rid of this pest.

None of the very largest representatives of the numerous monkey family exists in British East Africa. Two of the most interesting species in this protectorate are the destructive baboon and the beautiful colobus monkey. The range of this latter monkey, which is one of the most coveted hunting trophies as far as monkeys are concerned, extends from Abyssinia in the north down to the Kilima-Njaro, wherever the condition of the country is suitable to its requirements. The colobus love the dense tropical and subtropical forests, where they sometimes are found on the mountains at an altitude of six to eight thousand feet.

I have often noticed that this monkey never goes far away from water, and I once witnessed a most wonderful spectacle of a whole troop of these beautiful creatures as they were drinking from a rushing mountain stream which tumbled down from the large glaciers of Mt. Kenia. Big cedars and deciduous trees overhung the brook on both sides, so that in several places the branches formed perfect arches over the stream. From a good cover, some one hundred and fifty yards away, I had the pleasure of witnessing a regular performance by these graceful monkeys, which slid down like eels from the dizzy heights of the large cedars until they reached the clear water of the stream. Here they were washing their faces in the most cute way, and it appeared to me several times as if they had even been drinking out of their hands. Two of my men also thought that they saw the monkeys drink in this way. Although I am not absolutely sure that they actually drank out of the hands, if they did so, it was very much like the way in which the sons of the forest, the wild Wandorobo, generally drink. I had on this trip not shot any colobus monkeys as yet, but it is needless to say that it was impossible for me to disturb the peace and apparent joy of the company. After about half an hour of dancing around, jumping on each others' backs, and performing some quite remarkable equilibristic feats, the band suddenly disappeared among the crowns of the mighty trees.

The skin of the colobus monkey is beautifully marked, being, as a rule, perfectly black on the greater part of the body, with white sides of the face, large white fields, with much longer hair on the flanks, and with a long, white, and very bushy tail. Another characteristic of these monkeys is that they entirely lack the thumb on their hands, and are, therefore, often called by the zoölogists the " thumbless monkeys." It may here be remarked that there is a strange difference between the hair of this species of monkeys and that of all the rest of the family. Whereas each individual hair of the ordinary monkey distinctly shows different shades of color, those of the colobus monkeys are uniformly white or black.

On my last trip to Mt. Kenia my attention was one day called by a Wandorobo guide to an absolutely white colobus. I could not at first believe his story, but after a few minutes' search of the trees I actually found, among a troop of ordinary colobus monkeys, a very large specimen, which was absolutely snow-white, without a speck of black anywhere on its body or tail. This particular animal seemed to be very much more shy than the rest of the troop, and it took me almost an hour before I could get a shot at it, bringing it down from the top of an enormous cedar, from where it must have fallen over a hundred feet before it struck the ground. A few minutes afterward I secured a second specimen of white colobus monkey, but this one was somewhat smaller, and had a tiny, thin, white streak of grayish black hair in the middle of its back. This faint spot was about half an inch wide and somewhat over three inches long.

Very little is known, even by the natives, about the habits of this generally very shy monkey, for it lives only in the dense forest. It hardly ever does any damage to the crops of the natives, who may have their little " shambas " in the vicinity. The colobus monkeys live chiefly on buds, fruit, and certain insects, and they often go in troops of from twenty to one hundred at a time. It may, perhaps, be unusual, but I once found on the southwestern slopes of Mt. Kenia a place between two streams which seemed literally alive with these beautiful creatures, there being at least three to four hundred of them within a radius of a few hundred yards.

A great many attempts have been made to capture, tame, and bring the colobus to Europe and America, but all in vain. It seems as if the animal were too frail to survive the voyage, most of those shipped from East Africa having died before the vessel reached Port Said. I caught a beautiful young specimen in 1909, and had it for several days in camp. It became quite tame and even ate out of my hand. My hopes grew that it would be possible to get the monkey safely home to New York, when

ORDINARY COLOBUS MONKEYS.

TWO WHITE COLOBUS MONKEYS.
The right-hand one is a large female without a black spot on its body skin.
Both secured on Kenia.

I would have given it to our beautiful Bronx " Zoo," but, alas! after a few days it began to ail and refused to eat. I at once let it loose, thinking it would survive if left to return to the troop again. But, unfortunately, we found it dead the next morning, only a few hundred yards away from our camp.

The baboons are ugly, doglike monkeys, which run around in large troops. It is not an uncommon thing to see a hundred or more of them together at one time. Although most baboons are able to climb trees with the greatest ease, yet they very often are seen on the ground, and sometimes, even when pursued, they will go off at a great pace over the grass rather than to make for the nearest trees. This may only be a proof of intelligence on their part, for they have probably learned that the largest tree gives no protection from the white man's firearms. That they are well able to distinguish between the white hunter and natives has more than once attracted my attention.

It is very curious to observe a troop of these monkeys. They are able to change the expression of their faces in a most wonderful way, and who knows if this is not a " sign language " well understood by all baboons? When disturbed, and the troop goes off at great speed, the little ones ride on their mothers' backs, while the animals eject a series of short, barklike sounds. The color of the East African baboons is olive-green to yellowish brown. The callosities on the buttocks are very large and of a pinkish red color. As the " arms " and legs of this monkey are almost equal in length, this makes him really more fit to run on the ground than to live in trees.

The destructiveness of the baboon is very great and he is, therefore, much hated both by settlers and natives. His chief menu consists of roots, fruit, and tree-gum, but he seems to be equally fond of insects, birds' eggs, and small reptiles. It is fortunate for the agriculturist that the baboon has other enemies than man, for the favorite dish of the leopard is said to be the meat of baboons. These monkeys are very easily tamed, and soon follow their captors around like dogs. They are often taught to perform all sorts of tricks, and one of the cutest " shows," that I have seen, was exhibited in front of the hotel in Nairobi by two Hindoos, who had a small troop of well-trained baboons.

There are in East Africa two prominent species of the pig family, which are ordinarily met with by the sportsman. These are the Bush Pig and the still more common Wart Hog. Both of these animals are quite numerous in most parts of the Protectorate. The bush pig is hardly worth shooting, but the hideous-looking head of the wart hog, with its enormous tusks, makes it a rather interesting hunting trophy. The bush pig is not so often shot by the white man, for it appears to be more strictly nocturnal in its habits than the latter. It is also more fond of dense jungles and large forests, and, therefore, not often seen by the hunter, for the animal is very wary, has very fine hearing, and excellent scenting qualities. As it is living mostly in dense jungles, it is able to hear or scent the oncoming sportsman long before the latter catches a glimpse of his prey. The bush pig is somewhat smaller than the ordinary domesticated pig, and is of a reddish brown color. It has comparatively small tusks, which appear to be no larger than those of an ordinary hog. The animal does an immense amount of harm to the crops of both settlers and natives, the gardens of which it destroys in short order. It is fond of the sweet potatoes that many of the East African natives grow, and is the most destructive animal in this respect in the Protectorate. Combined efforts have fortunately, in many districts, now almost exterminated these undesirable nightly visitors.

On Mt. Kenia and in the forests of the Mau Escarpment there is said to exist a very large bush pig, of which all sorts of mysterious tales are told. This animal, generally called the " giant pig," is said by the natives to be of an almost black color and " as large as a zebra." Its skin is supposed to be covered with long bristles, and the beast carries enormous tusks. Very little is known about this animal, but I have been told by a settler that he actually saw this ferocious-looking beast only some eighty yards away at a time when he, unfortunately, had no gun at hand. It is said that a well-known English naturalist has promised a reward of £500 ($2,500) for the first perfect skin of the giant pig, which he wants to secure for his collection. I myself have found big tusks on Mt. Kenia which could have come from no other animal than a giant pig. One of these, which was broken off at the point, measured over twenty-two inches in length and almost eight inches in circumference at the base. As far as I know, there has been no authentic account of the life and habits of this animal, and there is at present no perfect skin of the giant pig in existence.

The common wart hog is larger than the ordinary bush

pig, and stands sometimes nearly three feet in height over the shoulder. The head is disproportionately large, with an exceedingly broad and flat forehead, which ends with an almost square muzzle. On each side of the face there are three strange-looking protuberances, or warts, and from these the pig derives its name. The largest of these warts are the two which project right under the eyes, where they grow out to a length of some five to six inches. Sometimes they are so long that the tips fall somewhat down, but otherwise they stand straight out at right angles from the side of the face. No animal could be more hideous-looking than the wart hog, with its almost cylindrical body, extremely thin legs, and enormous head. The wart hog carries tusks which sometimes attain a length of over twenty inches, although a good average tusk only measures from fifteen to eighteen inches on the curve. Strangely enough, in this species, it is the tusks of the upper jaw that are the longest. They curve in a semi-circle outward and upward until, I have been told, sometimes in very old specimens, the tips almost meet, forming a sort of arch over the nose.

The wart hog does not exclusively frequent swamps and damp places, as has often been asserted, but is more fond of perfectly dry plains and not too dense bush country. I believe it is quite a rare thing to find wart hogs around swamps, as I myself have hunted for weeks around such places as the Ol-Bolossat and other marches of the upper Rift Valley, but I have failed to find any wart hogs in these places. Although this ugly-looking beast is seen to feed along water courses and among the bush that generally lines the banks of rivers, yet it is often found quite far away from the nearest water. It seems to feed chiefly upon the roots of certain trees and bushes, and is fond of making big holes in the ground, in which it occasionally hides.

The wart hog lives in families of four to six, but old "tuskers" are often met with alone. It is the most comical sight to witness an excited family of wart hogs as they dash for cover, for they all turn their tails straight up in the air, in right angles with the line of their backs, and as the tails are bare, except for a little tuft at the extreme end, it looks as if the animals were supplied with whisk-brooms. This, I have several times noticed, is also the case with lions, for one of the lions that charged me came on with the tail held straight up in the air. It is as well the manner of the rhinos. The wart hog never seems to exhibit any particular courage, and even if wounded and cornered, hardly ever dares to charge its pursuer. However, cases have been known where wart hogs have been hunted with dogs, and where they have been able to rip up and kill several of the pack before the hunter could interfere.

One of the largest wart hogs I shot, I first saw lying down under a bush. I had been stalking it for a couple of minutes, when it must suddenly have gotten a whiff of our wind, for it rushed up and turned quickly around in different directions, sniffing the air. By this time I had come up to within seventy-five yards of the beast, which was an old male with large tusks, which glittered beautifully in the bright sunlight. As the animal turned its broadside to me I fired, aiming for the heart, as usual. Instantly the big wart hog ran off, as if shot out of a gun.

However, it soon began to encircle a large bush in the vicinity at a rapid pace. Six or seven times at least it ran madly round and round that bush, until it suddenly turned over and made several somersaults before it stretched itself out on the ground and expired. When cutting the animal up, I found that the bullet had pierced both lungs, and yet the animal was able to run for all those seconds at such a speed before it succumbed! The meat of old wart hogs has a very strong and disagreeable taste, but the chops of young ones are quite palatable even to the white man. Most of the natives, however, refuse to eat the meat of either bush pig or wart hog, and all orthodox Mohammedans cannot even be induced to touch the animal, being forbidden by their Koran to have anything to do with representatives of the pig family.

CHAPTER XIV

AFRICAN REPTILES AND BIRDS

AFRICA has not nearly as many reptiles as India and the Malayan Islands, although some of the largest and most poisonous snakes also inhabit the Dark Continent. Of all these, none is more dreaded than the puff adder. This deadly reptile is spread almost all over Africa, and is everywhere much feared and shunned by the natives. The puff adder has gotten its name from the fact that it is able to draw in a very large amount of air at one time, which causes a noticeable swelling of the body, and when it then suddenly lets the air escape it rushes out with a queer puffing or hissing sound, which may be heard for quite some distance.

It is a most hideous-looking creature, with a comparatively thick and short body and a broad, flat, triangular head, which is more clearly defined from the rest of the body than in most of the other snakes. Over the eyes and nose this repulsive-looking creature has a sort of horny shield, studded with straight-outstanding hard points. The nostrils are very small and, curiously enough, open straight upward, and very close to the wide mouth with its deadly fangs. The whole body is covered with comparatively large scales, which overlap each other like pointed shingles. The color is arranged in almost V-

227

shaped dark brown bands, with ends pointing backward, while the rest of the body is more of an ash-gray hue. The body ends in a short tail, which is exceedingly small in comparison with the size of the reptile.

This reptile seems to frequent not only sandy places, but also wooded country and forests. Very little authentic information is obtainable about the puff adder, but the natives of different districts have told me that it has a most curious way of striking what it wants to kill. Living on the smallest animals, he does not hesitate to attack horses, cattle, and even man, and its poison is so deadly that the largest animal will succumb a few hours after it has been bitten by a full-grown snake. People are said to die within a very few minutes from the time of the inoculation. I have killed two puff adders, both of which were lying near cattle-paths; and, strangely enough, both with their tails close to the path and the rest of the body forming almost a right angle with the same. The natives told me that they do this because, when they strike, they first lift the tail-end of the body and then, throwing this quickly down upon the ground, swing their heads around in a semicircle, thus striking the victim unexpectedly. Whether it is so or not is impossible to say, but I have heard this twice affirmed by different natives of widely separated districts.

In the southern part of Africa the natives feel very happy when they are able to locate a puff adder, for, after they have killed it, they extract the poison from its head and dip the points of their arrows in the deadly substance for the purpose of using them to kill both human enemies and wild beasts. Fortunately, the puff adder is not as common in British East Africa as it is in Uganda. In this latter country, as well as in the southern parts of the Sudan, it is very numerous and has often caused the death of natives by its fatal bite. In these last-named countries it also seems to grow somewhat larger and is not infrequently found to exceed six feet in length, with a girth of some twelve to fifteen inches.

A puff adder, which I found on one of the foothills of Mt. Kenia, seemed to be almost impossible to kill. I had passed close by the reptile's tail, stepping not more than two inches from the same, when the gun bearer, who was walking close behind me, saw the hideous creature, and begged me to shoot it with the gun. My first inclination was to do so, but, not wanting to spoil the beautifully marked skin, I secured one of the sticks of the porters, with which they support their loads from the shoulders. With this weapon I struck the snake over its head several times. I then lifted it up on the end of the cane and carried it for a while myself, as I could not induce any of the men to do it for me. They assured me that the snake would not die before sunset, unless I completely severed the head from the body. This I did not care to do, as I wanted to preserve the whole skin of the reptile; but when we arrived at our camping place about two hours later I put down the snake a few yards away from the place which I had selected for my tent, and got ready to take some photographs of the puff adder before it should be skinned.

Imagine my surprise when I came back with the camera and found that the snake was slowly crawling away from the place where I had put it! After having placed it again on a bare spot and taken a few photographs, I completely crushed the head with a stone and then told a couple of our " black taxidermists " to skin it. One of them came back in a few minutes to tell me that the snake was again worming away and that they did not dare to touch it. I then tied the snake with a heavy string to a stick driven into the ground, and, incredible as it sounds, it seemed still to be trying to wiggle away when I saw it last, just before sunset, and it was impossible to get any of the " skin men " to do anything with it that day.

The python is another snake quite frequently seen in British East Africa. The python is, perhaps, the most widely spread of all the species of snakes, for it is not only found in Africa, India, and Australia, but also southern Europe, in the West Indies, and the southwestern part of North America; indeed, it seems to be a denizen of all the warmer regions of the world, tropical and subtropical. The Indian python is the largest of the family. This huge reptile sometimes reaches the length of twenty-seven to thirty feet, with a girth of sometimes even more than two feet. Next to the Indian python in size comes the python which is found in the damp forests of West Africa, where it sometimes attains a length of over eighteen to twenty feet, with a circumference of just about as many inches. The body of this mighty reptile is somewhat depressed, the belly being more flat than is generally the case with snakes. The scales are very large and marked with dark brown, irregular spots of different sizes, most of which are connected by long, zigzag stripes running along each side of the body. The head is also well defined and the tail is short and stubby.

THE DEADLY PUFF ADDER.

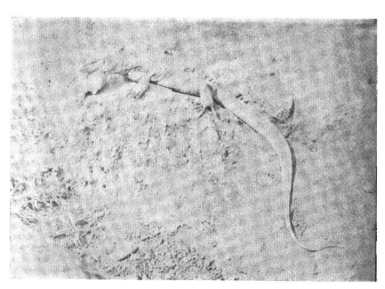

IGUANA, THE LARGEST OF AFRICAN LIZARDS.

This giant reptile is not as fond of open and arid country as many other snakes are, but seems to love damp but not too thick forests, where it is often seen lying on the large limbs of trees, from where it will fling itself upon its prey as it passes under the tree. The python is not afraid of water, but, on the contrary, is found swimming across lakes and rivers, and natives have assured me that the python often catches and devours fish, although I have no authentic proof that this is the case. The chief menu of the python consists of the smaller antelopes and half-grown goats and sheep, which the hideous monster first kills by crushing them between its coils. If the python cannot find antelopes, goats, or sheep, it will be content with birds of different kinds.

When the big reptile has seized its prey and squeezed it into a mass of tangled bone and flesh, it proceeds to swallow it whole, head first. It is a slow process, but is made easier by the ejection of a great quantity of saliva over the victim. This constitutes a kind of " grease," which makes it possible for the python to convey its prey through the throat into the intestines, which is done by the successive contracting of the segments of its body. When the snake has swallowed its prey, and particularly when this has been an antelope of considerable size, or a kid, it is extremely lazy and slow in its movements, but otherwise the big brute is very agile and fierce. The natives fear all kinds of snakes, and seem to have a tremendous respect for this reptile, although they know that it is not poisonous. I have heard from Lumbwa men that this snake has sometimes devoured little children, who have been caught by the python near the villages. It is, however, probably very rarely done, for the snake, in spite of its great strength, shares the fear of man with the rest of the animal creation.

The first python I ever saw in the jungle was killed under quite dramatic circumstances. We had left our camp one morning at a place on the Mau Escarpment, where we had spent the night at an altitude of over 7,000 feet. After about an hour's march through thick forest, we came into a more open country, where lots of charred tree trunks, many of which had fallen down, gave evidence of a previous fierce forest fire. Our march was somewhat hindered here by these fallen trees, over which we had to climb. Suddenly I stepped over something that made my foot slip, and which slid away from under my boot, but I did not think anything of it at the time. The first and second men behind me also passed the same obstruction without noticing anything particular, but the third man gave a tremendous yell, and as I quickly turned around I saw the head of a large python come hissing over the ground, as it seemed ready to throw itself over the terrified porter.

The rifle I carried that morning was the little Mann-licher, and, quicker than I can describe it, I fired at the head of the monster, hitting it squarely in its open mouth, as it was facing me at that moment. The bullet went clean through the head, and at such close distance of only about seven to eight yards, the velocity of the bullet almost exploded the whole head, and thus instantly killed the python. None of the porters wanted to venture into the grass to pull the reptile out, for they feared that it was still alive; so I went in myself, and grasping the python by its shattered head, I tried to pull it out, but its weight was too great, the wet grass making the skin so slippery that it was impossible to get a good hold of it.

When the men saw that I had grasped the reptile, they came to my aid. We then brought it out to a small place, from which the porters had mowed the grass with their knives. It was unfortunately too dark to photograph it, and as we had a long day's march before us, I did not want to stop and wait for the sun to rise; so we skinned the snake as quickly as possible and resumed our march. This python measured sixteen feet three inches before it was skinned and had a girth of nineteen and one half inches. Another python, which I later killed not far from Mombasa, on the way to the Shimba Hills, measured but eleven feet two inches in length and only seventeen and three quarter inches in circumference. This latter snake was hanging down from the large limb of a wild fig tree, some twenty feet from the ground, and right above a little native path which our caravan was following, the big head slowly swinging to and fro like a pendulum. I thought the snake was perhaps in the very act of throwing itself down upon some unsuspecting victim in the grass below. Suddenly the reptile caught sight of the caravan and quickly pulled its head back upon the limb, putting it beside a branch as if it wanted to hide itself from us. I was at the time carrying the .405 Winchester repeater, and gave it a bullet, which cut the spine about two inches back of the skull, causing its instant death; and, with a loud thud, it fell to the ground, much to the surprise and joy of the porters. The skin of this snake had the appearance of having been recently oiled, and several pieces of old skin, which still remained, showed that it had probably just exchanged this for the new skin.

In British East Africa snakes are fortunately not so very often found, for they never occur there in such abundance as they do in other countries, which have a more damp and hot climate. During the fourteen months that I have spent in East Africa I have only seen and killed two pythons, two puff adders, one long, green water snake, and another black and very poisonous snake, the name of which latter I do not know. This last snake was some five feet in length and almost uniformly black. It crawled into camp one Sunday morning, and the porters raised a tremendous "kelele," shouting at the top of their lungs, "Nyoka mbaya, nyoka mbaya, Bwana!" ("A poisonous snake, a poisonous snake, Sir!") This hateful reptile I also killed with a stick, as I did not want to spoil the skin with a bullet. The porters again refused to handle it until Mr. Lang and I had taken it up to show them that it was dead. Gripping its head firmly with my left hand, I took a little stick and pressed the point of one of the large fangs to see what would happen. I noticed now how quite a large drop of yellow substance was formed on the stick, evidently constituting the reptile's deadly poison. I regret that at the time I did not have any proper receptacle in which to preserve the poison, for it would have been very interesting to have had the substance analyzed afterwards. This snake we did not skin, but preserved it in alcohol for the museum.

Besides snakes there seem to be very few reptiles in British East Africa, with the exception of small iguanas,

CHAMELEON, WHICH CERTAINLY POSSESSES PROTECTIVE COLORATION.

A THREE-HORNED, SMALL, TREE LIZARD.

lizards and the chameleons, which latter are able to change their color instantly from dark green to bright red, or from ash-gray to an almost purple color. I have also seen a couple of small scorpions, one of which had the impudence to crawl into our tent, which the careless " boy " had left open, as there were no mosquitoes around. The sting from the tail of this scorpion is very painful, but does not prove fatal to grown-up people, although children sometimes have been known to succumb to its effect.

One of the mightiest of reptiles is the crocodile, which inhabits almost all the inland lakes and rivers of Africa. These hideous beasts, too well known to need describing, sometimes grow very audacious, and often attack, kill, and devour the natives, particularly old people and little children. The crocodiles on the Upper Nile are perfectly enormous, sometimes attaining a length of eighteen feet, and over. The strength of these beasts must be fabulous, for there have been authentic reports of how one single crocodile pulled down a big bull under water and killed him. One of the strangest things that has probably ever happened in this respect was the killing of a large bull rhinoceros by a single crocodile. This animal got hold of one of the hind legs of the rhino, and probably by twisting its mighty tail around some rocks in the river bottom, was able gradually to drag in the struggling quadruped in spite of all its strength and bulk. Farther and farther down into deep water the fighting couple went, until other reptiles of the same kind joined the chase, and soon killed and devoured the mighty beast. I should hardly have been able to believe this, if I had not myself seen three photographs taken of this remarkable scene.

One of the most pathetic stories that I have ever heard, and which I know is perfectly true, happened in the southern part of Africa a couple of years ago. A missionary, belonging to an English Protestant society, and who had been working among one of the inland tribes, was making his way down to the coast, where, in Delagoa Bay, he was to be married to his fiancée, who had come out from England to join him. With a small party of natives he had already been marching several days, when one morning they had to cross a shallow stream, mostly overgrown with reeds and rushes. This messenger of peace was armed only with a shotgun, for the purpose of securing game birds for his food, and, not suspecting any crocodiles or other dangerous beasts in the vicinity, he had been careless enough even to carry this gun unloaded. Just as he was about to step up out of the little stream, he was suddenly seized by a monstrous crocodile, which in a few seconds had completely severed both of his legs above the knees, and then disappeared into the water. The frightened natives scattered in all directions instead of coming to his aid, but the young man had courage and presence of mind enough to take up his notebook and in a hurry scribble a few words of farewell to his betrothed, while his life was rapidly ebbing away! When the porters afterwards returned to the place he was dead. Knowing his destination, the cowardly blacks brought the notebook and his other belongings down to the coast. The terrible grief and despair of the young woman, as she read the hastily scribbled lines, which simply ended with some blurred marks, is more easily imagined than described!

In British East Africa it is in the Athi and Tana Rivers and Lake Baringo that the sportsman finds the greatest number of crocodiles, as well as the largest. I must confess that I am possessed of such a hatred for these brutes that wherever I saw one I shot it, sometimes without even bothering to measure or skin it. One of these beasts killed on the shores of Lake Hannington, showed when we cut up his belly that his last meal had consisted of a couple of pink-colored flamingoes, but otherwise the crocodiles feed chiefly upon smaller animals and fish, which they are able to catch in the streams.

I once came to a certain village that had been terrorized for some time by a monstrous old crocodile, which had taken away a good many women and children, according to the stories told by the natives. They also affirmed that several times spears had been thrown at the big reptile, but all to no avail. This brute lived in a swamp formed by a small stream, and was often in hiding near the place where the women came to get water. As I asked them to show me the hiding place of the crocodile, no one wanted to venture near, but they pointed out some bushes in the distance, under which they had several times noticed the monster. With my powerful Mauser rifle in hand, I walked cautiously toward this place. When within some thirty yards of the dense, but low bushes, the crocodile surprised me by rushing out and making straight for me, with his big jaws wide open and glistening with the many sharp teeth! I fell on one knee to be near the ground, and opened fire. Before the dreaded reptile could close his mouth, I

17   237

had had time to shoot thrice, all three shots penetrating the animal from mouth to the end of the tail, and hashing it up in the most terrible way. This brute was over fourteen feet long. No sooner had the villagers seen that their hated enemy was killed than they set upon it with stones, clubs, and spears, almost hacking the thing to pieces, before I had the chance to measure it.

The wisest way to protect oneself from attacks of crocodiles, when crossing a river where the water is fairly deep, is first to fire a few shots into the stream. In this way I have several times with safety crossed rivers which were full of crocodiles, without any of them having put in appearance anywhere near the place. The only shots which will instantly kill a crocodile are those that either hit the brain, break the spine back of the neck, or else tear the heart literally to pieces. A bullet that simply goes through the heart will not hinder the monster from rushing back into the water and disappearing before it dies. The skin of the African crocodile is so much rougher and thicker than that of the American alligator, that it does not seem to have any commercial value, otherwise some enterprising person would be able in a short while to secure a great number of hides of these hideous reptiles from this part of Africa.

There are also a great number of game birds in the Protectorate. The meat of these constitutes a most palatable variation from that of the antelopes, but, strange to say, even the birds seem to be somewhat " dryer," and more devoid of fat than the kindred game birds of northern regions, just as the antelope meat is, as a rule, less

CROCODILE, SHOT AT LAKE HANNINGTON.
It had just devoured two pink flamingoes.

BUZZARDS IN THE ACT OF GETTING ON THE REMAINS OF A HARTEBEEST.

juicy and fat than that of deer, elk, or moose. The king of game birds is, in my opinion, the Giant Bustard. This stately bird, which is often seen on all the large plains of British East Africa, stands somewhat over four feet in height, and measures about nine feet across the wings. As the bird is generally found walking among the dry grass and stones of the plains, his coloring of dark grayish brown is indeed more protective than that of most mammals or birds. The bustards feed, like our turkey, mostly on insects, and their favorite food seems to be grasshoppers, but if these are scarce they will not refuse fruit and seeds.

They are very wary and capable of making out the hunter at so great a distance that it is practically impossible ever to get a chance at them with a shotgun. Their great size and thickness of feathers would also make a shotgun of no value, unless loaded with very heavy shot. The sportsman is indeed lucky if he can come within reasonable rifle range of these graceful birds, and two hundred and fifty to three hundred yards would almost be considered " close quarters " with them! When disturbed, the bustard often flies away only a short distance, generally to alight again almost straight in front of the on-coming hunter. Then it calmly walks away, picking at insects and worms, or whatever it chooses to eat, until the sportsman comes up to within some two hundred to three hundred yards, when the giant bird again takes a few long strides as if running to start off on its wings. During this short run it begins to flap with these, until it finally lifts itself majestically from the ground. In localities where bustards have been more often shot at, they will fly a great distance, when aroused, and usually not be seen any more that day. These birds seem to like to go by themselves, or at the most in pairs. I have never seen more than two together and very rarely even that.

One day, after some successful hunting near the beautiful Lake Elmenteita, we were returning to camp just a little after four in the afternoon, when I heard a queer, hissing sound somewhat behind and above my head. Turning around and looking up, I saw an enormous giant bustard flying at great speed at about two hundred yards' height from the ground. I happened to have the .405 Winchester in my hand at the time, and was lucky enough to hit the monstrous bird with my second shot, which brought it down with a crash. In measuring it we found that the spread between the wings was ten feet two inches, and it weighed a little over twenty-eight pounds. Although probably an old bird, to judge from the size, the flesh was delicious and more juicy than that of the East African birds in general. We took the skin off in such a way as to preserve it perfectly for the museum, while the meat was used for our table.

There is also a similar, but much smaller species of bustard, which is more frequently met with all over East Africa than his cousin, the giant bustard. These birds also seem to shun "society," as I, at least, have never seen more than two together. Most often only one bird is seen, walking along erect, except when picking up his food from the ground. All the bustards are very good walkers and will often try to run away at first, unless hotly pursued. The color of the smaller bustard is also of a grayish brown

FIVE OSTRICHES RUNNING AWAY AT HIGH SPEED AT SOME 300 YARDS.

HUGE MARABOU STORK.
Compare the size of the large porter on the ground with that of the bird.

hue, which is a good protective color, as the bird is generally found among dry grass and stones on the plains or among sparsely scattered mimosa trees. They have, in comparison, very long legs, but only three toes, like the ostrich.

The last-named bird has recently been put on the list of animals altogether protected, except on a special permit, which may be given to sportsmen who are accredited from some scientific institution. The reason for thus protecting the ostrich is the constantly growing ostrich feather industry of East Africa. For this purpose young ostriches are run down on horseback, corralled, and driven to the " shamba," or farm, where they soon become very tame and are kept in, strangely enough, by wire fences so frail-looking that it seemed to me that the powerful birds could easily make their escape if they wanted to, for they possess a great deal of strength in their legs. I have heard of at least one authentic case, where a wounded ostrich caused the death of a native by ripping up his stomach with a blow from one of his sharp-pointed toes.

One very often finds ostrich feathers on the ground, which have fallen off the wild birds. These the natives pick up and use in their caps and in a good many ornaments of war. The meat of one of the ostriches I shot on my first trip in 1906, when each sportsman was allowed to kill two of these birds, was too tough to be palatable, but it may be that the bird was a very old one. The legend that the ostrich never sits upon its nest, or broods over its eggs, is not true in the case of the East African ostrich at least, for I have twice seen female ostriches on their nests, each running away as soon as she became aware of me. One ostrich nest in the upper Rift Valley contained not less than eighteen huge eggs, nine of which were gathered in one heap, over which the bird was brooding. The other eggs, which evidently the mother bird could not cover, had been kicked away from the nest proper and were lying all around the same. The ostrich egg is not an unpalatable dish. Mr. Lang and I once had three hearty meals, consisting chiefly of the contents of one single ostrich egg, which is said to contain almost as much substance as two dozen ordinary hen's eggs.

Another and still more common game bird in East Africa is the guinea fowl, or " kanga," as the natives call it. This bird represents here the pheasant family, and seems to be spread all over the continent. Contrary to the habits of the bustard, the guinea fowls always are together in large flocks. I have repeatedly seen anywhere from twenty to one hundred birds at one time on the north-western plains of the Laikipia Plateau, and I once saw at least two hundred to two hundred and fifty together. One Saturday morning, after having discovered this enormous flock of guinea fowl close to our camp the previous night, I started out with a shotgun in hand just a little before daybreak. Anxious to secure some of the birds for food over Sunday, when I generally rested in camp, and closely followed by only one man, I started in the direction where we had seen the birds the evening before. We had only gone a few hundred yards from camp when we heard the whirring noise of the guinea fowl as they flew up all around us. Just as I got the gun ready to fire I saw

A PAIR OF FLAMINGOES.

They became so tame that the author could walk up to them within a few yards before they would stroll away, as seen in this picture.

PHOTOGRAPHING A CHARGING ANIMAL.

a regular cloud of the birds against the sky, into which flock I fired twice at random, for it was not light enough to take an accurate aim. Detailing two men to remain on the place until after the sun had risen, and then to pick up the birds that had been killed, we continued our trip for the day. Imagine my surprise when, on returning to the camp in the late afternoon, I found that the boys had picked up not less than twelve birds, which formed a very welcome and appetizing addition to our menu for Saturday night and Sunday.

There are several species of the guinea fowl in Africa, most of them distinguished by quite a high and bony helmet on top of the head and by stiff wattles, which stand out at an angle of about forty-five degrees from the beginning of the gap. The plumage of the common East African guinea fowl is blackish blue with small, almost round, white spots, while certain varieties have a couple of white feathers in each wing. There also exists a species of crested guinea fowl, although I was not fortunate enough to secure any of them during my trips.

Among other very common game birds are the delicious wild geese and ducks of different kinds, abundant in most of the rivers. Then the tiny snipe, and an innumerable number of quail, which sometimes succeed in frightening the men as they go buzzing up like skyrockets at their very feet. I never saw the men more surprised than when I succeeded in shooting down these swift quail before they had gotten more than a few yards away from where they rose out of the grass. There are certainly enough game birds in Africa to make this country a veritable paradise for any man fond of bird hunting, and when the great variety of beautiful winged creatures, like the flamingo, the crested crane, the hornbill, and other smaller birds, are taken into consideration, East Africa constitutes a very interesting field for the ornithologist, who, perhaps, does not care to hunt big game.

CHAPTER XV

THE NATIVES OF BRITISH EAST AFRICA

BRITISH EAST AFRICA is one of the most thinly populated districts of the Dark Continent, owing to the fact that great stretches of the country consist of barren, arid lands, and hundreds of square miles are nothing but deserts. On the other hand, the country comprises many high plateaus where there are hardly any people at all at the present time, although in these regions, lying at an altitude of from five thousand to eight thousand feet, there is plenty of water, good grazing lands, and fine forests. These parts of the country are particularly suitable for white settlers, as they have a splendid climate all the year round.

The coast is quite densely populated by the Swahili people, who for hundreds of years have been slaves of Arab and Portuguese masters. This tribe belongs to the great Bantu race of Negroes, which comprises most of the peoples of the whole of Central, East, and West Africa. The Swahili resembles greatly the common type of Negroes that live in the United States. They have, as a rule, very prominent cheek bones, heavy, thick, projecting lips, low foreheads, and curly hair, which the men generally wear short, sometimes shaving it into strange-looking figures. The women have their hair made into exceedingly small braids, which run like ridges along their heads, and sometimes end with a short "pigtail." Other women of the same race do not braid their hair at all, but let it stand out in big bunches all around the head.

These people have probably been taught by their early masters to build better houses than the inland tribes. They first put into the ground poles in a square or rectangle, then fasten crossbeams on to these with ropes made from creepers and tree bark, and, after having filled in with smaller twigs and branches, so that the whole resembles open basket work, they plaster the walls with clay or mud, which makes the houses fairly rain and wind proof. The roofs, sloping down at an angle of about forty-five degrees, are thatched with coarse, long grass, and not seldom covered on top with palm and banana leaves, which often are put on fresh before the rainy season begins.

When a Swahili couple go to housekeeping they certainly do not need a great many things, for the furniture of the house generally consists of a roughly made bed covered with boards, or with a network of bark ropes on which is laid grass and banana leaves; but "well-to-do" Swahili people have begun to use the more comfortable Hindoo bedsteads. One thing is sure: neither shoemakers, tailors, nor dressmakers would be able to make a living among these people, as they use very little covering, except, perhaps, the "better class." The common Swahili women only wear a little loin cloth and a cheap, brightly colored piece of calico, which they throw over their shoulders in much the same way as the East Indian women. The children, both boys and girls, run around naked during the first six or eight years, except in the cities, where they are now compelled to wear some kind of covering.

The men out in the country districts wear hardly anything at all except a little loin cloth, but in the cities they have adopted the Indian fashion of wearing muslin trousers, looking much like pointed pyjamas, or else long nightshirts, buttoned tightly around the neck and running down as far as the ankles. If they can afford it they have these shirts most beautifully embroidered. It is a strange-looking scene to watch a couple of hundred men in these long " nightshirts " coming out of a Mohammedan mosque, for instance, but I have heard the men say—and I believe it—that it is a most comfortable kind of clothing in a hot climate.

On my way out to British East Africa the first time, several of our fellow-passengers had described the Swahili to me as such a bad people that, at the time, I could hardly believe it possible. One of them, who had spent many years in East Africa, said: " You will find the Swahili a people composed mostly of lazy, lying thieves." I thought this statement terrible, but now, after many months' experience among them, I regret to say that it is not very much exaggerated, if at all. In the first place, as Mohammedans, they do not consider it at all wrong to lie to all not Mohammedans; and in the second place they do not seem to care even if they lie to their " own brethren." As to stealing, they seem to think, like the Greeks of old, that it is " all right " to do so as long as they are not caught. According to my experience, they are by far the most corrupt as well as the laziest of all the lazy inhabitants of British East Africa; for if the Swahili has his own way he will do nothing but eat and sleep, and, besides that, get his " fill " of " tembo," the Swahili name for the native palm wine, which is very intoxicating.

This palm wine is extracted in a most ingenious manner from the flower stalks of the cocoanut tree in the following way: As soon as a cocoanut tree is about to burst out with blossoms, they cut off the top of the flower stalk, and, with the help of the fibers, gourds are tied over the stalk and so fixed that the juice, which otherwise would produce the cocoanut, is forced to run into the gourds. These are then emptied as soon as they are full. A strong tree with several flower stalks will probably produce about two or three quarts a day. The contents of the gourds, when filled with this delicious, sweet sap, are then put away to ferment in the heat, and thus a very strong intoxicant is prepared. The beverage is exceedingly cheap, and, alas! only too much used by the natives.

The Swahilis are agriculturists, fishermen, common laborers, and caravan porters; they also raise poultry, partly for their own use and partly for trading purposes; but very few of them have energy and pluck enough to become merchants of any importance, like the Arabs and Hindoos.

When the young man wants to marry he has to buy his bride from her parents for sums ranging from five to one hundred dollars, according to her beauty and " station in life." A man is allowed to keep several wives, if he can afford to do so, for the government does not interfere in this respect, as the Mohammedan religion allows its followers to live in polygamy. It must be said, however, that plural marriages among the Swahili are not as common

Typical Swahili House on the Coast.

Hut of the Njamus-Nasai near Baringo.

to-day as they used to be, and where missionary influence is predominant they are disappearing altogether.

The Swahili young man can, if he has not all the ready cash necessary for buying his bride, do so on the " install-ment plan," if her father thinks that he is reliable enough to pay his debts. One of the gun bearers I employed had thus bought his wife, still owing his father-in-law seventy-five rupees, or twenty-five dollars. As he had not paid this at the stated time, the father-in-law went to Nairobi and took his daughter away in spite of her tears and protests, but he was honest enough to deposit the money, already paid for her, with the firm which had secured the gun bearer for me.

Farther back from the coast lives the Wanika tribe, which cultivates the ground to a certain extent, keeps herds of sheep and goats, and has a great many chickens. These people are also very fond of hunting, and they are said to be quite successful in killing even big game with bows and arrows. They live in grass huts in small com-munities, only two or three families building together, and when they are tired of one place, they simply pull up their stakes and move to another. Most of the men of this race go entirely naked, and the women wear nothing but a small, shirtlike loin cloth of either muslin, or skin, whereas the children run around in their " Adamitic " costumes.

Higher up the Uganda Railroad, after the great unin-habited Taru Desert has been crossed, live, on both sides of the line, the Wateita people, who are both herdsmen and agriculturists. In former days these people were quite wealthy; but, partly owing to the raids of the warlike

Masai, and perhaps chiefly as a result of the terrible rind-erpest, which took away thousands upon thousands of their cattle, and caused almost whole villages to die from starvation, they have now been reduced to comparative poverty. The Wateita people resemble very much the Wanika, but all their houses or huts are perfectly round, built of sticks and grass, and always clustered picturesquely together on the hilltops, where, in warlike times, it was more easy for them to defend themselves against their enemies. They belong to the great Bantu race, and live, very much like the inhabitants of the rest of the country, in polygamy, and in gross ignorance and superstition.

Northeast of the railroad, and farther inland, the trav-eler meets the industrious and courageous Wakamba people, who often successfully withstood the savage at-tacks of the Masai. The men of this tribe frequently used to file their teeth into sharp points, to appeal better to the weaker sex, but this makes them look very ugly and wild. Their chief weapon is a long swordlike knife, and bows and arrows, which latter they understand how to dip in a skillfully prepared and most deadly vegetable poison. Any man or beast even slightly scratched by one of these arrows will die in a very short time, as there is said to exist no means as yet discovered to neutralize the fatal effect of this poison.

The women are very lightly dressed, and they do not seem to wear any cloth at all, this being replaced by pieces of goat skin, which they understand how to make as soft as kid gloves. Of these skins they wear only two pieces; the one serves as a loin cloth, and the other is tied over the shoulder. The Wakamba are agriculturists, and have a good many cattle and fowls. They make good workmen, and some of the best caravan porters we had belonged to this tribe.

Following the railroad northwest of Nairobi the Kikuju territory begins, and, according to the statement of a gentleman who had been in this country many years, the splendid Kikuju race is probably destined to become predominating in the interior of British East Africa; for they are a great deal more industrious, clever and enterprising than any of the tribes of which I have spoken.

The Kikujus also live in round houses with thatched roofs, but the under part of these are made of solid boards of wood, generally cut from the cedar, which here grows in great abundance. The roof projects away out from the walls, and so far down that a tall man has hard work to crawl into his hut, the sides of which, in this way, are well protected against both rain and sun. The roof is supported by wooden poles, which run in double rows, crossing each other in such a way as to form a square in the middle, under which is the open fireplace. On each side of the entrance these poles divide the hut into three parts; the middle, and larger one, is taken up by the rude bed made of a big, slanting board, supported by poles about three feet from the ground; the room nearest the entrance is used as a storeroom for cooking pots, milk gourds, and so forth, whereas the other compartments contain the small, or sick, sheep and goats at night.

The Kikujus also live in polygamy. We heard of one man, a great chief, who had over one hundred wives. Each wife has her own house, but the first wife is the " boss " of the others. The male children are, as a rule, kept in the father's hut; but the girls live with their respective mothers. It is a strange thing that if a " well-to-do " man has only one wife, she will give him no rest until he has taken at least one more. This for the selfish reason that as long as she is the only wife she has to do all the work alone, as her husband could not keep any female servants. But if the man has two or more wives the work is divided among them, and the old " mamma " has the upper hand over the rest. The men themselves do not, as a rule, care to work in gardens or to carry wood and water, or milk the cows, but they herd the cattle, work as porters, and like to fight.

The chief arms of the Kikuju are a splendid knifelike sword called " panga," his knob stick, long spear, and his bow with poisoned arrows. The knob stick is one single piece of hard wood, cut thin at one end and then gradually increasing in size until it measures from ten to fifteen inches in circumference at the club end. These heavy weapons are most powerful, and men have told me that they have killed both human enemies and dangerous animals, such as leopards and even lions, with a single blow of the deadly knob stick. They are also experts in using their long, heavy spears, and are very clever with their bows. They secure the poison for the arrows by boiling the leaves and young shoots of a certain tree for a long time and then dip the arrows in the thick sediment. The fruit of this tree is perfectly delicious, and, strange to say, absolutely harmless to eat, being enjoyed greatly by both men and elephants. It resembles a small plum and is, when ripe, very juicy and of a rich purple color.

From time immemcrial the Kikuju race, which inhabits the highlands in the center of the Protectorate, has had frequent wars with the Masai tribe of the plains. Sometimes the Masai would be victorious, and carry away a great many cattle, sheep, and women from the Kikuju, but at other times they would be beaten, and the Kikujus would make up their former loss from the large Masai possessions. But of late these race wars and raids have, through the influence of the British government, fortunately entirely stopped.

The Kikuju people, both men and women, are very fond of wearing all sorts of ornaments in their ears. They cut the lobe of the ear, when the child is young, and insert heavy rings, or even stones, for the purpose of extending the lobe, until it finally widens so much that some of them succeed in putting in rings of wood or ivory the diameter of which is anywhere from six to eight inches. Besides this they make holes in the upper part of the ear and insert there pieces of wood or bamboo in such a way that these sticks very much resemble the ribs of an open fan. Both men and women wear bracelets of brass or iron wire, as well as necklaces of the same kind of material, and strings of glass beads. Anything may serve as a necklace for the Kikuju. Some, for instance, make them by putting on a string, or sinew of an animal, alternately the round roots of a little tree, and the hollow bones of birds, cut into equal lengths. Other ornaments are made of nuts and fruit pits, which are strung together in the same manner.

As loin ornaments the men wear a heavy brass wire from which numerous little iron or brass chains, varying from three to six inches in length, hang down. The women of "society" wear as similar decorations wide bead girdles, generally finished off by a string of shells. A stylish Kikuju girl is not even satisfied with all these things, for she wears, besides the just-mentioned ornaments, a number of diadems of beads around her head, heavy brass wire wound around the legs just below the knees, and, as long as she is unmarried, ankle rings of either brass or iron, on which again are strung numbers of heavy smaller rings, so that a "smart" Kikuju " society " woman—for such these are—wears ornaments of a total weight of from five to eight pounds, if not more.

The Kikuju houses are just about as " well furnished " as those of the previously mentioned tribes, the only addition being small wooden stools on three legs, cut out in one piece from the trunk of a cedar tree. A young Kikuju man has to buy his bride for the price of so many oxen, sheep and goats, ranging in value from five to one hundred and fifty dollars, according to her "beauty," strength, and grade of " society." The girl herself is generally not even asked whether or not she likes the man to whom she is going to be married. There have been many examples of liberty-loving Kikuju women killing themselves rather than become the wives of men they disliked.

Not very long ago a young Kikuju girl was sold by her father to a horrible old chief who already had over forty wives. She objected to this marriage, being already in love with a young but poor man, who for some time served in our caravan, but her objection was of no avail. Finally, when she heard that the old chief had already paid her price in live stock and was now coming to take her home by force, she ran away to the mission station in

Kijabe and implored the aid of the missionaries to save her from the brutal chief.

One day the parents succeeded in kidnaping their daughter from the mission station. Suddenly heartrending cries were heard from the bushes not far away, and running there one of the lady missionaries saw how the girl was being mercilessly beaten by her cruel parents and others, who tried to take her away by force. Instantly this courageous young American girl rushed at the assailants, grabbed the victim, and, tearing her away from the kidnapers, brought her back to the mission house, where she then was closely guarded.

The rascally old chief had, however, made up his mind to get the girl at any cost. He therefore applied to Nairobi for aid, and, strangely enough, the government supported him, and ordered the girl to be delivered to the chief, as he had already paid for her according to the law of his tribe. The missionaries now interviewed both the father of the girl and the old chief, and through their influence it was arranged that the father should return the cattle to the chief, who promised to leave the girl alone. In the meantime the young lover had been working hard so as to be able to buy his bride, and he succeeded finally with the help of others in bringing the required number of cattle and sheep to her father, after which the happy couple were married according to Kikuju rites.

Farther up along the line, in the Rift Valley, and on the Laikipia Plateau, live the Masai, who are perhaps the most intelligent and courageous people of East Africa, although extremely lazy and insolent. There has been a great deal of speculation as to the origin of this tribe, which a great many people have held to be a mixture of Negro and Ethiopian, but recent discoveries, however, have led to the almost certain conclusion that they belong to the Semitic race. Captain Merker, who has studied the Masai as has no one else, is of the opinion that they have the same origin as the Hebrew race of herdsmen, from whom the Masai have inherited a great many customs and ceremonies still in vogue. Some of the Masai men we met really made us think of the old patriarchs; especially a couple of chiefs, who had such pronounced Hebraic features that it was not difficult to believe that the Masai and the Israelites had sprung from a common ancestry. Among other things that seem to prove this, is the fact that the Masai, although having lived for centuries among idolatrous and polytheistic peoples, still adhere strictly to the monotheistic belief; further, they make a kind of atoning sacrifice, and all of their men above a certain age are circumcised in the same manner as the Jews.

The Masai tribe appear to be the most independent and liberty-loving of all African peoples. A young warrior would rather be killed than work as a slave, or even be induced to carry burdens as a caravan porter. He will serve as a herdsman, being an excellent and courageous defender of the cattle against all kinds of wild animals; and when intrusted with modern arms he certainly makes a splendid soldier. This tribe has from time immemorial been accustomed to be the rulers of East Central Africa, where it held all the other tribes in subjection—only the Kikujus being able at times to defend themselves with success against the Masai raiders. Enormous herds of fine cattle composed the riches of this tribe, but the terrible rinderpest killed off many thousands of their stock, so that to-day the tribe is not nearly as wealthy as it used to be. In former days they simply took from neighboring tribes, after bloody fights, what they wanted, but to-day they do not dare to attempt any more raidings, as they are well aware of the authority of the white man with his destructive firearms.

The Masai generally live in villages composed of a great number of huts, most of which are built closely together, and form either an oval or a circle. The backs of the huts are turned outward, and so form a wall, which is often strengthened and perfected by an almost impenetrable hedge of thorns. This wall is a safeguard against intruders of all kinds. The doors, or rather openings, of the houses are on the inside, facing each other, and the houses themselves are built of branches of trees and twigs which have been put together like a kind of open basketwork. When this is done the whole hut is coated over with layers of cow-dung mixed with clay, which makes it almost absolutely fire-and-wind proof. Most of the houses have no openings whatever besides the " door," so that almost all the smoke from the fire remains in the hut, causing different troubles to the eyes of the occupants. This is also the case with all the other tribes in East Africa.

The Masai do not cultivate the ground, but live almost exclusively from the products of their cattle, sheep and goats. They are very fond of good meat and fresh milk. This latter is poured into gourds which are cleaned out with a solution of charcoal, cows' urine and water, making the milk brought in an ordinary Masai gourd almost undrinkable for a white man.

The Masai women have to do all the work there is to be done, except herding the cattle and fighting the foe, whereas the older men generally stay at home to eat, smoke, and gamble. The youngsters when about eighteen years old are, with certain strange ceremonies, taken into the "soldier class" and serve as warriors or, as they call themselves, El Moran. These young men enjoy all sorts of privileges; almost naked, and tattooed with the traditional "war paint," these fellows run in batches from village to village, where they are received with open arms and allowed to indulge in all sorts of vice, and after a few days' feasting they receive as a special "peace offering" a fatted young bull or a couple of sheep. These they drive away to some far-off cave or other secluded place, but always near water, where they kill the animals, and eat their fill of the fresh meat. It was a former custom that when the young men were circumcised and became El Moran — which ceremony takes place about every four years — the new warriors should get into a fight with men of other tribes, and dip their spears in human blood, but to-day, of course, this is not tolerated by the British or German governments.

Even the Masai practice polygamy. Some of the chiefs have over fifty wives, and old "King" Lenana probably more than a hundred. The Masai women are, as among other tribes, simply bought from their fathers to become their husbands' wives, whether they like it or not. They adorn themselves very much like their Kikuju sisters, except that those who can afford it have an extra leg ornament of brass wire wound all the way from the knee down to the ankle in one piece. They also wear very

A Young Wanderobo, Ready to Shoot His Poisoned Arrow.

Masai El-Moran Warriors.
Two old chiefs are standing on the right.

large necklaces made of the same kind of wire, which is wound in ever-expanding circles until they project fully eight inches from the neck, looking very much like a wide shining collar.

The Masai use for protection and warfare almost exclusively their powerful spears, which they understand how to handle with great strength and skill. There is said to exist a secret organization among the different Masai tribes, the members of which pay homage to their old "king," Lenana. I have heard people who have lived among the Masai for many years say that one word from him would bring together thousands of these courageous young El Moran, who would willingly stake their lives in carrying out their chief's command. Many believe that with the present state of affairs in East Africa, should all the cunning and powerful Masai tribes rise simultaneously, they would probably be able to kill off every white person and all the government native soldiers in the Protectorate within twenty-four hours!

The Wanderobos are a wild jungle people, living in the forests of the middle and northern parts of the Protectorate. They are looked down upon by the Swahili, Kikuju, and Masai as "washenzi," or wild bush-people, which name they indeed deserve, for they have no chief, no tribal organization, and do not even live in villages. They are nomads, but without cattle or sheep, wandering around a great deal from place to place, staying where they happen to be able to kill some large animal, which they devour until nothing is left of the carcass even to attract the hyena, and then they move away again. These people are as near to "primitive man " as any race living, and yet, in spite of their wild life and habits, they possess a good deal of intelligence, and are the very best big-game trackers and hunters in East Africa. Among other interesting people in this Protectorate are the Galla, Lumbwa, Kavirondo, Nandi, Mbe, and other tribes, which are all more or less like the already mentioned natives.

Of these latter tribes, the Kavirondo is, in a commercial way, the most promising, for they are splendid agriculturists, and perhaps on the whole the hardest-working natives in British East Africa. They live all around the extreme western part of Victoria Nyanza, where the large Kavirondo Bay is almost in the center of their country. Strangely enough, it is not, as is usual, the men, but the women of the Kavirondo tribe who go around absolutely nude, even without the little loin cloth that otherwise the most scantily dressed native woman carries. Until the middle of 1909 one could see scores of these women, young and old, coming right down to the railroad stations, and there gazing at the foreigners as they passed, evidently without the slightest feeling of embarrassment, even if the tourist wanted to photograph them. Partly owing, I believe, to one of Mr. Roosevelt's expressions about the impropriety of this custom, they have now been forbidden to come up to the railroad stations, at least without some kind of covering.

When said that the women generally go around absolutely naked, it should be mentioned that the older ones carry a funny kind of " tail " of animals' hair, which hangs down from the center of the back and is held fast by a string around the waist. It is rather surprising to hear in connection with the strange fashions of the Kavirondo women that they are said to be the most chaste of all the native women of East Africa. They are now beginning, little by little, to put some clothing on. This tribe occupies the most fertile soil in the whole of the Protectorate; and I believe that in the near future the Kavirondo will make long strides in their upward march, as the men already begin to cultivate a taste for better clothing, furniture and houses, and are often anxious to be taught in the various mission schools. It is from this country that a great deal of wild coffee of good quality is secured, as well as a superior kind of ground nuts and the semsem oil seed. The Kavirondo are still very superstitious, and their " witch doctors " and " medicine men " do a flourishing business among the ignorant savages.

CHAPTER XVI

MISSIONARIES, SETTLERS, AND GOVERNMENT OFFICIALS

INTELLIGENT and self-sacrificing men and women who go out to live and work as missionaries among such tribes as those partly described in the previous chapter, certainly deserve a great deal of credit and commendation. For the people of East Africa are, without exception, in their native state revoltingly dirty, ignorant, superstitious, and cruel. At the same time they seem to be possessed of a great amount of false pride, one tribe thinking itself far superior not only to the other tribes of the country but also to the white man. Love, as we understand it, and tender compassion they seem not to know at all. Not only do they hate their enemies, which generally include all other tribes than theirs, but they are exceedingly cruel even to the people of their own household, often throwing out the old and sick people into the jungle to be devoured by carnivorous beasts.

One of the numerous superstitions of the natives is that if a person dies in a hut, this will bring great misfortune and grief to the other inhabitants. Therefore, as soon as they think that a member of the household is so sick that he or she is liable to die they carry the sick one out and often even tie him in the thorn bush a few hundred yards away from the village, so that he may be killed and eaten by lions, leopards, and hyenas. I know of one instance where an old woman was thus thrown out by her own son. The poor old soul had strength enough to free herself and crawl out of the bush, from whence she dragged herself to a neighboring village, where a second son of hers lived. As soon as this young brute saw the condition of his mother he, instead of trying to care for her, took a couple of other young men with him and dragged the unfortunate old woman out into the bush outside their village, where they mercilessly left her to the wild beasts. Again liberating herself, and exerting her utmost efforts, she succeeded in crawling to a nearby mission station, where she was most kindly received and where the missionaries built a special little hut for her near their own house. Imagine their joy and surprise when the old woman a few days later had recovered sufficiently to be able to be around! She subsequently became a Christian, and was still alive when I left Africa in February, 1910.

The position of woman in Africa is, as in almost all heathen countries, most deplorable. She has no rights whatsoever. She does not inherit with her brothers, and when a man dies who has a great deal of property and, therefore, a good many wives, these are inherited, with the rest of his belongings, by his sons if he has any, or else by the nearest male relative. A great deal of sickness and many curable diseases play great havoc among the tribes, where a little bit of care and instruction in the very rudiments of hygiene would improve their conditions greatly. Therefore, the whole of East Africa is in great need of missionary work, which should not only be evangelistic but also medical and industrial.

It is therefore a deplorable fact that many "globe trotters" and settlers in heathen lands often criticise and condemn foreign missions. Not only do they sneer at certain individual missionaries for their supposed inefficiency, ignorance, bigotry, and selfishness, but they also condemn mission work as a whole, maintaining that comparatively very little good is accomplished by these agencies, considering the great amount of money spent for mission work. They often say that not only certain unwise actions of the missionary are objectionable, but that even his very presence in the foreign fields is unnecessary, and that he only irritates the masses and provokes them to hostility toward the white merchant and his government. Further, it is asserted by the opponents of mission work that the missionary's influence tends to make the natives lazy, dishonest, and disrespectful toward their white masters.

The main reason why missionary work is so severely criticised by a great many travelers and settlers lies in the indifference they have toward the very Lord of missions Himself, and the missionary's Bible, which they dislike because it tells the truth about men and condemns corruption and sin. A number of years ago an old African queen had heard of mirrors, and believing that she was the most beautiful woman of her tribe, she ordered one of these strange things to be sent to her "palace." A mirror was bought and taken to the queen. But when she looked into it and beheld her frightful features, she became so infuriated that she not only threw the mirror on a stone and broke it, but also forbade, by death penalty, anyone in her kingdom to own a mirror. One single glance into the glass had convinced her of the wrong estimation of her beauty, and not wanting to be shown her true appearance she hated and destroyed the looking-glass.

It is a sad but well-known fact that many white settlers and travelers in heathen countries throw off all moral restraint, and live a life among the natives which is wholly unworthy of a civilized man, not to speak of a professing Christian. The missionaries, seeing this and hearing of it from the people among whom they work, necessarily have to reprove such people for their doings, and denounce them for the very sake of civilization and Christianity. Thus it is that unprincipled travelers and settlers conflict with missionaries and show the spirit of malice toward their work.

In the different heathen countries where it has been my privilege to travel—for instance, in India, Burma, China, Japan, Africa, and other places—I have always found the same thing. People who live questionable lives, and who do not care to represent any higher ideals, always condemn missionaries, just as the habitual drunkard and saloon-keeper hate temperance work. Yet, wherever I have found officials and settlers who were real gentlemen, and who made a point of setting a high example for the natives, they all highly respect the missionary and his work. The more such people have studied these difficult problems in the various heathen countries, the more they have learned to appreciate the true missionary and his unselfish work. Many wonderful testimonials to this effect have been publicly given by eminent American and British officials, as well as by heathen kings and prominent statesmen. To quote only a few well-known statements:

THE BIG GAME OF AFRICA

The late President William McKinley once publicly said in Carnegie Hall, among other things:

" I am glad of the opportunity to offer without stint my tribute of praise and respect to the missionary effort, which has wrought such wonderful triumphs for civilization. The story of Christian missions is one of thrilling interest and marvelous results . . . The noble, self-effacing, willing ministers of peace and good will should be classed with the world's heroes. . . . Who can estimate their value to the progress of nations? Their contribution to the onward and upward march of humanity is beyond all calculation. They have inculcated industry and taught various trades. They have promoted concords and unity, and brought races and nations closer together. They have made men better. They have increased the regard for home; have strengthened the sacred ties of family; have made the community well ordered and their work has been a potent influence in the development of law and the establishment of government."

The Hon. Theodore Roosevelt, one of the greatest Presidents this country ever had, says:

" It was once my privilege to see, close by, the mission work on Indian reservations in the West. I became so interested in it that I traveled all over the reservation to see what was being done, especially by the missionaries, because it needed no time at all to see that the great factors in the uplifting of the Indians were the men who were teaching them to be Christian citizens. When I came back I wished it had been in my power to convey my experiences to these people—very often well-meaning people —who speak about the inefficiency of foreign missions. I think if they could have realized but the tenth part of the work that had been done, they would understand that no more practical work, no more productive of fruit for civilization, could exist than the work being carried on by the men and women who give their lives to preaching the Gospel of Christ to mankind."

Colonel Denby, for a number of years the United States Minister to China, says:

"I have made a study of mission work in China for years. I took a man-of-war and visited almost every port in the Empire. At each one of the places I visited and inspected every mission station. They are all doing good work; they merit all the support that philanthropy can give them. I do not stint my commendation nor halt nor stammer about work that ought to be done at home instead of abroad. I make no comparisons. I unqualifiedly and in the strongest language that tongue can utter give to these men and women who are living and dying in China and in the Far East my full and unadulterated commendation. My doctrine is to tell, if I can, the simple truth about them, and when that is known, the caviling, the depreciation, and sneering which too often accompany comments on missionary work will disappear, they will stand before the world as they ought to stand, as benefactors of the people among whom their lives are spent, and the forerunners of the commerce of the world."

The Honorable John W. Foster, once Secretary of State, and successively Minister to Mexico, Russia, and Spain, who was asked by the Emperor of China to be Counselor of his Empire in making a treaty with Japan, says:

"My observation is that the mass of people in China do not object to missionaries . . . China stands in great need of Christianity. The teaching of Confucius, among the wisest of non-Christian philosophers, has had unlimited sway for twenty-five centuries; and this highest type of pagan ethics has produced a people the most superstitious, and a government the most corrupt and inefficient. Confucianism must be pronounced a failure. The hope of this people and its government is in Christianity."

General Lew Wallace, the celebrated author of Ben-Hur, formerly United States Minister to Turkey, testifies:

" When I went to Turkey I was prejudiced against missionaries, but my views of them and their work have completely changed. I found them to be an admirable body of men, doing a wonderful educational and civilizing work outside of their strictly religious work."

Lord John Lawrence, perhaps the greatest of all English Viceroys, affirms:

" Notwithstanding all that the English people have done to benefit India, the missionaries have done more than all other agencies combined."

At a large public meeting in Calcutta, Sir Augustus Rivers Thompson, then Lieutenant-Governor of Bengal, uttered these words:

" In my judgment Christian missionaries have done more real and lasting good to the people of India than all other agencies combined. They have been the salt of the country and the true savior of the Empire."

General Sir Charles Warren, at the time Governor of Natal, who was sent on a special mission of pacification to Zululand and Bechuanaland, reported:

" For the preservation of peace between the colonists and the natives, one missionary is worth more than a whole battalion of soldiers."

Sometime ago the British Consul at Mozambique delivered an address in Glasgow in which he, among other things, said:

" I must say that my ten years in Africa have convinced me that mission work is one of the most powerful and useful instruments we possess for the pacification of the country and suppression of the slave trade."

The great Chinese Statesman, the late Li Hung Chang, when he visited this country in 1906, said:

" The missionaries have not sought for pecuniary gains at the hands of our people. They have not been secret emissaries and diplomatic schemers. Their labors have no political significance, and the last, not the least, if I may be permitted to add, they have not interfered with, or usurped, the rights of the territorial authorities."

The lamented Marquis Ito, the greatest statesman Japan ever had, was not ashamed to say:

" Japan's progress and development are largely due to the influence of missionaries, exerted in the right directions, when Japan was first studying the outer world."

His Majesty Shulalongkorn, King of Siam, one of the most enlightened and progressive monarchs of the East, being a warm friend and supporter of missions in his kingdom, admits:

"American missionaries have done more to advance the welfare of my country and my people than any other foreign influence."

It would be very easy for me to print many more testimonials of the same character from a great many other prominent statesmen and governors, but this may suffice to confirm my assertion that high-minded and clear-sighted men the world over understand and appreciate the great value of missionary work, without which our own country, as well as Europe, would to-day still be worshiping idols and graven images, as our forefathers did.

On the other hand, I must frankly admit that there are a good many missionaries who, indeed, are inefficient, selfish, ignorant, and lazy. Such men would probably do better as tailors, shoemakers, clerks, and teachers in their respective home lands; and I dare say that such people have many times unnecessarily provoked both white men and natives; they have been a hindrance to the very cause they were sent out to further. The different missionary societies know and deplore this very much indeed. But to judge from such missionaries, and to condemn the great body of noble men and women whose only aim in life is to elevate, help, and advance the conditions of native tribes the world over, is just as unreasonable and absurd as to say that the Americans are no good, that they are drunkards, crooks, and thieves, because there are *some* such people in our great land!

As to the influence of mission work among the tribes of Central Africa, may I here mention what, for instance, Sir Harry Johnston, a former Commissioner to East

Africa and Uganda, said in his report to the home government:

"All the difference between the Uganda of 1900 and the bloody, harassed, and barbarous days of King Mtesa and his son, Mwaggo, is really extraordinary, and the larger share in this improvement is undoubtedly due to the teaching of the missionaries. I do honestly consider that the work of the great missions in the Uganda Protectorate has achieved most satisfactory results. It cannot be said that the natives of the Uganda Protectorate have been spoiled by Christianity; they have been greatly improved, and have, in the adoption of this religion, lost neither manliness nor straightforwardness."

When this prominent colonizer once received a deputation from the Basoga people, as he passed through their country, he closed his address to them with these words:

"Long ago we English were like the Kavirondo (a people which are much despised by the more intelligent and civilized Basoga), and we wore no clothes and smeared our bodies with paint, but when we learned Christianity from the Romans, we changed and became great. We want you to learn Christianity, and to follow in our steps, and you, too, will be great."

In regard to the settlers of British East Africa, I regret to say that many of them are of an inferior type of people, whose general conduct is very offensive to decent white men and a reproach not only to Christianity, but also to civilization in the eyes of the heathen and Mohammedan. Many of them will not hesitate to maltreat the natives, to live openly in the most licentious manner, so much so that in some instances they have, through their immoral conduct, incensed the natives to riot and murder as a retaliation. That such men are the avowed enemies of missionaries and everything connected with Christianity, no one can wonder. On the other hand, it must be also acknowledged that there are a good many settlers in East Africa who are of an entirely different type, and whose very presence and conduct are a blessing to the land. All of those that it was my privilege to meet of this latter class had nothing but unstinted praise for the missionary efforts, and they cheerfully acknowledged the great benefit the country derived from their presence and labors.

I am also happy to say that the great number of government officials with whom I came in contact seemed to belong to the last-named class. They were of that high-minded, hard-working and efficient kind which reflects credit and honor upon the great government which employs them. They were greatly respected among both settlers and natives, and their work highly appreciated by the missionaries. These government officials, again, were of one accord in commending the labor of the missionaries, and willingly acknowledged how great a part they play in the pacification and general uplifting of the country.

Among these splendid British officials I may mention H. M. Commissioner, Mr. C. Ainsworth of the Kisumu Province, the most populous district of British East Africa, who, with his American wife, resides at Port Florence, on the shores of Victoria Nyanza, and whose guest I had the pleasure of being during the first two days of this year. Other men of the same type are the District Commissioners, Messrs. H. B. Partington of the Lumbwa District, and C. Collier of the Laikipia-Masai Reserve, who are certainly two of the ablest men in British East Africa. With these last-named three officials I have had several long conversations about the work of missionaries, and they have all agreed in that regard that the missionaries in their respective districts are doing a splendid work for the betterment and enlightening of the people.

Four years elapsed between my first and last visit to Africa. I must say, for the sake of truth and for the encouragement of all well-wishers of missionary enterprise, that I noticed a very marked improvement in the behavior and appearance of the natives among whom faithful and efficient missionaries have been laboring. It is often said by the critics that native converts, generally called "mission boys," are inferior to those who still remain heathen, as if to say that the influence of Christianity upon these natives would have a bad effect. I want to say here in explanation of this that a great many young heathen, who have understood the advantage of the teachings of mission schools, go to these schools for a few terms and study enough to learn to read and write and to be trained a little in domestic sciences. When this is accomplished they leave the mission, in many cases without ever having accepted Christianity. They are then generally called " mission boys," and by many people supposed to be native converts.

In many instances some of these "mission boys" are certainly greater rascals than the absolutely ignorant

273

heathen, for they have come into touch with civilization enough to be more up to all sorts of tricks than the wild jungle people; but to blame missionaries for this is certainly most unreasonable. During my three different expeditions to East Africa I had a good many " mission boys " in my caravan. Some of these had never been converted, not even professedly so, and behaved in such a way that they had to be dismissed from the service. Others, who had been recommended to me by the missionaries as Christian converts, certainly showed a wonderful difference in character and behavior, and to one or two of them I felt that I could intrust anything I had on earth, sure that they would not defraud me of a penny's worth.

In my opinion the only hope for Africa lies in the thorough evangelization of its people by faithful, self-sacrificing missionaries, who do not only live and teach a practical gospel, but also are intelligent enough to train the negro along industrial lines, and to teach him to better himself commercially, morally, socially, and religiously, until every one of the savage tribes of the Dark Continent has learned to know Him, who is indeed the Light of the World.

CHAPTER XVII

HINTS ON PHOTOGRAPHY AND THE PRESERVING
OF TROPHIES

NOTHING is more interesting than to bring home a number of good photographs after an extended hunting trip, wherever it may have been. Not only is the sportsman thus enabled to show relatives and friends photographs of the wild animals, their haunts, savage people, and the different scenes of the countries visited, but he also has a chance of living his adventures over again as he looks upon his pictures. And again, while the big-game pictures and photographs of wild people and scenery are interesting to look upon, there are also all kinds of pictures of camp life and little every-day occurrences in the jungle. These things make the country seem more real, particularly to those who have not had the privilege of visiting the same.

Wild animal photography and hunting could and should go hand in hand, for without the first the hunter has no substantial proof, except for his trophies, of the things he may tell of when he comes home. The taking of pictures of wild and dangerous game certainly requires just as much of skill and courage as that of hunting these animals. Besides this, it takes a great deal more of patience and requires much more time. Personally, I

275

regret now that I did not take more time for my photography in the jungle than I did, but, as I was anxious to return to America at a certain time from the three different African trips, I always wanted to accomplish with the utmost speed what I had started out to do.

Sometimes the " camera hunter " must spend whole days and weeks in order to get a single good photograph of certain animals. A German doctor, whom I met on the shores of Victoria Nyanza, showed me some wonderful pictures of the wild life of the hippo, which he assured me had taken him all of five weeks to secure, and of all the different exposures, having used up more than six dozen films and plates, only five negatives were really first-class!

To watch a wild animal when it thinks it is unobserved is certainly one of the most interesting things the hunter can do. I have for hours repeatedly watched herds of zebra, hartebeest, and Grant's gazelle from quite close quarters, and it was a great pleasure to see how the animals fed, played, and fought together, absolutely unconscious of the presence of man. During such times of watching, the different characteristics of the several animals appear very marked indeed. Of the different game of the plains none is more curious than the wildebeest, as before stated, but the zebra, Grant's gazelle, Thomson's gazelle, and the impala are very interesting in their own way, although perhaps not as lively and " full of fun " as seem to be the curious-looking wildebeest. I deplore not having found leisure enough to watch these animals more often with a view of minutely describing afterwards their peculiar way of feeding, playing, and drinking.

The dangers and the excitement that accompany wild

animal photography can hardly be exaggerated, particularly if the naturalist goes out without any white man for his protection and help. No matter how courageous the native gun bearer or askari may be, the hunter never can depend upon him entirely. I once had a gun bearer who, with the greatest courage, stood by me as I encountered a lion charge, and yet the very same man was one of the first to run away when, another time, on Mt. Kenia, we were charged by a herd of elephants! I was unfortunate myself in this respect in having been out on my shooting trips without the company of any white hunter, although on my first expedition I had Mr. Lang as taxidermist. He generally had to remain in camp to take care of all the skins, and so I had to stalk the animals with camera and gun alone. The danger is, however, very much minimized if the wild-animal photographer has with him a white man who is accustomed to jungle life, and is a fearless fellow and a good shot. Mr. Radcliffe Dugmore was in that respect fortunate in having young Mr. Clark with him, who generally stood guard with his rifle while Dugmore took the pictures. Thus he secured a collection which certainly far surpasses anything that has hitherto been brought home from the jungles of Africa.

As before mentioned, the big-game photographer needs particularly three things for his success: first, plenty of time; second, unlimited patience; and third, a good outfit. I say plenty of time, because, as already stated, it will often be necessary for the photographer to spend days and weeks in the securing of a single good negative of a special animal. Often he will have to construct his cover one day and wait for two days or more, until the animals are so accustomed to the same that he will be able to take his picture from as close a distance as he desires. Then again, he may find that after he has been able to take a few pictures of the object in question, most of these, or possibly all, are complete failures on account of too poor light, too short exposure, or some defect in film or plate, which latter I myself had to contend with on several occasions. This was particularly annoying to me in a roll of films which I used on the Laikipia Plateau in photographing a big bull giraffe. For, in some way still unaccounted for, three of the most important exposures of the roll were so much sunstruck as to spoil almost entirely the effect of the picture. After such an experience it may be weeks before the sportsman has an equally good chance at the same kind of animal, and, therefore, time is one of the first considerations in big-animal photography.

The patience required is certainly more than the average man is possessed of, for time and again the animal will not appear in the place at the time wanted, or some unfortunate crack from stepping on a branch, or other noise, may scare the shy beast away before the sportsman has a chance to use his camera. It is very often the case with night photography that a miserable hyena or jackal will snap the string and set off the camera which was placed and fixed for the king of beasts, and thus the photographer has to set and reset his apparatus perhaps a dozen times during several nights before he is able to get a single good photograph of a lion in the act of springing on its prey or coming down to drink at a stream. Another thing that requires patience in this kind of big game photography is the motionless endurance of mosquitoes and other insects, when one is standing behind a light cover for the sake of immortalizing some wild beast.

With the two first-named qualities at his disposal the most important question is that of the outfit. It is true in the way of a camera as it is with the gun, that it is not possible to have one camera which is equally well fitted for all kinds of work. The big-game hunter should, therefore, have at least two or three photographic apparatus of different construction.

On one of my trips I brought with me the large Zeiss telephoto camera, which is very expensive and quite heavy to carry around. This apparatus would take pictures at several hundred yards with perfect accuracy, if I was only fortunate enough always to use the right focus and exposure. But if the animal or other object that was being photographed was within a hundred yards or less, this was an exceedingly difficult task, as I simply had to judge the distance and then set the focus accordingly. Of course this telephoto camera is also fitted with a removable ground glass for the purpose of accurate focusing, but in nine cases out of ten the photographer of live game has no time to put in the ground glass, throw the focusing cloth over his head, focus, remove these things, and insert his plate or film for the exposure, and I, therefore, had to judge the distance the best way I could when I saw the animal coming. This feat in Africa is particularly difficult, and one is generally apt to underestimate it, especially in the beginning.

I was fortunate enough to be able to take twelve photographs of two rhinos, which first lay down and then stood up together, after which one of them charged me.

Of these twelve exposures only four were really clear, first-class negatives, which are reproduced in the chapter on the rhino. Then, another thing against this otherwise so excellent apparatus is that the slightest vibration of the hand or the tripod makes the picture blurred, and the lens requires a good deal of light, and that from the right direction, if a very short exposure is to be successful.

If I should go out to Africa again I would take an American-made camera—the naturalist's Graflex—which is made by the kodak company in Rochester. This camera is even more expensive than the Zeiss, costing, when new, with the best kind of tripod, two film holders and case, about $500, but it is, without a doubt, the best camera outfit in existence for wild-animal photography. It is advisable to take two film or plate holders to enable the photographer to make quicker changes when at work in the field. Otherwise the changing of the film roll may spoil his chances for another exposure, wanted in a hurry. It was with such camera outfit that both Mr. Kermit Roosevelt and Mr. Dugmore achieved their wonderful success in photographing wild beasts, both at night and in the daytime, and Dr. Chapman uses the same apparatus in his bird photography. This excellent camera is also a little heavier and larger than the Zeiss telephoto apparatus, but it has that wonderful advantage, common to all the Graflex cameras, that the photographer is able to focus on a ground glass, where he sees the image right-side up and without any focusing cloth over his head, until the very moment that he " snaps " the picture. He is thus not obliged to do any guessing at all as to the exact distance or time of exposure, but is sure of getting the object sharp at least nine times out of ten.

It is also advisable to take a smaller camera, with possibly a wide-angle lens, for photographing scenery, villages, and similar objects, for which purpose some people like to take a panoramic camera. I should also think it would be possible to fix a small and light camera with a " universal lens " under the barrel of the gun, and at the very end of the same, with some kind of an attachment which would make it possible for the photographer to " snap," for instance, a charging animal at a few yards distance, and then, without changing the position of the gun, kill the oncoming beast. If I go back to Africa again I shall certainly try this method, as it would enable the hunter to wait with comparative safety until the very last moment to see whether the animal means mischief or not before he would have to shoot to save his life.

Another important question to decide is whether it is advisable to take films or dry plates, or both. During one of my expeditions, when I had both kinds almost equally divided, it so happened that one of the porters, who carried a box with some of our best, already developed negatives, dropped the same in crossing a river, when he stumbled over some stones. The result was that the heavy box hit one of these, and a great many of the negatives were broken and ruined, which was a great loss to us, indeed. On the other hand, dry plates will, as a rule, keep better in the tropics, but if the films are carefully put up in sealed tin boxes they will keep for fully five to six months in any climate, particularly if one is careful to develop the rolls as quickly as possible after the exposures.

THE BIG GAME OF AFRICA

In British East Africa, where on all the high plateaus the game is most plentiful and the sportsman has plenty of clear water, cool enough for photography, I always used to develop my negatives every day or two, although the air was dry enough not to spoil the film rolls, even if the developing had been put off for a few weeks. It is, however, much the safer plan to develop the negatives, if possible, the very same evening after they have been exposed. Thus the photographer knows at once what success he has had, will more easily understand the reason for his failures, and will, in this way, be less apt to make mistakes in the future.

This is particularly easy as far as films are concerned, as the photographer is then able to develop the same in daylight with the developing machine or developing tank, which I have used with great success and pleasure on all my African trips. For the dry plates and for individual film rolls, that need to have the different negatives developed at different lengths of time, a small photographer's tent of dark brown or dark green material, and possibly lined with red, is very useful. Another thing which should not be forgotten is the practical little green umbrella tent, with its " windows," through which the photographs are taken. This little tent is easily carried and very quickly put up. It is almost invisible to the animals at only a few yards' distance, if carefully placed among some bush, or else screened off a little with branches and grass.

As to the exposures, it is well to remember for the beginner that they must be a great deal longer than he is generally inclined to think, as the moisture in the air makes the light in reality not as strong as it appears to be. I

SOME OF THE AUTHOR'S TROPHIES AT KIJABE R. R. STATION IN 1906.
Note the relative size of the elephant tusks.

AUTHOR'S "LION CAMP" ON THE SOTIK.

have heard from a good many sportsmen that in the beginning ninety per cent of their negatives were underexposed until they got accustomed to judge more accurately the intensity of the light. Nowadays anything in the way of developing papers, hypo, and other chemicals of fairly good quality are obtainable in Nairobi at a slightly advanced price.

Another very important feature of the sportsman's life in the jungle is the skillful preserving of his trophies. A great many skins which sportsmen have taken home from different parts of the world are so badly taken off and so poorly cured that I have heard taxidermists, like the celebrated Roland Ward in Piccadilly, London, say that they very often had to piece the skins out with parts of other skins. The sportsman who goes out to Africa without the slightest knowledge of taxidermy will probably experience that a high percentage of the trophies he brings home have been spoiled by careless handling by the native gun bearers. These men, although most of them know perfectly well how to prepare the trophy, at least so that it will not spoil in shipment, are so lazy that they will not, as a rule, take the trouble to do this properly, unless " Bwana mkubwa " is able to show them how to do it or else closely watches their work.

These men, unless differently instructed, will invariably cut up the head and neck skin on the throat side, and thus spoil the trophy entirely both for the private collection and the museum. The proper way is to cut it up all along the back of the neck. If the animals are to be mounted whole or in part, or are to be given away to museums, it is very necessary to carefully measure the different parts of the animal before the skin is taken off. For nowadays the mounting is not done by "stuffing," as formerly, but in such way that a carefully proportioned plaster cast is made, over which the skin of the animal is then drawn and sewed together. For this purpose it is necessary to take a number of measurements, such as, for instance (1), the full length of the animal from tip of nose to end of tail; (2) measurements of the neck behind the ears; (3) the neck by the shoulders; (4) height of the animal at the withers; (5) the same at pelvis; (6) the girth of chest; (7) the same of the belly; (8) the size of the legs at the body; (9) at the knee; and (10) just above the hoofs. From such measurements, carefully and tightly taken, a cast can be made of exactly the same shape and size as the identical animal, the skin of which is to be mounted.

In skinning smaller mammals it is not necessary to cut open the legs, but just to make a slit on the chest and belly and on the top of the neck, as by so doing the whole animal can be skinned without any more cutting. The skins of larger animals are sometimes taken off in sections so as to make them easier to cure, preserve, and transport, but this is not necessary. I have myself brought home to New York City several skins of rhinos, eland, and giraffes, which were beautifully prepared by Mr. Lang and his black helpers in one single piece. This, of course, requires the supervision of a skilled taxidermist and a great deal of care and hard work, for the heavy hides have to be cut thin with large knives from the thickness of an inch and more to that of an ordinary antelope or deer skin.

The hides of wild animals are generally prepared in

three different ways. One method, pursued by the natives the world over, consists in cutting the skin of the animal up all the way from the mouth to the tail on the underside. Then it is cut open on the inside of the legs, and afterwards simply pegged out to dry in the sun. During the dry seasons this method is, in most instances, safe, but the skins are ruined for mounting and are very troublesome to transport, because they are stiff and heavy. A much better way to do, although it requires a great deal more care and work, is to have the thicker parts of the skins cut thin and then the skin stretched out on the ground and rubbed over with a mixture of one third of alum to two thirds of white salt. For the hairy side a thin coat of arsenical soap will suffice to protect it from parasites. The third method is the one which Mr. Selous most highly recommends and which I have also successfully tried myself. After the animal has been skinned, all fleshy parts and fat are most carefully cut away, the lips cut thin, the ears turned inside out, and the cartilage cleaned from all meat and fat, after which the skin is stretched out by hand on the ground or else sewed on to pegs, to be kept more stretched. The inside of the skin is then rubbed over with a thin, uniform coat of arsenical soap, which also with advantage is applied to the hairy parts for the sake of bugs and insects.

Besides such trophies as skins of fur animals and antelopes, tusks, horns, and heads of elephants, rhinos, hippos, giraffes, and other large beasts, the feet of certain of these animals are very valuable trophies. They can be made up into umbrella stands, cigar boxes, inkstands, card cases, and other souvenirs, and are very much valued by relatives and friends at home. Beautiful walking sticks and riding whips, as well as table tops, which look very much like polished agate, can be made from the skins of rhinos and hippos, and I have even seen most beautifully made bowls and card receivers pressed out of the skins of these pachyderms.

Each sportsman should feel that he is not only out in the wilderness for the sake of his own recreation and pleasure, but also for the sake of serving science and humanity at large. For, even in our enlightened day, it is quite possible to discover new species of animals, as has been my good fortune on several occasions, and also to enrich the interesting and profitable knowledge of natural history by the experiences in the jungles. Not only is it our duty and pleasure as sportsmen to make careful observations of the life of the big-game animals, to preserve them and the record of their habits by the use of photography, and by the careful preservation of the hunting trophies for ourselves and our contemporaries, but we ought to do this also for the benefit of coming generations, who will probably not be able to find much big game in any part of the world.

CHAPTER XVIII

GENERAL OUTFIT AND ROUTE OF TRAVEL

BIG-game hunting, and particularly the pursuing of powerful and dangerous animals, such as the elephant, buffalo, lion, rhinoceros, leopard, with either camera or gun, is certainly one of the most fascinating pastimes the lover of Nature and animal life can have. It not only brings the hunter into the closest touch with the wonderful animal creation, but also enables him to enjoy the most varied scenes of Nature. It takes him over seemingly endless plains, with their vast herds of all sorts of game, and into the stillness and majesty of the virgin forest, where the grandest of all game, the elephant, loves to roam. It takes him up to the cool hills and high plateaus with their crystal-clear, rushing mountain streams, as well as to the hot and mosquito-infested lowlands and swamps with their deadly climates.

The outfit, therefore, of the big-game hunter must of necessity be well chosen, and so carefully selected that with the minimum of bulk he will have the maximum of safety, comfort, and pleasure. On the proper and not too cumbersome outfit depends not only the big-game hunter's comfort, health, safety, and pleasure, but also, to a very large extent, his success. On my first trip to Africa, in 1906, I met a man who had gone out to do some big-game hunting and who ridiculed the idea of having a mosquito-proof tent, a proper bed and bedstead, emergency rations, etc. *He* was going to do without such "unnecessary" things, would rough it instead, and so with "less trouble" and in shorter time bag all the game he wanted. But he landed worn out and sick in the Nairobi hospital a few weeks later, and had to return home without the coveted trophies. Another young man, a German baron, made the opposite mistake of taking so many really unnecessary things, including whole boxes of beer and wine, that he was greatly hampered thereby, and thus also failed to attain what he had set out to accomplish within the limits of his time.

The outfit should, therefore, include only the things really useful and exclude everything that civilized man can dispense with without in any way depriving himself of what is absolutely necessary for his health, pleasure, and success. For the true big-game hunter does not go into the wilderness to live sumptuously but to enjoy a complete rest and change from the products of "over-civilization" and the whirl and rush of business, to have a chance to study wild animal life, and experience a certain amount of hardships in obtaining his coveted trophies, the memory of which in after years will belong to the happiest moments of his life.

To those who intend to go out to Africa for the sake of photography and big-game shooting, but who as yet have had no experience in tropical countries, I here venture to give a few hints which may be useful to follow:

1. *The tent* is one of the most important parts of the outfit and should for East Africa, where all of the outfit

has to be carried on porters' heads or backs, be so small that, with fly and poles, packed in a waterproof tent bag, it does not weigh much more than sixty pounds, when dry. When packed wet, a tent will generally weigh fully ten to twenty pounds more, which makes it very heavy to be carried by one porter. If the tent is larger, one man carries the inner tent and ground sheets and another the fly, poles and stakes. I have found the former way much handier, for it will allow the hunter to have an inner tent seven feet high by six feet wide and seven feet long, with waterproof ground cloth sewed on all around and a fly extending to the ground seven and a half feet long by twelve feet long at the bottom.

Such a tent gives ample room for one person, and in an emergency can easily accommodate two. Both ends of the inner tent should be provided with mosquito nets; the rear end with a large " window," and the front with a loose net to be lifted up, when any one goes in or out, or else have the net fastened all around the edges of the tent's " door," with an opening in the middle, which may be closed with a string in the same fashion as a lady's sewing bag. A tent thus made gives perfect protection from mosquitoes, flies, ticks, ants, lizards, snakes, and all kinds of " creeping things," with which the tropics swarm. The waterproof ground cloth, sewed on to the tent, gives excellent protection from the dampness of the ground, or even water, in which it is sometimes necessary to pitch the tent after or during a heavy rain storm. An extra " dining room extension," to be buttoned on to the fly in front, is very useful and can be carried, with its pole, as an extra cover for the sleeping bag, or complete bed, which generally does not make more than half a load. This extension should not reach quite down to the ground, thus allowing for more circulation of air. Of the different materials that I have tried for tents, nothing seems to be better than the green, medium-weight, imported water-proofed canvas.

The smaller sized tent is much to be preferred, when there is a great deal of continuous marching to be done, as it is very quickly put up and taken down. If the hunter plans to remain in the same camp for several days, he simply lets his men put up a " grass shade house " in front of the tent to serve as a dining room and resting place, such house being much cooler than even a double tent, and, if reasonably well made, will not let any rain through.

Of course, if the sportsman only intends to visit the healthy portions and high plateaus of British East Africa, the mosquito net is not so much a necessity; but it will always prove a source of great comfort, if the hunter sometimes wants to rest in the daytime without having to be bothered with flies, wasps, or spiders, of which there are great numbers.

2. *Provisions* in sufficient quantity should be taken from home, as the local supply is very much inferior, and things like the splendidly prepared American breakfast foods, such as Puffed Rice, Shredded Wheat, Force, and other kinds cannot be obtained in East Africa at present. A reasonable amount of these breakfast foods will be found very useful, particularly as nowadays good fresh milk can often be obtained from settlers and natives. It is also important to take a few pounds of the so-called dehydrated fruits and vegetables, so light to carry and

really necessary with the different kinds of meat which the hunter usually secures in abundance. In any tropical country it is not good to live too much on a meat diet, and as fresh vegetables very rarely can be obtained in Africa, these dehydrated peas, spinach, cranberries, and a good many other varieties serve as most excellent substitutes.

A few small tins of different potted meats, perhaps half a dozen for each month one expects to be out on the shooting trip, should be carried, as sometimes in going through farms, or thickly settled countries, no game can be procured for a few days at a time. Another very useful article is the " Erbswurst " for soup, the emergency food of the German army, some kind of meat extract for beef tea, as well as Borden's condensed, unsweetened milk, far superior to anything obtainable in East Africa. Other food stuffs, such as tea, coffee, sugar, rice, and flour, can be obtained in good quality locally.

3. *The personal clothing* is another very important part of the big-game hunter's outfit. Beginning with the necessary sun helmet, which can advantageously be obtained at Port Said on the way out, at least one rather heavy hunting suit should be taken, for the high plateaus are, in the early mornings and in the evenings, very cold. The mercury falls on these plateaus, although lying right under the equator, often below the freezing point. Then several pairs of Khaki or other dull-colored riding breeches, woolen shirts, light and heavy, all of some dark green or brownish shades, which seem to blend best with all kinds of country. A coat is generally worn only in the early morning hours, between five and eight, or after the

return to camp in the evening. Otherwise most hunters go around in their flannel or Khaki shirts.

4. *Good boots* are very essential, and should be of strong but soft waterproof skin, with very heavy soles, some of which should be studded with hobnails to prevent slipping on the dry grass. It is also advisable to take at least one pair of boots with heavy rubber soles for silent stalking on hard and rocky ground. Mr. F. C. Selous, the famous African elephant hunter, used such rubber-soled boots exclusively on his last African trip and found them very satisfactory. Others again, including ex-President Roosevelt, do not fancy them much. Over the boots, unless they reach almost up to the knee, it is good to wear either strong canvas or leather leggings, or the unrivaled English puttees, which are practically both water and snake proof, and can be obtained in Mombasa or Nairobi.

5. *Underclothes* should be of the same kind as are used at home during fall and spring. A cummerband or two should not be forgotten, even if not regularly used. Many people, including physicians, recommend only woolen underclothes for the tropics, but I myself have with great comfort and safety used ordinary cotton underclothes and linen mesh, which certainly are much cooler and seem to absorb moisture better than anything else.

6. *Stockings* should be of medium weight, of whatever material used; but as the extremes of heat and cold of the various districts are very great, it may be wise to carry a few pairs of extra heavy and also very light stockings.

Experience has shown that for a four months' trip in the jungle it is not necessary to take more than six changes of underclothes, one dozen and a half pairs of socks, four pairs of trousers or breeches, one light and one heavy coat, four pairs of boots, two pairs of puttees, cummerbands, handkerchiefs, and a small but well-stocked sewing bag; all of which, with the exception of the boots, will go into a small, air-tight tin or steel uniform case, best bought in England, but also procurable at Port Said or Nairobi. This light tin box will also hold the necessary toilet articles and yet only weigh about sixty pounds or under. For the boots and soiled clothes (which as a rule are washed every day or two by the personal servant or "boy"), as well as clothes not dry, a waterproof canvas bag with lockbar is the best. This bag, which also may contain a pair of rubber boots and an extra rain coat, is generally added to the camp chair, or table, to form another load.

7. *Camp furniture* and *kitchen utensils* should contain at least a collapsible cot with sleeping bag, a camp table and ditto chair or two, a complete aluminum cooking outfit in a waterproof canvas bag, a simple collapsible grill, ditto baking oven, and one or two bread forms. A couple of the so-called "South African water bags" of canvas—a most useful addition to one's camp outfit—a few canvas pails and wash basins, and possibly a canvas bath tub, and the hunter has everything really necessary to his health and comfort in as small a bulk as possible.

8. *A small emergency tent* is another very useful article to take along. This could be of a pyramid shape, with but one collapsible pole in the center and with waterproof ground cloth sewed on all around, about six and a half feet high by six and a half feet square at the bottom. This tent, preferably with a pole of bicycle tubing in three sections, rolls up into a very small parcel and need not weigh

more than twenty-five pounds, cover and all. It should always be carried while tracking big game, such as elephants, lions, and buffaloes, as one never knows how far from the main camp the chase may lead. Without such an emergency tent the hunter would often either lose much time, and possibly the game, by having to return to camp for the night, or else experience the discomforts and dangers of having to sleep in the jungle without any shelter —which is neither pleasant nor safe. Besides this little tent, it is wise always to let a man carry a small bag or a tin containing emergency rations of bread, biscuits, tinned meat, cocoa or tea, and sugar enough for two days, in case it is found expedient to follow the beast very far from the permanent camp. Had I always done this myself it would have saved me many a disappointment and unnecessary exposure.

9. *The question of armament* is one about which each hunter seems to have his own ideas; but one thing is sure, that just as it is impossible for a tailor to make a suit of clothes that will fit all sizes of men, just as impossible is it for a gun maker to turn out a weapon which is equally serviceable for all sorts of game. The small-caliber guns, like the marvelous little .256 Mannlicher-Shoenaur, with its flat trajectory, long range and enormous penetration, come nearest to perfection no doubt, for I have myself not only killed such game as wildebeest, leopard, and zebra at from two hundred to five hundred yards with that gun, but also with *only one shot at each* instantly killed a charging rhinoceros and two elephants. Yet I should hesitate to go against a charging lion with such a gun, unless I was close enough to be sure of a head shot, for the bullet is

too small and light to stop such a beast at once, even if shot through the heart.

To be well equipped with guns there should be one small bore, such as the popular Mannlicher just mentioned, a heavier magazine rifle, such as the powerful .405 Winchester—a splendid " lion killer "—or a nine- or eleven-millimeter Mauser or Mannlicher rifle, and then perhaps a double-barreled .450 cordite Express, such as Colonel Roosevelt has used with great success on his African trip. If the hunter is a strong and powerfully built man, he may use even a double-barreled .577 cordite Express—without doubt the most potent shoulder weapon made—firing not less than one hundred grains of cordite and a bullet weighing seven hundred and fifty grains, giving the gun a tremendous penetration. But the weight of this gun of fourteen to fifteen pounds, and the rather " unpleasant " recoil of the shot, makes it impossible for anyone but a heavily set man to use it.

Once in 1906, when suddenly charged by a female rhinoceros on the western slopes of Mt. Kenia, I fired with this kind of gun at very close quarters, the muzzle of the gun being perhaps not more than four yards away from the rhino's forehead. The bullet passed right through the brute's head, plowed through the whole neck, smashed the lungs, and was cut out by my taxidermist from the very center of the rhino's heart!

A small caliber, high-power gun, although perfectly sufficient to kill any animal instantly, if shot through its head, is not powerful enough to stop a big charging beast, if fired at any other part of its body, whereas the tremendous shock of for instance, a bullet from the .577 Express would stop and turn any beast at once, even if the most vital part of its body was missed. Therefore, when hunting such dangerous game as the elephant, rhino, lion, or buffalo, the sportsman should always, for safety's sake, take along a big-bore, high-power rifle in reserve for a final shot at close quarters. The heavy rifle is generally carried by a gun bearer, who is supposed to walk close behind the hunter.

Some men never want the " trouble " of carrying any kind of gun themselves, except just when they want to fire at an animal, their gun bearers always carrying the guns behind them. In this way many a rare animal has escaped before the " sportsman " has had time to take the rifle from his gun bearer and fire, and not a few hunters have thus been killed by suddenly charging animals in dense bush or high grass. I myself would have been killed on at least three different occasions, had I not carried the gun myself and been ready to fire instantly, once not even having time to bring the rifle up to the shoulder. By sheer luck I hit the rhino's head and killed it instantly, less than three yards from the muzzle of the gun, which was only the small .256 Mannlicher.

10. *A good shotgun* is a very useful weapon in Africa, as the country swarms with game birds of all kinds, from the giant bustard, with a spread of wing measuring ten feet and more, to the tiny snipe and quail, so delicious for the table. Among other game birds there are ducks, geese, guinea fowl, and partridges, the meat of which forms a very much appreciated change from the venison, and the rather tough zebra and rhino meat. Such a gun, loaded with buckshot, is one of the best weapons at night for leopards,

hyenas, and even lions, at close quarters. A German officer, with whom I traveled home from Africa in 1910, told me that he had killed not less than two lions and fourteen leopards at night with a double-barreled, twelve-gauge shotgun during the last six years, and another of my German fellow passengers corroborated his statements. I myself once killed a hunting leopard with a twelve-gauge shotgun, when I was out bird shooting near Lake Baringo in 1906, to which I already have referred in the chapter on leopards.

A good many sportsmen also carry a heavy revolver or automatic pistol for use in an emergency at close quarters. A young settler in British East Africa who had been badly mauled by a wounded lion, at which he had emptied his gun, but which rushed at him before he could reload, told me that if he had carried his revolver at the time he would not have been mauled. As it was, his life was only saved by the courage of one of his servants, who killed the lion on his very body by a well-aimed shot through its head.

Some hunters like to use a telescope on their guns for long-range shots on the plains, and I have a couple of times with advantage also used the Maxim gun silencer, which was fitted to the .256 Mannlicher.

On landing in Mombasa or Kilindini an import duty of ten per cent *ad valorem* is levied on all articles brought into the country, except on personal wearing apparel and already used cameras. Guns and ammunition are generally charged for at the local value, which is usually equivalent to some twenty-five per cent advance on their cost in Europe or America.

THE BIG GAME OF AFRICA

There are different ways of reaching British East Africa. The quickest route is via Marseilles or Naples by either the French or the German line, and from there via Port Said, the Suez Canal, and the Red Sea to Mombasa or Kilindini. Of these two direct lines the German East African line is by far the better of the two, having much larger and better fitted steamers for the tropics. The trip from Naples to Mombasa or Kilindini occupies from fifteen to sixteen days and costs about four hundred dollars first class from Naples and return, so that the cost of the whole trip from New York to Kilindini and return, via Naples, would be approximately six hundred to eight hundred dollars, according to the size and location of the stateroom. At Naples there are always good and direct connections with New York by large and excellent steamers of the North German Lloyd, the Hamburg-American and the White Star Line.

CHAPTER XIX

RETROSPECT AND CONCLUSION

In reviewing what has been said about the big game of the Dark Continent, it is evident that British East Africa is the most wonderful shooting country in the world, not only in regard to the large number of different species obtainable, their gameness, and value as trophies, but also as to its healthfulness and easiness of reach. Thanks to the Uganda Railroad, many government roads and bridges, and a network of well-defined native paths, most parts of the country are now easily, comfortably, and safely reached, so that even ladies may greatly enjoy a short sojourn in the Protectorate.

It was my privilege to meet ex-President Roosevelt again, when the Camp Fire Club of America gave a luncheon to him, shortly after his return to this country. On this occasion Colonel Roosevelt gave a most interesting and instructive address about big-game shooting in East Africa. Among other things, he said in substance:

" We need not read with envy of the wonderful chances for big-game shooting that our forefathers had in centuries past, when they hunted with the bow and arrow in the wilds of Europe, nor do we need to wonder at the accounts of the marvelous opportunities for great sport that the Egyptian, Babylonian, Greek, Roman, and afterwards

299

European rulers had, at the time when wild bison and bears, lions, and much other big game roamed around in great numbers even in Europe, for British East Africa is a much more wonderful game country than any which those rulers ever laid their eyes upon! We have out there a much greater variety of species, as well as much larger and fiercer animals, often gathering in herds much mightier than anything ever seen in either Europe or India. The herds of American bison and elk were certainly wonderful in our own country a few decades ago, but out there in East Africa the vast herds of antelopes even surpass these, and that right now in our present time. I wish that all sportsmen in this country, who are able to do so, would go out to British East Africa and enjoy for a while the marvelous opportunities for big-game shooting which that country still offers. . . ."

I heartily agree with Colonel Roosevelt's remarkable utterances, and believe that every fearless and able-bodied sportsman, who is fond of big-game shooting, and who can afford it, should go out to British East Africa as soon as possible. For there is no question that the enormous herds of game even there are quickly diminishing before the advancing army of settlers, hunters, and naturalists, who now yearly visit the country. I regret to say that it is my firm opinion, formed both from reports of several old African hunters as well as from my own observations in the field during my three expeditions to Africa, that the big game there is rapidly being shot off. " Record heads " of most of the game it is almost impossible to secure any more; large bull elephants with tusks weighing more than one hundred pounds apiece are extremely rare, and rhinos with horns of even twenty-four inches and more hardly ever encountered, unless the hunter goes very far away from the ordinary hunting districts. In certain localities, where large elephant herds with magnificent tuskers used to roam around only a few years ago, not an elephant is seen to-day, and where the mighty pachyderms still exist in British East Africa, as on Mt. Kenia, the Aberdare Mountains, Mt. Elgon, and in the southwestern part of the Protectorate, they are very shy and wary, and even tuskers with ivory of one hundred pounds a pair are scarce. The lion is getting more and more rare and shy, and is much less frequently encountered during the daytime than only a few years ago, and big black-maned ones are extremely hard to secure. This is also the case with the cunning leopard, which seems to have learned by experience to distinguish between the black savage and the white man with his far-reaching and destructive guns.

I do not believe that the native hunters are a menace to the wild game, for even in centuries past, when they did exactly what they pleased without any restrictions or control on the part of the white man, the game increased all the time. Although some of the tribes are extremely fond of hunting and live chiefly from the game they secure, yet even they do not seem to be able to check the natural increase of the game. The African is, with few exceptions, much too lazy to be very destructive to the animals, for he will only kill what he needs for food and his scanty clothing, or to secure the coveted ivory for trading purposes. Yet his methods of hunting and his armament are so primitive and poor that without firearms he never could do much harm to the game. In

German and Portuguese East Africa, where at times the natives have been allowed to carry firearms, this was different, but in most of the countries controlled by European governments, including British East Africa, he is, fortunately, not allowed to carry firearms. It is, therefore, only with the advent of the white sportsman and settler with their destructive modern weapons that the natural increase of game has been checked, and some of the finest of the animals threatened with total extinction.

Yet, in spite of all this, British East Africa is to-day the most remarkable game country in the world. On its vast plains the sportsman will still find countless numbers of different kinds of hartebeest, topi, Grant's and Thomson's gazelles, lion, wart hog, wildebeest, water buck, giraffe, zebra, and occasionally eland, rhino and hippo, in and near the rivers. In open bush or parklike country he will meet zebra, Jackson's hartebeest, impala, oryx, eland, roan, sable, wart hog, giraffe, rhino, reed buck, water buck, baboons, bush pig, and many of the smaller antelopes. In the big, dense forests he may secure elephant, bush pig, bongo, rhino, bush buck, possibly the giant pig, and a great number of different kinds of monkeys and smaller fur animals, while almost everywhere there is an abundance of birds, big and small, not to speak of the reptiles previously referred to.

From the above it is evident that whereas certain animals, like the elephant, bongo, bush pig and monkeys, are found only in the forests, and other game, like the gnu, topi, and Thomson's gazelle, are all denizens of the plains, a great number of the choicest game animals are found both on the plains and in open bush and forest country. Among these the most important are the lion, giraffe, hartebeest, zebra, wart hog, Grant's gazelle, oryx, eland, roan, sable, rhino, leopard, baboons, and a number of smaller antelopes. The best kind of country, therefore, to hunt in, is, without doubt, those places where the plains merge into open bush or parklike country and where clumps of bushes are mingled with larger shade trees. This kind of country is also much more suitable for observing animals at close quarters. There the naturalist-sportsman is more apt to secure good photographs of live big game, and there it is possible to stalk the wild animals successfully with both camera and gun, and this is one of the most interesting feats of big-game hunting.

It is not too much to say that from one hundred and fifty to two hundred shooting parties, and sometimes even more, now yearly go out to British East Africa in search of big game. If it is estimated that each hunting party during the sojourn in the land only kills on an average fifty animals—some have perhaps felled from two to three hundred and more, even without counting the many animals which were wounded but not secured by the party, and which afterwards succumbed to their wounds—this would make from two hundred parties not less than ten thousand animals slaughtered yearly! Add to this that each adult lion or leopard kills an animal almost every night, no one can wonder that game grows more and more scarce and wary, and that fine heads and large tusks will soon be impossible to obtain.

The sportsman who is able to do so should, therefore,

as before remarked, go out to these wonderful shooting grounds just as soon as possible, if he wants to see the vast game herds before they dwindle away more perceptibly. I regret to say that it is perfectly true that a good many hunters so ruthlessly and wantonly destroy game, wounding hundreds of animals at long distance without even bothering to follow them up, that they indeed do not deserve to be classed as sportsmen. It should be the duty of each man, who goes out to Africa for a shoot, most scrupulously to observe the game laws and to do all he can to discourage the slaughter of game animals by others. As Colonel Roosevelt so fitly remarked: "No sportsman should kill game unless:

" First, it is an exceptionally fine head;

" Second, it is intended to be preserved for scientific purposes;

" Third, it is shot in real—not pretended—self-defense."

If this is complied with by all true sportsmen, and such people as wantonly and cruelly destroy game were made to feel that they in this respect are nothing but " criminals," much will be accomplished in the right direction and the standard of big-game hunting be raised. Thus, and with large and suitable game preserves, British East Africa will still for decades hold its own as the world's finest hunting ground.

My book is finished, but as I have written these pages, they have made me live all over again my wanderings, hardships, and many narrow escapes! They have revived in my memory the many pleasant evenings when, after days of excitement and danger, failure or success, the whole safari gathered around the big camp-fire, where naked savages delighted to perform their weird war dances, and where I listened to their tales of adventure, love, and fight, lulled to sleep by the crackling of the logs and the mournful howls of the hyena or the magnificent roars of the lion!

APPENDIX

I. THE KI-SWAHILI LANGUAGE

THE Ki-Swahili language, of the Bantu group, is not only spoken by the Swahili coast people of British and German East Africa, but has for hundreds of years been used by the Arab merchants and slave traders on their safaris into the interior. There is hardly a tribe of any size at all in the whole of British East Africa, German East Africa, British Central Africa, Uganda, and even the Congo, of which not a few people at least understand enough of Ki-Swahili to be able to serve fairly well as guides, gun-bearers and interpreters.

The language generally spoken by these inland tribes is, of course, a very corrupt form of Ki-Swahili. In this respect it corresponds to the " pidgin-English " spoken by the Chinamen in Hong Kong and other places in the East where many English-speaking people live. The ordinary illiterate caravan porter, even when a Swahili, speaks almost exclusively this " pidgin-Swahili," partly because he knows no better, but also because he is aware that the average European, or the savage inlander, will then more easily understand him.

When I arrived the first time in Africa I had, by hard work, during the last three weeks of the voyage, acquired a rude knowledge of Ki-Swahili, enough to enable me to get along very nicely with the porters without an interpreter. When arriving the second and third time in Africa, I had learned to speak the language more correctly and grammatically, but found that I often had to speak in the pidgin dialect to be quicker understood by the porters of the different tribes in my caravan.

APPENDIX

In the following lessons, which any man with average intelligence will be able to learn in much less time than it requires to go from New York to Mombasa, enough of this mostly used pidgin-Swahili will be taught to enable the sportsman to communicate directly with his guides, gun-bearers, and porters, even if these do not understand a word of English. To anyone who has the time, patience, and ambition to learn the language more correctly—which ought not to take an average man more than five or six months, giving to it about two hours a day—I most strongly recommend the two following publications: "Swahili Exercises" by Edward Steere, a most excellent and concise introduction to the Ki-Swahili language, and, to those who understand German, I would recommend as a still better grammar, "Praktische Suaheli Grammatik," by Prof. Dr. C. Velten. This latter book has the advantage of having a splendid dictionary at the end and is, perhaps, somewhat more thorough than the smaller English publication.

Introduction

The pronunciation of the Swahili words is very much like that of Italian or Spanish. So, for instance, *a* is pronounced like *a* in *father; e* like *e* in *fret; i* as *i* in *pin; o* as *o* in *for; u* as *u* in *lung; y* as *y* in *yet.*

The consonants are pronounced almost exactly as in English.

To compare the correct Ki-Swahili with the pidgin dialect, let us, for instance, mention the word for *my,* which, in its simplest form is *-angu,* preceded by the consonant prefix, peculiar to the word of the "owned" object. For instance my wife is *bibi wangu;* but my knife, *kisu changu;* my sail, *tanga langu;* my house, *nyumba yangu;* my place, *pahali pangu.* This shows that the same English word, my, may be expressed by either *wangu, changu, langu, yangu,* or *pangu,* according to the word to which it belongs. The illiterate porter, however will generally use the form *wangu* or *yangu* with all these words with the

possible exception sometimes of the words beginning with *Ki-*
or *Ch-*, and this only for the sake of euphony.

The same is the case with the adjectives and prefixes to the
verbs. Take, for instance, the word for our large, *-kubwa;* a
large man, *mtu mkubwa;* a large knife, *kisu kikubwa;* or take
the verb, *kata,* cut, for instance; he cuts is *a-na-kata;* it (the
knife) cuts, *ki-na-kata.* The Swahili will, however, understand
you equally well if you simply say *kisu mkubwa a-na-kata,* the
big knife, instead of the correct *kisu kikubwa ki-na-kata.*

The following lessons will give this pidgin-Swahili as it is
mostly used in the " safari language " of the porters. This is
exactly what the hunter really needs and wants on his shooting
expedition, which he will enjoy twice as much, if he is able to
communicate directly with his own men, as well as with the
chieftains and guides from tribes which he may meet on his
inland expedition. Not only will he thus enjoy his outing more,
but is also much less apt to be deceived by his men and guides.

After the lessons follows a key to the translations of the
different exercises, so that the reader will be able to determine
whether his own translations are correct or not. This key should
not be used, however, indiscriminately, but only after the student
has first written out his own translations of the different exercises, both in English and Swahili. At the end is a vocabulary,
containing in alphabetical order all the words that have occurred
in the lessons, and a good many more.

Lesson I

1. The Swahili knows no articles whatever; *mtu,* therefore,
means man, as well as the man, or a man; *mtoto,* a, or the child.

2. The adjectives always follow the word they refer to, and
take different prefixes according to the eight different classes,
to which the noun may belong, but we will here treat them all
as belonging to the first class, that of the living beings.

3. In the same way the personal prefixes, pronouns, and the

verbs will be treated, as most of the substantives, that the sportsman is likely to use, belong to this class anyhow.

4. The personal prefixes for the verbs are, *Ni-, U-, A-, Tu-, M-,* and *Wa-;* I, Thou, He (she or it), We, You, and They.

5. The tense prefixes for the verbs are, *-na-* for the present tense, *-li-* or *-me-* for past, and *-ta-* for future. Thus, for instance, of the verb, *piga,* shoot, beat, we have: *Ni-na-piga,* I shoot; *Ni-li-piga,* I shot; *Ni-me-piga,* I have shot; *Ni-ta-piga,* I shall shoot. In writing or in printing, the forms of the verbs are always written in one word, *Ninapiga,* but in the first two lessons they are separated, so as to make it easier for the beginner to find the different forms at a glance.

6. The Swahili has no special interrogative form of the verb, but expresses the question by a different tone of voice. For instance, *Mtu hapa,* may mean: A man is here, or *Is* a man here? according to the way of pronouncing the words. If an interrogative is used, it is always placed after the word it refers to, except, perhaps, when it stands in a longer sentence and belongs to several nouns, when it may begin the sentence. For instance, *wapi,* where; Where is the man? in Swahili, *Mtu wapi?* Where are the man and the woman? *Wapi mtu na bibi?*

7. Is or are, as a general rule, are omitted in the sentence, unless they are especially accentuated. In such case, both is and are are expressed by *ni* for all persons, singular and plural, and *si* for the negative is not, or are not; therefore, The man *is* here, *Mtu ni hapa;* The man *is* not here, *Mtu si hapa.*

8. The second person imperative of all regular verbs in Swahili is, as in English, exactly like their infinitive form; thus, *piga* means shoot (to shoot), and shoot! When in English *to* is put before the infinitive form, the *Swahili* uses *ku.* To shoot, therefore, is in Swahili, *ku-piga.*

Vocabulary

bwana, *sir, master.*
chakula, *food, meal.*
bunduki, *gun.*

bibi, *wife, women, miss.*
bilauri, *glass.*
leta, *bring.*

310

hema, *tent.*
kahava, *coffee.*
boy, *servant, butler.*
chai, *tea.*
chumvi, *salt.*
majani, *grass.*
kisu, *knife.*
maji, *water.*
masiwa, *milk.*
mkate, *bread.*
safari, *travel, caravan, trip.*
tembo, *elephant.*
sukari, *sugar.*
mtoto, *child, baby.*
nyama, *animal, meat.*
simba, *lion.*
nyumba, *house, home.*
mtu, *man.*
sahani, *plate.*

ona, *see, find.*
penda, *love.*
taka, *want, like.*
piga, *shoot, beat.*
piga hema, *pitch the tent.*
wapi, *where.*
tayari, *ready.*
sasa hivi, *instantly, just now.*
ema (=yema), *good, all right.*
hapa, *here.*
sasa, *now.*
katika, *in, on, by, at.*
sana, *very, very much.*
hapana, *no, not.*
kali, *sharp, cruel, dangerous.*
ndio, *yes.*
karibu, *near.*
na, *and, with.*
-kubwa, *large, great.*

Exercises

Translate into English:

A.[1] 1. Mtu mkubwa a-me-piga simba. 2. Bibi a-na-penda mtoto. 3. Boy, kisu wapi? 4. Katika nyumba, Bwana. 5. Leta kisu na bunduki hapa! 6. Ndio, Bwana. 7. Ni-me-ona tembo mkubwa katika majani. 8. Safari wapi? 9. Hapa karibu, Bwana! 10. Leta chakula, boy; kisu, sahani na bilauri! 11. Simba nyama kali. 12. Piga hema hapa! 13. Ni-na-taka chai, sukari na masiwa, siagi, mkate na chumvi! 14. Boy, leta maji hapa! 15. Ndio, Bwana, sasa hivi. 16. Bunduki si katika nyumba, ni hapa katika hema. 17. Bwana na bibi ni hapa katika majani na wa-na-taka chakula. 18. Chakula tayari, boy? 19. Ndio, sasa tayari! 20. Bwana kali a-na-piga sana boy. 21. Leta bunduki, ni-na-ona simba hapa karibu! 22. Tembo a-na-taka maji. 23. Ni-me-ona mtu mkubwa katika hema hapa na a-me-piga nyama kwa bunduki. 24. Wapi sukari, mkate, chai na masiwa? 25. Chakula hapa, Bwana!

---

[1] The letters in front of the exercises refer to the keys for the same at the end of the chapter.

APPENDIX

Translate into Swahili:

B. 1. The man saw a lion near the house. 2. Butler, bring the food; I want tea, bread, butter and milk right away! 3. Yes, Sir, the food is ready in the house. 4. All right! 5. Where is the caravan now? 6. Near by, Sir, near by! 7. I see an elephant in the water. 8. No, Sir, it is not an elephant. 9. Where are the gun, the knife and the tent? 10. Here, Sir! 11. The food is not good, bring a plate and a knife! 12. I want to shoot the lion right away! 13. Where is the lion now? 14. Near by in the grass by the water. 15. The child saw the women in the house. 16. Sir, the food is now ready; coffee, sugar and milk with bread. 17. I want very much water, milk and a knife. 18. Have you seen the women here? 19. No, Sir, the women are not here; they are in the tent. 20. Do you want the food right away? Yes, bring (it) here now. 21. The elephant and the lion are dangerous animals. 22. Butler, put up the tent here and bring the water! 23. I see an animal in the grass, bring at once the gun and the knife! 24. Yes, Sir, they are here! 25. All right, butler, now I want the caravan.

LESSON II

1. The plurals of substantives are formed by different prefixes before the root of the word, but as there are not less than eight different classes, each requiring its particular prefix, and as it is very difficult to know to which of these classes the different words belong, the following lists will always give the plural of each substantive, except where the plural is the same as the singular, as is done also in the vocabulary.

2. The adjectives and prefixes before the verbs as well as those before the different pronouns, will all be treated as belonging to the first class, as before mentioned.

3. The adjectives are given here in their simplest form; for singular, prefix *m-*, for plural, *wa-* (the proper prefixes for the first class); for instance, *Mtu mrefu*, a tall man; *watu warefu*, tall men.

4. The possessive case is expressed by the particle *wa* for

the first class; for instance, The European's wife, *Bibi wa Msungu.* The master's knife, *Kisu wa Bwana.*

Vocabulary

kisu, visu, *knife.*
mtu, watu, *man.*
mtoto, watoto, *child.*
kitendo, vitendo, *action.*
mshale, mishale, *arrow.*
kitanda, vitanda, *bedstead.*
kitabu, vitabu, *book.*
mzigo, mizigo, *burden.*
kiti, viti, *chair.*
kitana, vitana, *comb.*
mpishi, wapishi, *cook.*
-gumu, *hard.*
-zito, *heavy.*
-dogo, *little.*
-refu, *long.*
-pya, *new.*
-zima, *sound, well.*
-tamu, *sweet.*
-nene, *thick.*
sema, *say, speak.*
safisha, *clean.*
kamata, *take hold of.*
kikombe, vikombe, *cup.*
mlango, milango, *door.*
mzungo, wasungo, *white man.*
mkono, mikono, *hand.*
kipini, vipini, *handle.*
kilima, vilima, *hill.*

kiboko, viboko, *hippopotamus.*
kioo, vioo, *mirror.*
-kubwa, *large, great.*
-zuri, *good, beautiful.*
-pana, *broad.*
-kavu, *dry.*
-tupu, *empty.*
-baya, *bad.*
ku-ogopa, *to fear.*
ku-fanya, *to do.*
ku-la, *to eat.*
ngapi, *how many?*
-moja, *one.*
-bili, or wili, *two.*
-tatu, *three.*
-nne, *four.*
-tano, *five.*
-sitta, *six.*
nini, *what?*
wangu, *my, mine.*
wako, *your, yours.*
wake, *his, hers, its.*
nina, *I have.*
una, *you (thou) have.*
ana, *he has.*
tuna, *we have.*
mna, *you have.*
wana, *they have.*

Exercises

Translate into English:

C. 1. Watu warefu wa-me-leta visu hapa. 2. Mtoto a-na vitanda tatu katika nyumba. 3. Leta sasa hivi mishale tano! 4. U-na-sema nini? 5. Ni-na-sema, ni-na-taka chakula wangu katika hema wangu sasa. 6. Ndio, Bwana mkubwa, ni-ta-leta! 7. Mpishi mnene a-me-safisha vikombe wangu. 8. Mzungo mkubwa a-me-ona bibi wako hapa karibu. 9. U-na-ogopa mtu mrefu? 10. Mlango wa nyumba wangu mzito. 11. Boy, kikombe wangu si safi! 12. Ndio, Bwana, ni-ta-safisha! 13. Safari a-na-fanya nini sasa? 14. A-na-kula cha-kula katika hema, chakula wa nyama wa kiboko mnene, Bwana. 15. Kipini wa kisu si nzuri. 16. Watu ngapi katika safari wako? 17. Ni-na watu watano sasa. 18. Mtoto wangu si mzima. 19. Kahawa wangu si tamu, nataka sukari na masiwa katika kikombe. 20. Ni-me-ona tembo moja, simba wawili na viboko watano, na ni-me-piga tembo, simba moja na kiboko moja. 21. Bunduki wangu wapi? Ni safi? Ndio, Bwana, ni-me-safisha. 22. Mzigo wako mzito? Hapana, Bwana, ni nzuri. 23. Watoto watano wapi? Hapa, katika majani na wa-na-kula nyama, chai, masiwa na mkate. 24. Mtoto, safisha mikono wako sasa hivi na leta kitana hapa! 25. U-me-ona kitabu mpya katika mlango? Ndio, Bwana, ni-ta-leta?

Translate into Swahili:

D. 1. My child has a beautiful book in (his) hand. 2. Three ele-phants and four hippos are in the water. 3. How many lions have you shot? 4. I have shot four lions with my gun, and my boy shot one with an arrow. 5. What did your wife say? 6. She said she wanted very much the meal just now. 7. Boy, bring the mirror and the comb! 8. I see a white man in the door of my house; what does he want? 9. Your action is bad, my child. 10. Is your tea sweet? No, bring (me) the sugar! 11. Take hold of the tent and put it up here! 12. Yes, sir, they have six loads. 13. Boy, what are you doing here? Sir, I am cleaning your gun and knife. 14. All right, where is the gun bearer? In the tent, sir, and he is eating his food now. 15. Do you fear a lion? 16. Take hold of the handle and bring it here! 17. Is the load heavy now? No, Sir, it is light. 18. Bring three men here right away! 19. How many chairs are in the tent now? 20. We have four chairs, two bedsteads and one mirror. 21. How many hills are there here? 22. I see five; one very large and four small. 23. My child has five fine buttons. 24. Your actions are not good, my men. 25. Where have you pitched my tent? Is it near the water?

THE KI–SWAHILI LANGUAGE

LESSON III

1. The verb has, as before remarked, four simple tenses in its positive form; the present, *na;* the imperfect, *li;* the perfect, *me;* and the future, *ta.*

2. The negative forms of the verbs have only three tenses and are expressed both by different prefixes and in the present tense also by a change in the verb itself. The personal negative prefixes are: *si, hu, ha, hatu, ham, kawa;* meaning literally: I not, You (lit. thou) not, He (she or it) not, We not, They not. Of the verb *ku-piga* (to shoot), for instance, the simple forms are the following:

Present.

Positive Form.	Negative Form.
ninapiga (or napiga), *I shoot.*	sipigi, *I do not shoot.*
unapiga, *you shoot.*	hupigi, *you do not shoot.*
anapiga, *he (she) shoots.*	hapigi, *he (she) does not shoot.*
tunapiga, *we shoot.*	hatupigi, *we do not shoot.*
mnapiga, *you shoot.*	hampigi, *you do not shoot.*
wanapiga, *they shoot.*	hawapigi, *they do not shoot.*

Imperfect.

nilipiga, *I shot.*	sikupiga, *I did not shoot.*

Perfect.

nimepiga, *I have shot.*	sikupiga, *I have not shot.*

Future.

nitapiga, *I will shoot.*	sitapiga, *I will not shoot.*

Imperative.

piga, *shoot!* (sing.).	usipigi, *do not shoot!* (sing.).
pigeni, *shoot!* (plural).	msipigi, *do not shoot!* (plural).

315

APPENDIX

Vocabulary

ku-jibu, *to answer.*
ku-fika, *to arrive.*
ku-uliza, *to ask.*
ku-amsha, *to awaken.*
ku-nunua, *to buy.*
ku-sayidia, *to help.*
ku-jua, *to know.*
ku-chukua, *to carry.*
ku-panda, *to climb up.*
ku-rudi, *to come, or go back.*
ku-pika, *to cook.*
ku-lia, *to cry.*
ku-anguka, *to fall.*
ku-funga, *to bind.*
ku-ua, *to kill.*
ku-pima, *to measure.*
ku-simama, *to stand.*
ku-pa, *to give.*
ku-tasama, *to see, look for.*

mnyampara, *caravan-headman.*
askari, *soldier.*
kifaru, *rhinoceros.*
mamba, *crocodile.*
kongoni, *hartebeest.*
pofu, *eland.*
mpagazi, *caravan porter.*
-vivu, *lazy, idle.*
leo, *to-day.*
jana, *yesterday.*
kesho, *to-morrow.*
labda, *perhaps.*
karibu ya, *near by.*
chini ya, *below.*
juu ya, *above.*
ndani ya, *inside.*
huko, *there.*
ngosi, *skin.*
pembe, *horn, corner.*

Translate into English:

E. 1. Boy, sema mnyampara kusayidia mpagazi kuchukua mzigo. 2. Mzungu amefika katika campi; anataka kununua chakula. 3. Ah, sitaki kuuza sasa. 4. Mnyampara na gun bearer rudeni hapa, nataka (or ninataka) kupiga kongoni. 5. Wapagazi wavivu sana. 6. Uliza askari hapa wapi kisu wangu. 7. Bwana, askari anasema hajui. 8. Safari atafika huko leo? Sijui, Bwana, labda. 9. Katika maji hapa ninaona mamba na viboko. 10. Mny-ampara, leta wapagazi sasa hivi; nataka (or ninataka) kupiga kifaru, na watu watachukua ngozi na pembe. 11. Panda juu ya kilima na tasama, labda myama huko. 12. Ndio Bwana, natasama (nina-tasama) simba na kifaru huko karibu ya kilima. 13. Nataka kun-unua chakula wa watu. 14. Kesho tutafanya safari. 15. Wapi gun bearer na boy sasa? 16. Uliza boy anafanya nini. 17. Bwana, anasema anasafisha bunduki. 18. Ema, sema mpishi nataka kula chakula. 19. Unataka nini, Bwana? 20. Nataka chai, mkata, siagi, nyama na chumvi! 21. Bibi wangu wapi? Ndani ya nyumba,

Bwana. 22. Chini ya milima huko naona pofu. 23. Boy, sayidia gun bearer kusafisha bunduki. 24. Mpishi atapika chakula sasa? 25. Mtu mnoja ameanguka hapa.

Translate into Swahili:

F. 1. Gun bearer, tell my men to climb up the hill and kill the hartebeest. 2. Measure the lion at once! 3. Near by the water I see an elephant standing. (Sw. he stands.) 4. Boy, bring the rifle and the knife and tell the gun bearer to come here! 5. Yes, Sir, he is coming now. 6. Headman, where are the porters? 7. Perhaps I will go back to Nairobi to-morrow. 8. Boy, is the food ready now? 9. No, Sir, there is no food here now. 10. Shall I go and buy? 11. No, I do not want you to go, tell the headman to buy. 12. Where is the hartebeest now, gun bearer? 13. I do not know, Sir, perhaps it has fallen! 14. No, Mabruki, I see the animal near · the large hill. 15. Have you seen a lion to-day? 16. No, Sir, I have not seen any animal. 17. Is the soldier here now? 18. I do not know, Sir! 19. Awaken the porters at once, I want to help the European there! 20. The cook is inside the tent, ask if the meal is ready. 21. A bad man will not help his wife. 22. He will perhaps arrive here to-morrow, I do not know. 23. Have you cleaned the gun and the knife? 24. Yes, Sir, they are ready now. 25. Very well, eat the food right away.

Lesson IV

1. The Swahili verb also uses an *objective prefix* to denote the one, which receives the action of the verb; this prefix is inserted between the tense prefix and the verb-root. The objective prefixes are: *-Ni-, -ku-, -m-, -tu-, -wa-, -wa-;* Me, you (thee), him (her, it), us, you, them. You beat me, *U-na-ni-piga;* I have beaten them, *Ni-me-wa-piga;* they will beat us, *Wa-ta-tu-piga,* the syllables being written together: *Unanipiga, Nimewapiga,* and *Watatupiga.*

2. This objective prefix is also used instead of the lacking definite article: for instance, he beats a man, *anapiga mtu;* but,

he beats the man, *anampiga mtu*. We shall shoot the Lion, *Tutampiga simba*. If the verb begins with a vowel, a -*w*- is inserted between the objective -*m*- and the verb, for the sake of euphony; thus, for instance, instead of saying *alimona*, he saw him, the Swahili says *alimwona*, etc.

3. Two of the most common irregular verbs are *ku-ja*, to come, and *ku-wenda*, to go, abbreviated to *kwenda*. These verbs are always used with the infinitive mark, like all monosyllable verbs. Hence, he comes, *anakuja;* they go, *wanakwenda;* we will come, *tutakuja*, etc. The imperative of these verbs is also irregular; for instance: Come! *Njoo!* Come! (plural) *Njooni!* Go! *Nenda!* Go! (plural) *Nendeni!*

4. One of the most useful of the many compound forms of the verb is the form for " if." For all persons and tenses this form is the same; it is -*ngali*-, inserted immediately behind the personal prefixes. It denotes that if a person does something, another thing is bound to follow; for instance, *Ningaliwapiga* (ni-ngali-wa-piga) *wangalikimbia* (wa-ngali-kim-bia) may mean: If I beat them, if I had beaten, would beat, or shall beat them, they will, would have, or might run away.

5. If can also be expressed by *kama*, which generally starts the sentence; If you buy food, give (it) to me, *Kama unanunua posho, nipe* (an irregular form for *nikupa*).

Vocabulary

mbwa, *dog.*
kiboko, bibako, *hippo.*
posho, *porter's food.*
-refu, *long.*
labda, *perhaps.*
campi, *camp.*
mto, *river.*
killa, *all, every.*
upesi, *fast, quick.*
ku-sikia, *to hear, listen.*
ku-ambia, *to tell, narrate.*
ku-weza, *to be able to.*

ku-safiri, *to travel, march.*
ku-andika, *to write, engage.*
ku-pa, *to give, present.*
sana, *much, very much.*
huyu, *this.*
hawa, *these.*
mti, miti, *tree.*
mingi, *many.*
gani? *what kind?*
mimi, *I, I myself.*
ingine, *another.*
yule, *that.*

ku-taka, *want, like*.
ku-tasama, *to see, behold*.
ku-funga, *to tie, bind*.
ku-kimbia, *to run, run away*.

wale, *those*.
kazi, *work, labor*.
choroa, *oryx, antelope*.
sikitika, *sorry, sad*.

Exercises

Translate into English:

G. 1. Umetasema simba hapa? 2. Ndio, nimemtasama karibu ya milima huko. 3. Waliwajibu watu sasa hivi. 4. Tutampiga mtoto mbaya ndani ya hema kesho. 5. Umewatasama nyama huko? 6. Ndio, Bwana, ninawaona sasa kongoni, simba na kifaru. 7. Ni, karibu? 8. Hapana, si karibu, Bwana. 9. Ungalitaka chakula sasa, ningalikuleta. 10. Kama kifaru angalikwenda, singalimpiga. 11. Njoni hapa, killa watu, nitawakupa posho chini ya mti mkubwa huko. 12. Hungalisafisha bunduki, ningalikupiga. 13. Watu hawa si wazuri. 14. Sikumpiga simba leo karibu ya mlima huko. 15. Ungalimwona tembo karibu, nisema sasa hivi. 16. Nataka kwenda kupiga nyama mingi sasa. 17. Watu wanakula nini, mnyampara? Ah, Bwana, chakula mingi leo, nyama wa kongoni na choroa. 18. Watu wanataka posho sasa? 19. Wangalikuja tungaliwakupa pesa. 20. Unataka nini, boy? 21. Bwana, mimi nataka kazi. 22. Kazi gani unataka? 23. Ah, Bwana, nataka kazi wa gun bearer ao kirongozi. 24. Nimewaandika killa watu wangu, sasa sitaki ingine. 25. Mimi sikitika sana, Bwana, mimi najua kazi mingi, niandika!

Translate into Swahili:

H. 1. I shall beat the dog, if it does not come. 2. The hippo has come up above the water. 3. Can you see him, boy? 4. No, Sir, I cannot! 5. Do you want to shoot him right away? 6. Yes, bring me the big gun and the long knife. 7. Yes, Sir, they are here now. 8. Where (are) the porters? Are they near the camp? 9. Go and ask the headman. 10. He says he does not know where (they are) now, Sir. 11. Bind the little rhino with rope, he will run away! 12. Come up here, all (you) people, I want to see you. 13. I want to leave camp to-morrow and go to the big river. 14. All right, Sir, we will make all things ready. 15. Is the caravan not here, headman? I want them to arrive at once! 16. He said he had not shot a lion. 17. I told him to run very fast, but he would not! 18. Is he lazy or is he not well? 19. I do not know, Sir, I believe he was eating his food. 20. We will not shoot animals here, they have run away. 21. Listen, if you will come here, I shall give you food. 22. If you hear the lion, tell me at once! 23. Porters, do not kill the little hippo, bind him! 24. Sir, they do not come here, they do not like to help the gun bearer! 25. Tell them if they do not come, I shall not give them food to-morrow.

LESSON V

1. The personal pronouns are: *Mimi*, I; *wewe*, you, or thou, (always used in addressing a person); *yeye*, he (she or it); *sisi*, we; *nyinyi*, you; *wao*, they.

2. The possessive pronouns for the first class are: *Wangu*, my, mine; *wako*, thy, thine; *wake*, his (her, its); *wetu*, our; *wenu*, your; *wao*, their. For instance, *Bibi wangu*, my wife, or the wife is mine. *Wapagazi wetu*, our porters. *Tembo wake*, his elephant.

3. The interrogatives are: *Nani*, who? *Lini*, when? *Nini*, what? *Gani*, what kind? *Ngapi*, how many? *Wapi*, where? They stand after the word they refer to; for instance, *Simba wapi?* Where is the lion? *Wapagazi gani ninyi?* What kind of porters are you?

4. The interrogative Which? is in singular *Yupi?* in plural *Wapi?* For instance, *Mtu yupi?* Which man? *Tembo yupi wako?* Which elephant is yours?

5. Most of the numerals up to ten may be prefixed like adjectives, but they are also often used without any prefix, which is better than to add the wrong one. Half is *nuss; kumi na nuss*, ten and a half, etc.

1, *moja.*	7, *saba.*
2, *wili,* or *bili.*	8, *nane.*
3, *tatu.*	9, *tissa,* or *kenda.*
4, *nne.*	10, *kumi.*
5, *tano.*	11, *kumi na moja.*
6, *sita.*	12, *kumi na bili.*

13, *kumi na tatu*, etc.	70, *sabaini.*
20, *asherini.*	80, *themanini.*
21, *asherini na moja.*	90, *tissini.*
22, *asherini na bili*, etc.	100, *mia, mia moja.*
30, *thalathini.*	200, *mia mbili.*
31, *thalathini na moja*, etc.	300, *mia tatu,* etc.
40, *arbaini.*	1,000, *elfu.*
50, *khamsini.*	2,000, *elfu mbili.*
60, *sittini.*	10,000, *lakhi.*

6. The time is expressed by *saa*, watch; *saa sitta*, six o'clock; *saa nane na nuss,* half past eight, etc. The Swahili time is six hours behind in reckoning; for instance, *Saa sitta* is 12 o'clock; *saa saba,* one o'clock; *saa kumi,* four o'clock, etc. The question, What time is it, is expressed by *Saa ngapi.* For instance, *Saa ngapi sasa?* What time is it now? *Saa tissa!* It is nine o'clock, or according to European reckoning, three P. M.

Exercises

Translate into English:

I. 1. Mimi tayari sasa hivi. 2. Ambia mtu huyu nikuleta mikate sitta! 3. Wapagazi wangapi unataka, Bwana? 4. Mimi? Ninataka (nataka) watu kumi na saba. 5. Umekuja lini? 6. Mimi, nilikuja jana, saa tatu na nuss. 7. Bibi huyu nani? Bibi wangu, Bwana. 8. Watu, nyinyi wabaya sana. 9. Sisi? Ah, hapana, Bwana! 10. Ulitasama nyama mingi, gun bearer? 11. Ndio, niliwatasama kongoni sitta, vifaru tatu na simba moja. 12. Killa nyama wanasimama karibu ya milima huko. 13. Tutakwenda wakupiga, Bwana? 14. Ndio, nitakuja sasa hivi. Leta watu asherini na tano! 15. Tembo wangu mkubwa sana na ameanguka karibu ya campini. 16. Yeye mbaya sana, anataka mkupiga, Bwana! 17. Mpagazi, umefanya nini sasa? 18. Mimi? Sifanyi kitu (a thing). 19. Bunduki gani hapa? Bunduki mkubwa wa tembo na 'faru. 20. Unataka nini, Bwana? Sitaki kitu! 21. Wapagazi kumi na mbili walinisema, hawataka kwenda kesho, Bwana, si wazima. 22. Waambia kwenda sasa hivi ndani ya hema woa na pumzika. 23. Visu ngapi katika campi, Boy. 24. Sijui, Bwana, labda tissa. 25. Leta killa hapa!

APPENDIX

Translate into Swahili:

J. 1. How many animals have you shot? 2. I have killed six lions, seven elephants, four hippos, two leopards, three giraffes, twenty-five hartebeests, and twelve rhinos. 3. All the people are coming back to camp. 4. Tell them to rest to-morrow. 5. I will eat my food now, boy, bring (it) at once. 6. Go quickly and shoot that animal. 7. What animal, Sir, I do not see anything? 8. A big river is near our camp, bring water at once. 9. Headman, tell twelve men to help carry the heavy skin to camp. 10. Very well, Sir, they are coming at eight o'clock (2 p.m.). 11. If your load is very heavy, ask two men to help you. 12. I do not know where the porters are now. 13. Are they down by the river? 14. We do not see them. 15. If you do not run, I shall beat you! 16. I am not able to run, Sir, I am not well. 17. This porter has beaten two Masai warriors. 18. Now they will perhaps kill him. 19. Where is my guide? 20. I wish to know how many loads of food are in camp. 21. What kind of a headman are you? 22. You do not know anything. 23. What do you want? 24. I want my food, Sir, the headman did not give me. 25. Tell the gun bearer to give me my big gun right away.

Lesson VI

I. The comparative of the adjectives is generally formed by adding *zayidi ya*, more than, to the adjective; for instance, *Tembo nyama mkubwa zayidi ya simba*, The elephant is an animal larger than the lion. *Mpagazi huyu mbaya zayidi ya yule*, This porter is worse (more bad) than that.

2. The superlative is mostly expressed by putting the words *sana*, very much, or *kabisa*, exceedingly, after the adjective. For instance, *Tembo mkubwa kabisa katika killa nyama*, The elephant is the largest of all animals. *Mpishi huyu nzuri sana*, This cook is the very best.

3. The ordinal numbers are expressed by putting *wa* in front of the number. For instance, *Mtu wa tatu*, the third man. *Nilimpiga leo simba wa saba*, I shot to-day the seventh lion.

4. The verb *ku-wa*, to be, is in many respects irregular; it is

322

not used in the present tense, as before remarked, but, if it must be expressed, *ni* signifies am, is, and are, and *si*, am not, is not, and are not.

Imperfect.

nilikuwa (regular), *I was.*   sikuwa (regular), *I was not.*

Perfect.

nimekuwa (regular), *I have been.*   sikuwa (regular), *I have not been.*

Future.

nitakuwa (regular), *I shall be.*   sitakuwa (regular), *I shall not be.*

Imperative.

uwe! *be!*   usiwe! *be not!*
mwe! *be!* (plural).   msiwe! *be not!* (plural).

5. The verb to have is expressed by *ku-wan-na*, literally to be with, and forms the imperfect, perfect, and future tenses exactly as the verb *kuwa*, only adding *-na* at the end. For instance, *Nimekuwa-na*, I have had; *tutakuwa-na*, we shall have; *hatutakuwa-na*, we shall not have, etc. The present is formed by simply adding the *-na* to the personal verb-prefixes *Ni, u, a,* etc., as before remarked; and the imperative of *ku-wa* is not used at all.

Vocabulary

siku, *day.*
nguo, *clothes.*
kofia, *hat.*
kilemba, vilemba, *turban.*
shirti, *shirt.*
suruali, *trousers.*
suruali ndogo, *drawers.*
socks, *socks, stockings.*
bakuli, mabakuli, *basin.*

kibanda, vibanda, *hut, house.*
kitambaa, vitam, *towel, rag.*
sabuni, *soap.*
kijiko, vijiko, *spoon.*
uma, nyuma, *fork.*
ku-osha, *to wash.*
ku-oga, *to bathe.*
ku-anika, *to dry in the sun.*
mafuta, *fat, grease.*

ndoo, *bucket*.
kamba, *rope, twine*.
mshipi, mishipi, *belt*.
kiatu, viatu, *boot, shoe*.
koti, *coat*.

risassi, *cartridge*.
nguvu, *strong*.
ku-jenga, *to build*.
ku-shona, *to sew*.
ashanti, *thanks!*

Exercises

Translate into English:

K. 1. Mpagazi huko nguvu zayidi ya huyu. 2. Simba kali zayidi ya kiboko. 3. Anika ngoo wango leo nzuri sayidi ya yana!
4. Ndio, Bwana, nimefanya nzuri kabisa leo! 5. Umeosha suruali
na koti wangu sasa, boy? 6. Killa nguo tayari, niliosha yana.
7. Socks wangu nzuri kabisa. 8. Mtu huyu nguvu sana na anakula
mingi. 9. Sema mpagazi wa tano atakuja hapa. 10. Nimekuwa
mzima yana, lakini leo siwezi. 11. Mnyampara huyu ni mtu wa
sitta katika hema hapa. 12. Una risassi mingi wa bunduki mkubwa, gun bearer? 13. Hapana, Bwana, si mingi sasa, lazimo kununnua ingine katika Nairobi. 14. Ndio, kesho nitanunnua risassi,
viatu na mshipi. 15. Uwe nguvu sasa na mpiga mpagazi huyu!
16. Ah, hapana, mnyampara, Bwana wangu hataki. 17. Hatuta-
kuwana posho wa killa watu, kama hatununnui zayidi leo. 18. Ypi
amejenga kibanda huko? 19. Sijui, labda Mzungo yule katika
campi. 20. Boy, safisha sasa hivi sahani kwa sabuni, na kijiko na
uma. 21. Ndoo na bakuli wapi? Nataka kuoga. 22. Leta suruali
ndogo, viatu mkubwa na kofia, mimi nataka kwenda kupiga nyama.
23. Killa kitu tayari, Bwana. 24. Ema, boy, sasa umefanya nzuri
sana, nitakukupa rupia moja. 25. Ah, wewe nzuri kabisa, Bwana
Mkubwa, ahsanti sana!

Translate into Swahili:

L. 1. Where are my clothes, boy? Bring here the trousers,
drawers, socks, small shoes and the hat. 2. I will at once go out to
shoot animals. 3. What kind of animals do you like the most?
4. I have told you that I want very much another lion, an elephant
and a kongoni. 5. Very well, all the animals are here near by, but
a lion, I do not know. 6. Tie the knife to my belt and give me many
cartridges, gun bearer! 7. Where is the long rope? We had it yesterday in the tent, but I do not know now where it is. 8. I believe

the headman has taken the rope into his tent. 9. When did you arrive in camp, porter? 10. I have been here the whole day, Sir. 11. Headman, has this man been here all the day? 12. I do not know, Sir, I have not seen him. 13. Porter, you are very bad, I will not have you in my caravan. 14. Go and take your food and run away. . 15. If you do not go at once, I shall send the soldier to beat you! 16. Yes, Sir, I have been very bad, but now I shall be good. 17. All right, go and do your work now. 18. What work shall I do? 19. Help the headman to make the loads ready, we shall march on to-morrow. 20. Boy, bring here water, soap and a towel, I will now bathe. 21. When I have bathed, I want my food at once. 22. See that the plate, fork, spoon and knife are very clean. 23. Have you not had your food to-day, guide? 24. Yes, thank you very much, I have eaten my posho. 25. Go now and sleep.

Lesson VII

1. The passive forms of the verbs are made by the insertion of a -w- between the last two letters of the verb, but are otherwise exactly like the active tenses. For instance, *Ninapiga*, I love; *Ninapigwa*, I am being loved; *Amepiga*, he has shot; *amepigwa*, he has been shot, etc. *Kongoni ameuwa na simba*, the hartebeest was killed by the lion. *Wapagazi wamepigwa na askari*, the porters have been beaten by the soldier.

2. The Swahili is very fond of a special narrative tense, which includes the idea of "and" with a past tense; this narrative tense is expressed by inserting -ka- between the personal prefix and the verb. For instance, *Akakuja, akasema mimi tayari,* and he came and he said I am ready. *Tukakuja tukaona kifaru na tukampiga,* and we came and we found a rhino, and we shot him.

3. The infinitives of verbs are often used as substantives and are in English translated by the present participle or by the infinitive with to. For instance, *Nataka kupiga*, I like shooting, or to shoot. *Gunbearer anapenda kusafisha bunduki*, the gunbearer likes the cleaning of guns, or to clean guns.

APPENDIX

4. The syllable -*ni* attached to a substantive denotes in, at, around, by. For instance, *campi*, camp; *campini*, in, at, around, or by the camp.

5. Most of the adverbs can be used as prepositions by adding the syllable *ya* to the word. For instance, *Juu*, above; *juu ya nyumba*, above the house, etc.

Adverbs and Conjugations.

juu, *on top, above.*
mbele, *before, in front.*
yakini, *certainly.*
hatta, *until, even.*
mbali, *far, far off.*
nyuma, *after, behind.*
chini, *below, at bottom.*
yamikini, *possibly.*
halisi, *exactly.*
upesi, *fast, quickly.*
zamani, *formerly.*
marra moja, *immediately.*
mwisho, *lastly.*

zayidi, *more.*
sasa hivi, *instantly.*
njé, *outside.*
kweli, *truly, sincerely.*
polepole, *gently, slowly.*
ndani, *inside, within.*
tu, *merely, only.*
karibu, *near.*
marra nyingi, *often.*
halafu, *presently, soon.*
ema (pron. yema), *well, all right.*

---

na, *and, also.*
na-na, *both, and.*
ao-ao, *either, or.*
lakini, *however, but.*
illi, *in order that.*
hatta, *till.*

kwamba, *although.*
illa, *except.*
kama, kwamba, *if, that, how that.*
wala-wala, *neither, nor.*
na, kwa, *to, with, together.*

Exercises

Translate into English:

M. 1. Nimeambiwa kama mpagazi alimpiga mnyampara katika campi (or campini). 2. Nikamsema askari kumkamata mpagazi na kumpiga. 3. Sijui kama ninapendwa na watu wangu, lakini ninasadiki. 4. Boy wangu anasema kama ameona kifaru amemwua kongoni. 5. Akamwambia gun bearer kama walikimbia wapagazi watano. 6. Ni mbaya kupigwa na mtu mkali. 7. Mto mkubwa si mbali ya campini, karibu sana, Bwana. 8. Fanyeni kazi wao polepole sasa! 9. Njooni upesi na sayideni mnyampara ndani ya hema yake sasa hivi! 10. Tasama maji chini ya ngozi wa simba, ni mbaya kabisa. 11. Wapagazi hawa ni wavivu sana, hawanataka kufanya kazi wao nzuri. 12. Unataka kupiga nyama wakubwa? Ndio, kweli, nataka sana. 13. Tutakwenda sasa wapi? 14. Tutafika miti wakubwa chini ya milima huko leo? 15. Ah, hapana, Bwana, njia mbali kabisa; labda tutafika kesho. 16. Wapi ngozi wa nyama, Mabruki, ni njé wa nyumba katika maji? 17. Mabruki hajui, mimi nitakwenda na tasama, Bwana! 18. Zamani wewe ulifanya kazi wako nzuri lakini sasa mbaya. 19. Ao wewe ni mwivu sana ao si mzima, sijui. 20. Wala mimi na bibi wangu, wala wapagazi tunajua njia huko. 21. Njoo hapa, illi nitakusema tutafanya nini sasa. 22. Walimwambia marra nyingi kama yeye mbaya, lakini hataki asikia. 23. Mizigo ngapi wa posho una sasa campini? Tatu tu, Bwana. 24. Simama hapa hatta mimi nakuja. 25. Na tembo na kifaru ni nyama wakubwa sana, na wakali kabisa.

Translate into Swahili:

N. 1. My headman is very much beloved by all the porters in the caravan. 2. He is a very good man and I like him very much. 3. The gun bearer came and told me to-day that we have not many cartridges in the camp. 4. And he said he would like to go and buy cartridges in Nairobi. 5. And he went and came back and gave me seventy-five. 6. Have you heard what this fellow has done, when he came in the tent yesterday? 7. No, what did he do? He is certainly not a bad man. 8. Truly, he is now not good and he likes to fight often with the men. 9. We are not much beloved by these people, but know we that we are good (to them). 10. Formerly there were many lions and rhinos here, but the foreigners have shot (at) them much. 11. They have all run away to the hills, where it is bad to go. 12. If what you say is true, we shall go with the caravan to-morrow. 13. Very well, Sir, I shall make all the men ready to-day. 14. We have not much posho now in camp. All the meat has been finished. 15. If we go out to shoot game to-day, you will tell ten men to go with us. 16. I and my best men shall go in front with the guns, and the caravan will go behind (us). 17. Very well, we shall do what you say, Sir! 18. In the camp

is now much water and grass, although it is on top of the hill.
19. Will they arrive soon from the river? 20. We do not know,
but think they will come to-morrow. 21. Where is the Masai
guide? I have not seen him to-day. 22. Here he is, Sir, he has eaten
his food in the big tent. 23. Tell the truth (truthfully), do you
know the path to the nearest water? 24. Yes, I am guide, I know
all the paths here. 25. We will reach the water to-morrow, but
it is quite far from here.

Lesson VIII

1. By prefixing *m-*, *pa-*, and *ku-* for the syllable *-na* (with),
the following much used words are formed: *Mna*, here is (or,
is there here?); *pana* and *kuna*, there is (or, is there there?);
their negative form is, *Hamna*, here is not, or are not; *hapana*
and *hakuna*, there is not, or are not. These words are also used
in the form of a question, *Mna nyama*, are here wild animals?
The answer *Mna* means there are! *Hamna*, there are none!
Hapana matunda, there is no fruit there. *Hapana* also stands
for no and not.

2. The usual Swahili greeting is a combination of the personal verb prefixes and the word *jambo*, circumstance, matter.
So, for instance, *sijambo*, I am well (literally I have nothing the
matter with me); *hujambo*, you are well, or are you well? etc.;
hatujambo, we are well, or are we well; *hawajambo?* are they
well, all according to the tone of voice.

3. When Swahili people meet, they generally greet each
other in the following way: *Hujambo?* How do you do? *Sijambo!* I am well! or *Siwezi!* I am ill! Then they say *Hali
gani?* How are you? to which they answer either *Ema sana*,
very well, or *Siwezi*, I am not well.

Among interjections and other useful words are:

4. *Baado*, afterwards, which is used for all sorts of expressions. For instance, if you ask: Is the food ready now? if it is
not, the man will probably say *Baado, Bwana!* meaning Not yet,

it will be though, presently! Or if you ask: Have you finished your work? *Umekwisha kazi wako?* and he answers: *Baado!* it means that it is not yet finished, but that he is going to finish it some time. *Baado* corresponds in this respect to the Spanish " *la manjana*," or to the Russian " *ce chass*," freely translated, " some time in the future."

5. The word *bass*, or *bassi*, enough, is used also for " stop that! " If, for instance, two men are fighting, a " *bassi* " from the Bwana will put an instant stop to it. If the boy is pouring in tea or water for you, and you do not want any more, *bass* is the word to use to imply that you have had enough.

6. To signify something in the distance, the Swahili uses the word *kulé*, which literally means there. If the object is about one hundred yards off or a little more, he says, " *kulé!* " (with the accent sharply on the " e ") but pronounced in an ordinary pitch of voice. If the object referred to is half a mile away, he says again " *kulé!* " but in a much higher pitch of voice, and dwelling much longer on the é. Should the animal or whatever the man is pointing out, be very far away, like distant hills, the Swahili will again use his " *kulé!* " but with the voice at the very highest pitch, and at the same time dwell so long on the "e," that it sounds as if he had at least ten " e's " in his " ku- léééééééééé " to pronounce. It is, therefore, really necessary to note in what pitch the word is pronounced, so as to be able to " judge the distance."

7. The exclamation *Hodi!* (possibly translated hello! and pronounced with great stress on the " o "), must always be used before any tent or house, not one's own, is entered. It is very improper, and betrays in the eyes of the Swahili the greatest ignorance and bad breeding to enter without first calling, " *Hodi!* " The answer is generally simply, " *Karibu!* " Come near, come in! Then the stranger says, " *Salaam!* " Hail, or peace, if the occupant is Indian or Arab, or even an " educated " Swahili, otherwise he uses the regular greeting with *Hujambo!* etc.

8. When an honored guest comes in, all the people in the

room generally get up to greet him; if he wants to prevent this —which he should do according to "etiquette"—he says: "*Starehe, starehe!*" Don't trouble yourselves! or Sit down, don't move!

9. Good-bye is *Kwa heri!* and have a good night, or sleep well, *lala nzuri!*

10. Some adjectives are taken from the Arabic and are always indeclinable; the most important of these are:

amini, *faithful.*
halali, *lawful.*
haramu, *forbidden.*
rahisi, *cheap, easy.*
salama, *safe, harmless.*
sahihi, *correct, faultless.*

ghali, *expensive.*
hodari, *clever, able.*
lazimo, *compulsory.*
rathi, *content.*
safi, *clean, pure.*
sunne, *advisable.*

11. The Swahili verbs may be made reciprocal simply by changing the final -*a* into -*ana;* of, for instance, *piga,* is formed *pigana,* shoot—or beat each other; of *ku-penda,* love, *ku-pendana,* love each other, etc. *Wapagasi wasayidiana kwa mizigo,* Porters, help each other with the loads!

ku-kubali, *to accept.*
ku-patana, *to agree.*
ku-sadiki, *to believe.*
ku-vunja, *to break.*
ku-angalia, *to take care of.*
ku-danganya, *to cheat.*
ku-panda, *to climb up.*
ku-shinda, *to conquer, beat.*
ku-pindua, *to overturn.*
ku-kataa, *to refuse.*
ku-ngoja, *to wait.*
ku-onana, *to meet.*
ku-chinja, *to kill for food.*
ku-sahau, *to forget.*
ku-isha, *to finish.*

ku-shtaki, *to accuse.*
ku-sumbua, *to annoy.*
ku-chemka, *to boil.*
ku-teketeza, *to burn.*
ku-kamata, *to take hold of.*
ku-chagua, *to choose.*
ku-karibia, *to come near.*
ku-fikiri, *to consider.*
ku-omba, *to pray.*
ku-kaa, *to remain.*
ku-tafuta, *to search for.*
ku-tangulia, *to go before.*
ku-ruka, *to fly.*
ku-samehe, *to forgive.*
ku-tumaa, *to hope.*

gari, magari, *railroad, carriage.*
mrima, *coast.*
barua, *letter.*
meza, *table.*
njaa, *hunger.*
bandera, *flag, banner.*
fimbo, *cane, stick.*
inchi, *country, land.*
mbu, *mosquito.*
bakshish, *present.*

mchele, *rice.*
barra, *interior land.*
nyani, *monkey.*
leso, *handkerchief.*
kiu, *thirst.*
asali, *honey.*
darubini, *fieldglasses.*
kuni, *firewood.*
pofu, *eland.*
serkali, *government.*

Exercises

Translate into English:

O. 1. Nasadiki sitaki kukubali kazi wako leo. 2. Boy wangu anakushinda sana, Juma. 3. Mbu mingi hapa, Bwana, watakusumbua, usipigi hema wako chini ya mti mkubwa. 4. Panda kilima kule na tafuta nyama. 5. Kama unawaona, njoo marra moja na niambia. 6. Gun bearer akakwenda, akatasama, akawaona, akamwambia Bwana wake. 7. Yeye akakwenda akawapiga kongoni wawili na pofu moja, akakuwa rathi sana. 8. Sikusikia kama mpishi amekwisha kuchemka masiwa. Unajua wewe? 9. Baado, Bwana, lakini nitakwenda kutasama! 10. Ah, badoo kabisa, Bwana, labda tayari halafu nussu saa, sijui. 11. Anatangulia nani huko? 12. Unanitaka kwenda kuuliza, Bwana? 13. Ah, hapana kitu, Ali, nenda nikuleta askari moja na wapagazi sitta. 14. Kwa sababu nataka wakupeleke katika Nairobi. 15. Barua wako wapi, watu wanataka kwenda sasa? 16. Mna nyani katika inchi wa Kenia? Mna mingi kabisa, Bwana. 17. Nina njaa na kiu sana leo, leta upesi chakula, kama ni tayari. 18. Kamata leso na bandera na peleka hemani. 19. El-moran, unataka asali? Ah, sitaki, Bwana, sikuli asali. 20. Juu ya meza nini, boy? Fimbo wako na darubini, Bwana. 21. Hodi! Karibu! Salaam! Salaam! Haligani? Ema sana! 22. Starehe, starehe, mimi nataka kaa kitako! 23. Msipigana njiani na msipumziki, hatta mtafika bomani. 24. Wapagazi wameleta kuni mingi sasa? Ndio, Bwana, wameleta mingi kabisa na tutafanya moto mkubwa sasa hivi. 25. Ema sana, halafu wasema watu msifanyi kelele, nataka kulala. Kwa heri, Bwana Mkubwa, lala nzuri!

APPENDIX

Translate into Swahili:

P. 1. God will accept our prayer (*sala*); He will forgive and forget. 2. Do not annoy the animals, they will run away! 3. I will consider what you say. 4. Wait (plur.) here two hours, until the other porters arrive! 5. Do not remain here, because the water is very bad. 6. Turn the rhino over now, we must skin it at once. 7. Sir, the men refuse to carry their loads up this hill, what shall I do? 8. Tell them that if they do their work well, I shall give them presents when we arrive in camp. 9. But if they will not obey, tell the soldiers to bind them, and I will send them to the government fort. 10. That will be enough, Sir, now they obey at once. 11. What flies there, Mabruki? 12. Very large birds (*ndege*), and they are fighting each other. 13. Shall I shoot them for the cook? 14. Are there any lions here, guide? No, Sir, but there are elephants yonder, near the big mountain. 15. Good morning, Ali, how are you? 16. I am very well, Sir, and you? 17. My faithful cook is safe in camp to-day, the lion did not kill him. 18. This food is not cheap, it is very expensive, I don't want it. 19. To shoot here is forbidden. 20. Tell the soldier to take hold of the beast. 21. Shall he kill it for food? Yes, and give it to the cook. 22. I want the whole caravan to go to the railroad to bring the skins and heads there and to buy food. 23. We must have sixty-five loads for the porters, and rice, sugar and milk for me. 24. After ten days I will finish my trip and go to the coast, but I will return here another year (*mwaka*) again. 25. This trip was very fine; I have shot many big animals, lions, elephants, rhinos, hippos, crocodiles, monkeys, giraffes, pigs, leopards, elands, hartebeests, gnus, and large birds, and all the time I was well. Now good-bye, all my men, good-bye.

Safari wa Bwana X

Translate into English:

Bwana X. alitoka America, akakwenda Mombasa katika meli na alifika Nairobi kwa gari. Huko akaandika safari mkubwa, akakamata Ali wa mnyampara; boy wake Mohammed, mtu wa mrima, gun bearer wawili, mpishi moja, askari sitta na wapagazi khamsini. Bwana alitaka kwenda Laikipia, kwa sababu alitaka kupiga nyama mingi na wakubwa. Akakaa siku sitta tu katika

Nairobi, halafu killa safari akakwenda katika Fort Hall. Karibu wake aliwapiga kiboko na mamba watatu. Kama safari akafika Laikipia, wakafanya kampi mkubwa sana. Killa siku Bwana alikwenda kuwinda nyama, akawapiga mingi; simba, tembo, vifaru, choroa, wapofu, twiga, nyati, nyani, fissi, chui, na ndege mingi na wakubwa. Katika Laikipia jua si kali sana, maji nzuri, na mbu hapana. Bwana alikuwa mzima sana na rathi kabisa, kwa sababu aliweza kurudi na ngozi na pembe mingi. Halafu alikaa Mombasa siku nne tu, akarudi Ulaya katika meli mkubwa. Akafika nyumba wake, akawaona bibi na watoto wake wazima, akafuraha sana akamwambia ahsanti kwa Muungu.

II. KEY TO THE EXERCISES

A. 1. The big man has shot a lion. 2. The woman loves (her) child. 3. Butler, where is the knife? 4. In the house, Sir. 5. Bring the knife and the gun here. 6. Yes, Sir. 7. I have seen a large elephant in the grass. 8. Where is the caravan? 9. Here, near by, Sir. 10. Bring the food, butler; a knife, plate and a glass. 11. The lion is a dangerous animal. 12. Put the tent up here! 13. I want tea, sugar and milk, butter, bread and salt! 14. Butler, bring the water here. 15. Yes, Sir, instantly. 16. The gun is not in the house, it is here in the tent. 17. The master and (his) wife are here in the grass and want (their) food. 18. Is the meal ready, butler? 19. Yes, it is ready now. 20. The severe master has beaten (his) boy much. 21. Bring the gun, I see a lion here near by. 22. The elephant likes water. 23. I have seen a big man here in the tent, and he has shot an animal with the gun. 24. Where is the sugar, bread, tea and milk? 25. The food is here, Sir.

B. 1. Mtu aliona simba karibu ya nyumba. 2. Boy, leta chakula; nataka chai, mkate, siagi na masiwa sasa hivi. 3. Ndio, Bwana, chakula tayari katika nyumba. 4. Ema! 5. Safari wapi sasa? 6. Karibu, Bwana, karibu! 7. Naono (or ninaoma) tembo katika maji. 8. Hapana, Bwana, si tembo. 9. Wapi bunduki, kisu na hema? 10. Hapa, Bwana. 11. Chakula si nzuri, leta sahani na kisu. 12. Nataka kupiga simba sasa hivi. 13. Wapi simba sasa? 14. Karibu katika majani katika maji. 15. Mtoto aliona bibi katika nyumba. 16. Bwana, chakula tayari sasa; kahawa, sukari na masiwa kwa mkate. 17. Nataka sana maji, masiwa na kisu. 18. Umeona bibi hapa? 19. Hapana, Bwana, bibi si hapa; ni katika hema. 20. Unataka chakula sasa hivi? Ndio, leta hapa sasa. 21. Tembo na simba ni nyama kali. 22. Boy, piga hema hapa na leta maji. 23. Naona nyama katika majani, leta sasa hivi

334

bunduki na kisu. 24. Ndio, Bwana, ni hapa. 25. Ema, boy, sasa nataka safari.

C. 1. The tall people have brought the knives here. 2. The child has three bedsteads in the house. 3. Bring at once five arrows. 4. What do you say? 5. I say, I want my food in my tent now. 6. Yes, Great Master, I will bring (it). 7. The stout cooks have cleaned my cups. 8. The big foreigner has seen his wife here near by. 9. Do you fear the tall man? 10. The door of my house is heavy. 11. Butler, my cup is not clean. 12. Yes, Sir, I will clean (it). 13. What is the caravan doing now? 14. Eating (their) food in the tent; the food is of the meat of the thick hippopotamus, Sir. 15. The knife's handle is not beautiful. 16. How many people are in your caravan? 17. I have five people now. 18. My child is not well. 19. My coffee is not sweet, I want sugar and milk in the cup. 20. I have seen one elephant, two lions and five hippos, and I have shot the elephant, one lion and one hippo. 21. Where is my gun? Is it clean? Yes, Sir, I have cleaned (it). 22. Is your load heavy? No, Sir, it is fine. 23. Where are the five children? Here in the grass, and they are eating meat, tea, milk and bread. 24. Child, clean your hands instantly and bring the comb here. 25. Have you seen the new book by the door? Yes, Sir, I will bring (it).

D. 1. Mtoto wangu ana kitabu nzuri katika mkono. 2. Tembo watatu na viboko wanne ni katika maji. 3. Simba ngapi umepiga? 4. Nimepiga simba wanne kwa bunduki wangu na boy wangu amepiga moja kwa mshale. 5. Alisema bibi wako? 6. Alisema anataka chakula sasa hivi. 7. Boy, leta kioo na kitana. 8. Natasama Mzungu katika mlango wa nyumba wangu; anataka nini? 9. Kitendo wako mbaya, mtoto wangu. 10. Chai wako ni tamu? Hapana, leta sukari! 11. Kamata hema na piga hapa! 12. Ndio, Bwana, wana mizigo sitta. 13. Boy, unafanya nini hapa? Bwana, ninasafisha bunduki na kisu wangu. 14. Ema, gunbearer wapi? Katika hema, Bwana, na anakula chakula wake sasa. 15. Unaogopa simba? 16. Kamata kipini na leta hapa! 17. Mzigo mzito sasa? Hapana, Bwana, ni upesi. 18. Leta wato watatu sasa hivi! 19. Vitu ngapi katika hema sasa? 20. Tuna vitu wanne, vitanda wiwili na kioo moja. 21. Vilima ngapi hapa? 22. Ninaona tano;

335

moja mkubwa sana na nne ndogo. 23. Mtoto wangu ana vifungo watano wazuri. 24. Vitendo wao si wazuri, watu wangu! 25. Umepiga hema wangu wapi? Ni karibu ya maji?

E. 1. Boy, tell the caravan headman to help the porter to carry the load. 2. A European has arrived in the camp; he wants to buy food. 3. Oh, I don't want to sell now. 4. Headmen and gun-bearer, come here, I want to shoot a hartebeest. 5. The porters are very lazy. 6. Ask the soldier here where my knife is. 7. Sir, the soldier says he does not know. 8. Will the caravan reach there to-day? I do not know, Sir, perhaps. 9. Near the water here I see a crocodile and hippos. 10. Headmen, bring the porters right away. I want to shoot the rhino, and the people shall carry the skin and the horn. 11. Climb up on the hill and look around, perhaps there are animals there. 12. Yes, Sir, I see a lion and a rhino there near the hill. 13. I want to buy food for the people. 14. To-morrow we shall go on with the caravan. 15. Where are the gun bearer and the boy now? 16. Ask the boy what he is doing. 17. Sir, he says he is cleaning the gun. 18. Very well, tell the cook that I want to eat the food. 19. What do you want, Sir? 20. I want tea, bread, butter, meat and salt. 21. Where is my wife? In the house, Sir. 22. Down at the mountain over there I see an eland. 23. Boy, help the gun bearer to clean the guns. 24. Shall the cook cook the food now? 25. One man has fallen down here.

F. 1. Gun bearer, sema watu wangu kupanda kilima na kuua kongoni. 2. Pima simba sasa hivi! 3. Karibu ya maji naona tembo anasimama. 4. Boy, leta bunduki na kisu na sema gun bearer kwenda hapa! 5. Ndio, Bwana, anakuja sasa. 6. Mnyampara, wapagazi wapi? 7. Labda nitarudi katika Nairobi kesho. 8. Boy, chakula tayari sasa? 9. Hapana, Bwana, si chakula hapa sasa. 10. Utakwenda kununnua? 11. Hapana, sitaki wewe kwenda, sema mnyampara kununnua! 12. Kongoni sasa wapi, gun bearer? 13. Sijui, Bwana, labda ameanguka. 14. Hapana, Mabruki, naona nyama karibu ya kilima mkubwa. 15. Umeona simba leo? 16. Hapana ona nyama. 17. Askari hapa sasa? 18. Sijui, Bwana. 19. Amsha wapagazi sasa hivi, nataka kusayidia Mzungu huko. 20. Mpishi ni ndani ya hema; uliza kama chakula tayari! 21.

336

Mtu mbaya hataki kusayidia bibi wake. 22. Atafika hapa kesho, labda, sijui. 23. Umesafisha bunduki na kisu. 24. Ndio, Bwana, ni tayari sasa. 25. Ema, kula chakula sasa hivi.

G. 1. Did you see a lion here? 2. Yes, I have seen him near the mountain there. 3. They answered the people right away. 4. We will beat the naughty child in the tent to-morrow. 5. Have you seen the animals there? 6. Yes, Sir, I am seeing now a hartebeest, a lion and a rhino. 7. Are they near? 8. No, Sir, they are not near. 9. If you want the meal now, I will bring it. 10. If the rhino goes away I will not shoot him. 11. Come here, all ye people, I will give you posho under the big tree there. 12. If you do not clean the gun, I will hit you. 13. These people are not good. 14. I did not shoot the lion to-day near the mountain there. 15. If you see the elephant near by, tell me right away. 16. I want to go and shoot many animals now. 17. What are the people eating, headman? Oh, Sir, there is lots of food to-day, meat of hartebeest and oryx. 18. Do the people want the posho now? 19. If they come we will give them money: 20. What do you want, boy? 21. Sir, I want work. 22. What kind of work do you want? 23. Oh, Sir, I want work as gunbearer or guide. 24. I have engaged all my people, now I don't want another. 25. I am very sorry, Sir, I know many kinds of work; engage me.

H. 1. Nitampiga mbwa kama hangalikuja. 2. Kiboko alikuja juu ya maji. 3. Unaweza kumwona, boy. 4. Hapana, Bwana, siwezi! 5. Unataka kumpiga sasa hivi? 6. Ndio, nileta bunbuki mkubwa na kisu mrefu! 7. Ndio, Bwana, ni hapa sasa. 8. Wapagazi wapi? Ni karibu ya kampi? 9. Nenda na mwuliza mnyampara. 10. Bwana, alisema hajui wapi sasa. 11. Mfunga kifaru ndogo kwa kamba, ataka kukimbia! 12. Njooni hapa, killa watu, nataka wakuona! 13. Nataka kuacha kampi kesho na kwenda katika mto mkubwa. 14. Ema, Bwana, tutafanya killa kitu tayari. 15. Safari si hapa, mnyampara? Wanataka kufika sasa hivi. 16. Alisema hukupiga simba. 17. Nilimwambia kukimbia upesi sana, lakini hakutaka. 18. Yeye mvivu ao hawezi? 19. Sijui, Bwana, nasadiki alikula chakula wake. 20. Hatutapiga nyama hapa, wamekimbia. 21. Sikia, ungalikuja hapa ningalikukupa posho. 22. Kama ungalisikia simba, nisema marra moja! 23. Wapagazi, msimwui kiboko ndogo, mfungeni! 24. Bwana, hawakuʃa hapa, hawataka kumsayidi gun bearer. 25. Waambia kama hawangali-kuja, singaliwakupa chakula kesho.

I. 1. I am ready right away. 2. Tell that man to bring me six loaves of bread. 3. How many porters do you want, Sir? 4. I? I want seventeen. 5. When have you come? 6. I? I came yes-terday, half past three (9:30 a. m.). 7. Who is this woman? My wife, Sir. 8. Men, you are very bad. 9. We? Oh, no, Sir! 10. Did you see many animals, gun bearer? 11. Yes, I saw six harte-beests, three rhinos and one lion. 12. All the animals were stand-ing near the mountain there. 13. Shall we go to shoot them, Sir? 14. Yes, I will come at once; bring twenty-five people. 15. My elephant is very large, and he has fallen near the camp. 16. He is very bad, I want to beat him, Sir. 17. Porter, what are you doing now? 18. I? I am not doing anything. 19. What kind of gun is here? The big gun for elephants and rhinos. 20. What do you want, Sir? I don't want anything. 21. Twenty-two porters told me they don't want to march to-morrow, Sir, they are not well. 22. Tell them to go instantly into their tent and rest. 23. How many knives are there in camp, boy? 24. I do not know, Sir, perhaps nine. 25. Bring them all here.

J. 1. Nyama ngapi umepiga? 2. Nimepiga simba sitta, tembo saba, viboko wanne, chui wawili, twiga watatu, kongoni asherini na tano na vifaru kumi na mbili. 3. Killa watu wanarudi kampini. 4. Waambia kupumzika kesho. 5. Nataka kula chakula sasa, boy, leta sasa hivi! 6. Nenda upesi na piga nyama yule. 7. Nyama nani? Huoni kitu. 8. Mto kbubwa ni karibu ya kampi yetu, leta maji marra moja! 9. Mnyampara, ambia wato kumi na mbili kus-ayidi kuchukua ngozi mzito katika kampini. 10. Ema, Bwana, wanakuja saa nane. 11. Kama mzigo wako mzito sana, uliza watu wawili kukusayidi. 12. Sijui wapi watu sasa. 13. Ni chini ya mto? 14. Hatuwaoni. 15. Hungalikimbia ningalikupiga! 16. Siwezi kukimbia, Bwana, si mzima. 17. Mpagazi huyu amewapiga El-moran wa Masai wawili. 18. Sasa watamwua labda. 19. Kiron-gozi wangu wapi? 20. Nataka kujua mizgo wa psoho ngapi katika kampi. 21. Mnyampara gani, wewe? 22. Hujui kitu! 23. Unataka nini? 24. Nataka chakula wangu, Bwana, mnyampara hakupupa. 25. Ambia gun bearer kunileta bunduki wangu mkubwa sasa hivi.

K. 1. The porter over there is stronger than this man. 2. The lion is more dangerous than the hippo. 3. Dry my clothes to-day better than yesterday. 4. Yes, Sir, I have done it very well to-day. 5. Have you washed my trousers and coat now, boy? 6. All the clothes are ready, I washed them yesterday. 7. My socks are very fine. 8. This man is very strong and he is eating much. 9. Tell the fifth porter to come (that he will come) here. 10. I was well yesterday, but to-day I am sick. 11. This headman is the sixth man in the tent here. 12. Have you many cartridges for the big gun, gunbearer? 13. No, Sir, there are not many now. It is necessary to buy others in Nairobi. 14. Yes, to-morrow I will buy cartridges, shoes and a belt. 15. Be strong now, and beat this porter. 16. Oh, no, headman, my master does not like it. 17. We shall not have food for all the people if we do not buy more to-day. 18. Who is building a house there? 19. I do not know, perhaps that white man in the camp. 20. Boy, clean the plate instantly with soap and also the spoon and the fork. 21. Where are the bucket and the basin? I want to bathe. 22. Bring the drawers, the big boots and the hat, I want to go out and shoot animals. 23. Everything is ready, Sir. 24. Very well, boy, now you have done very well. I will give you one rupee. 25. Oh, you are exceedingly kind, great master, thank you very much.

L. 1. Nguo wangu wapi, boy? Leta suruali, suruali ndogo, socks, viatu ndogo na kofia! 2. Nataka kwenda kupiga nyama sasa hivi. 3. Nyama gani unataka sana? 4. Nimekuwambia kama nataka sana simba ingine, tembo na kongoni. 5. Ema, nyama yote ni hapa karibu, lakini simba, sijui. 6. Funga kisu katika mshipi wangu na nipe (nikupa) risassi mingi, gun bearer. 7. Kamba mrefu wapi? Tulikuwana yana katika hema, lakini sijui sasa wapi. 8. Nasadiki mnyampara amekamata kamba katika hema yake. 9. Umefika kampi lini, mpagazi? 10. Nilikuwa hapa killa siku, Bwana. 11. Mnyampara, mtu huyu alikuwa hapa killa siku? 12. Sijui, Bwana, simkuona. 13. Mpagazi, wewe mbaya sana, sikutaki katika sa fari wangu. 14. Nenda, kamata posho yako no kimbia! 15. Hungalikwenda sasa hivi, ningalipeleka askari kukupiga. 16.

Ndio, Bwana, nilikuwa mbaya sana, lakini sasa nitakuwa nzuri sana! 17. Ema, nenda na fanya kazi wako sasa! 18. Kazi gani utafanya? 19. Msayidia mnyampara kufanya mizigo tayari, tutasafiri kesho. 20. Boy, leta hapa maji, sabuni na kitambaa, nataka kuoga sasa. 21. Ningalioga ningalitaka chakula marra moja! 22. Tasama kama sahani, uma, kijiko na kisu ni safi sana! 23. Huku-wana posho wako leo, kirongozi? 24. Ndio, ahsanti sana, nimekula posho wangu. 25. Sasa nenda na lala!

M. 1. I have been told that a porter beat the headman in camp. 2. Tell the soldier to get hold of the porter and beat him. 3. I do not know if I am liked by my people, but I think so. 4. My boy says that he has seen a rhinoceros kill the hartebeest. 5. Tell the gun bearer that five porters ran away. 6. It is bad to be beaten by this severe man. 7. The big river is not far from camp, it is very near, Sir. 8. Do your work very carefully now. 9. Come quickly (plur.) and help the headman in his tent right away. 10. Behold the water under the lion skin, it is exceedingly bad. 11. These porters are very lazy, they do not want to do their work well. 12. Do you want to shoot the big animals? Yes, truly, I want very much (to do so). 13. Where shall we go now? 14. Will we arrive at the big trees at the foot of the mountain over there? 15. Oh, no, Sir, the road is very far, perhaps we will reach (it) to-morrow. 16. Where are the animal skins, Mabruki? Are they outside the house in the water? 17. Mabruki does not know, I will go out and see, Sir. 18. Formerly you did your work well, but now, poorly. 19. Either you are very lazy or you are not well, I do not know. 20. Neither I and my wife nor the porters know the road there. 21. Come here in order that I may tell you what you shall do now. 22. I have told him many times that he is bad, but he does not want to obey. 23. How many loads of posho have you now in camp? Only three, Sir. 24. Stay here until I come. 25. Both the elephant and rhino are very big animals, and they are exceedingly fierce.

N. 1. Mnyampara wangu anapendwa sana na killa wapagazi katika safari. 2. Yeye mtu nzuri sana, na nitampenda sana. 3. Gun bearer alikuja akanisema leo kama hatukuwana risassi mingi katika kampi. 4. Akasema akataka kwenda kununua risassi katika Nairobi. 5. Akakwenda akarudi akanikupa sabini na tano. 6. Umesikia amefaya nini huyu, kama alikuja katika hema yana? 7. Hapana, ulifanya nini? Yeye si mtu mbaya. 8. Kweli, sasa si nzuri na anataka sana kupigana kwa watu marra nyingi. 9. Hatupendwa sasa na watu hawa, lakini tunajua sisi tunakuwa nzuri. 10. Zamani hapa simba na vifaru mingi, lakini Wazungu wamewapiga sana. 11. Wamekimbia yote katika mlima, wapi kwenda ni mbaya. 12. Kama ungalisema kweli, tutasafiri kesho. 13. Ema, Bwana, nitafanya killa watu tayari leo. 14. Hatukuwana posho mingi kampi ni sasa, nyama yote amekwisha. 15. Kama tungalikwenda kupiga nyama leo, ungaliwambia watu kumi kwenda na sisi. 16. Mimi na watu wangu wazuri sana tutatangulia kwa bunduki na safari atakwenda nyuma. 17. Ema, tutafanya unasema nini. 18. Katika kampini sasa maji na majani mingi, kwamba ni juu ya kilima. 19. Watafika karibu katika mtoni? 20. Hatujui, lakini tunasadiki watakuja kesho. 21. Kirongozi wa Masai wapi? Simkumwona leo. 22. Yeye hapa, Bwana, anakula posho wake katika hema mkubwa. 23. Sema kweli, unajua njia katika maji karibu sana? 24. Ndio, mimi kirongozi, najua killa njia hapa. 25. Tutafika maji kesho, lakini mbali kwa hapa.

O. 1. I believe I will not accept your work to-day. 2. My boy exceeds (beats) you by far, Juma. 3. There are many mosquitoes here, Sir. They will annoy you, don't put your tent under the big tree. 4. Climb up on the hill over there, and look out for game. 5. If you see any, come at once and tell me. 6. And the gunbearer went and looked around and saw them and told his master. 7. And he went and he shot two kongoni and one eland, and he was very well satisfied. 8. I have not heard if the cook has finished to boil (boiling) the milk. Do you know? 9. Not yet, Sir, but I will go and see. 10. Oh, not for a long while, Sir, perhaps it is ready after half an hour, I do not know. 11. Who is going ahead there? 12. Do you want me to go and ask, Sir? 13. Oh, no matter, Ali, go and bring me one soldier and six porters. 14. Because I want to send them to Nairobi. 15. Where is your letter, the people want to go now. 16. Are there monkeys in the district of Kenia? There are exceedingly many, Sir. 17. I have great hunger and thirst, bring the food quickly if it is ready. 18. Take the handkerchief and the flag and put them in the tent. 19. Warrior, do you want some honey? Oh, I don't want it, Sir, I do not eat honey. 20. What is on the table, boy? Your cane and the fieldglasses, Sir. 21. Hello! Come in! Hail! Peace! How are you? Very well. 22. Don't bother, don't move. I want to sit down. 23. Do not fight with each other on the road, and do not rest until you reach the fort. 24. Have the porters brought lots of firewood now? Yes, Sir, they have brought exceedingly much, and we will make a big fire right away. 25. Very well, afterwards tell the people not to make any noise, I want to sleep. Good-bye, Great Master, sleep well.

P. 1. Muungu atakubali sala wetu; atasamehe na atasahau. 2. Usiwasumbua nyama! Watakimbia. 3. Nitafikiri unasema nini. 4. Ngojeni hapa saa mbili, hatta wapagazi ingine watafika! 5. Usikai hapa, kwa sababu maji mbaja sana. 6. Pindua kifaru sasa, lazimo tunamchuna marra moja! 7. Bwana, watu wanakataa kuchukua mizigo wao yuu ya kilima ule, utafanja nini? 8. Waambia kama tunafanya kazi wao nzuri, nitawakupa bakshishi, kama tungalifika kampini. 9. Lakini kama hawataka sikia, wasema askari wafunga na nitawapeleka katika boma wa serkali. 10. Bassi, Bwana, sasa watasikia marra moja! 11. Anaruka huko, Mabruki? 12. Ndege (birds) wakubwa sana na wanapigana. 13. Utawapiga kwa mpishi? 14. Kirongozi, mna simba hapa? Hapana, Bwana, lakini tembo karibu ya milima mkubwa kule. 15. Hujambo, Ali, haligani? 16. Sijambo sana, nawe? 17. Mpishi wangu amini ni salama katika kampi leo, simba hamkuua. 18. Posho huyu si rahisi, ni gahali sana, sitaki! 19. Kupiga hapa, haramu. 20. Ambia askari kumkamata nyama! 21. Atamchinja? Ndio, na mkupa mpishi. 22. Nataka killa safari kwenda na garri kupeleka ngozi na kitchwa huko na kununnua posho. 23. Lazimo sisi kuwana mizigo sittini na tano kwa wapagazi, na mchele, sukari na maziwa kwa mimi. 24. Halafu siku kumi nitakwisha safari wangu na kwenda katika mrima, lakini nitarudi hapa mwaka ingini tena. 25. Safari huyu nzuri sana; nitawapiga nyama wakubwa mingi, simba, tembo, vifaru, viboko, mamba, nyani, twiga, nguruwe, chui, pofu, kongoni, nyumbo, na ndege wakubwa, na killa siku nilikuwa mzima. Sasa kwa heri, killa watu wangu, kwa heri!

III. SWAHILI–ENGLISH VOCABULARY[1]

A

Abadan, *always, constantly.*
Acha, ku-, *to leave, let go, allow.*
Adabu, *good manners, politeness.*
Adui, *enemy.*
Afu, ku-, *to save, to deliver.*
Aga, ku-, *to take leave of, to agree with.*
Ahsanti, *thanks, thank you.*
Aina, *kind.*
Akali, *some few, some.*
Akili, *intelligence, wits.*
Alama, *mark.*
Allah, *God.*
Amani, *peace, safety.*
Ambia, ku-, *to tell, to say to.*
Amerikano, *American sheeting.*
Amini, or Aminifu, *trustworthy, faithful.*
Amka, ku-, *to awake.*
Amsha, ku-, *to waken, cause to awake.*
Andika, ku-, *to describe, write, employ.*
Angalia, ku-, *to look attentively, observe, beware of.*
Angika, ku-, *to hang up, hang against a wall.*
Anguka, ku-, *to fall down.*
Anika, ku-, *to spread out to dry.*
Anza, ku-, *to begin.*

Ao, *or.*
Ao—ao, *either—or.*
Apisha, ku-, *to make to swear, to adjure.*
Ariaa, *lower! let out the rope!*
Asali, *sirup, honey.*
Askari, *soldier.*
Assubui, *in the morning.*
Aza, ku-, *to ponder, think.*
Azizi, *rarity, curiosity.*

B

Baa, mabaa, *worthless person, reprobate, disaster.*
Baado, *afterwards.*
Baba, *father.*
Badili, ku-, *to change, exchange, alter.*
Bado, *not yet, afterwards.*
Bado kidogo, *soon.*
Bahari, *sea.*
Bakuli, mabakuli, *basin.*
Balaa, *sorrow.*
Bamba, mabamba, *plate.*
Bandera, *flag.*
Banzi, mabanzi, *splint, a small thin piece of wood.*
Bara, or barra, *wild country, inland.*
Barafu, *ice, snow.*
Baraka, *blessing, progress.*

---

[1] See Lesson II, paragraph 1, and its vocabulary.

Barasi, *disease*.

Baruti, *gunpowder*.

Bass, or bassi, *enough, it will do*.

Bastola, *pistol*.

Bata, mabata, *duck*.

Batili, ku-, *to annul, to reduce to nothing*.

-baya, *bad*.

Bega, mabega, *shoulder*.

Biashara, *trade, commerce*.

Bibi, *wife, woman*.

Bilauri, *drinking glass*.

Billa, *except by*.

Bin, *son (Arab)*.

Binti, *daughter*.

Bithaa, *goods, merchandise*.

-bovu, *rotten, bad, malicious*.

Boga, maboga, *pumpkin, vegetables*.

Boma, maboma, *rampart, fort, government building*.

Boni, *ostrich*.

Boriti, *rafter, thick pole*.

Boy, *butler, servant*.

Bubu, mabubu, *dumb*.

Buli, mabuli, *teapot*.

Bunduki, *gun*.

Buni, *coffee berry*.

Burre, *for nothing, in vain*.

Bustani, *garden*.

Busu, *kiss*.

Busu, ku-, *to kiss*.

Bwana, *master, lord, sir*.

-bili, or -wili, *two*.

C

Campi, campini, *camp, at, by or in the camp*.

Chacha, ku-, *to ferment*.

Chafu, machafu, *cheek*.

Chai, *tea*.

Chakaa, ku-, *to become worn out*.

Chakula, *food, meal*.

Changanya, ku-, *to mix*.

Chango, vyango, *peg to hang things upon*.

Chavu, vyavu, *net*.

Cheka, ku-, *to laugh, laugh at*.

Cheo, vyeo, *measurement, length, breadth, station*.

Cherevu, *cunning, subtlety*.

Cheti, vyeti, *bill, passport*.

Cheza, ku-, *to play, dance*.

Chimba, ku-, *to dig*.

Chini, *down, bottom, below*.

Chini ya, *under, below*.

Chinja, ku-, *to cut, slaughter animals, kill for food*.

Chiti, *note of hand, note of any kind*.

Choka, ku-, *to become tired*.

Choma, ku-, *to stab, stick, prick, dazzle*.

Chombo, vyombo, *vessel, pot*.

Choroa, *oryx*.

Chovu, *weary, tired*.

Chui, *leopard*.

Chukia, ku-, *to be disgusted at, hate*.

Chukiza, ku-, *to disgust, offend*.

Chukua, ku-, *to carry*.

Chula, vyula, *frog*.

Chuma, vyuma, *iron, a piece of iron*.

Chumba, vyumba, *room*.

Chumvi, *salt*.

Chuna, ku-, *to skin, to flay*.

Chunga, ku-, *to pasture, tend animals*.

Chungu, vyungu, *earthen cooking pot*.

Chungu, *heap, pile*.

-chungu, *bitter*.

Chuo, vyuo, *book*.

D

Dacha, ku-, *to drop.*

Dafu, madafu, *cocoanut, for drinking.*

Damu, *blood.*

Danganya, ku-, *to cheat, humbug, impose upon.*

Daraja, *step, staircase, bridge.*

Dari, *roof, upper floor.*

Darubini, *field glass, telescope.*

Dau, madau, *native sailboat.*

Dawa, *medicine.*

Desturi, *custom, customs.*

Dini, *religion, worship.*

Dira, *compass.*

Dirisha, madirisha, *window.*

Dobi, *washerman.*

-dogo, *little, small, young.*

Donda, madonda, *large sores.*

Dondoro, *Dyker's antelope.*

Doti, *loin cloth.*

Dudu, madudu, *insect, insects.*

Duka, maduka, *shop, store.*

Dun, *a fine.*

Duni, *below, less, inferior.*

Dunia, *the world, this world.*

E

-ekundu, *red.*

-ema, *good, kind, all right.*

-embamba, *narrow, thin, slim.*

Embe, *mango.*

Enda, kw-, *to go.*

-eupe, *white, clear, clean.*

-eusi, *black, dark colored.*

F

Fa, ku-, *to die, perish, fade away.*

Fagia, ku-, *to sweep.*

Fakiri, *a poor person, beggar.*

Fanya, ku-, *to make, do, mend.*

Fayida, *profit, gain, interest.*

Fetha, *silver, money.*

Ficha, ku-, *to hide.*

Figa, mafiga, *fire-stones (to support the cooking pot).*

Fika, ku-, *to arrive.*

Fikiri, ku-, *to consider.*

Fimbo, *stick.*

Fisi, *hyena.*

Frasi, *horse, mare.*

Fuja, ku-, *to waste, leak.*

Fuko, mafuko, *a large bag.*

Fukuza, ku-, *to drive away, chase.*

Fundi, *skilled workman, teacher.*

Funga, ku-, *fasten, tie, bind, imprison.*

Fungua, ku-, *unfasten, open, let loose.*

Funua, ku-, *to uncover, open a book.*

Funza, *maggot, jigger.*

Fupa, mafupa, *large bone.*

-fupi, *short.*

Furaha, *joy, pleasure.*

Fusi, *rubbish.*

Futa, ku-, *to wipe.*

Fuzi, mafuzi, *shoulder.*

G

Galawa, *canoe.*

Gani? *what? what kind?*

Gari, magari, *carriage.*

Gawanya, ku-, *to divide, to share.*

-geni, *foreign, strange.*

Gereza, *fort, prison.*

Geuza, ku-, *to change, turn.*

Ghafala, *suddenly.*

Ghali, *dear.*

Ghatabu, *anger, passion.*

Giza, *darkness.*

Gombana, ku-, *to quarrel.*

Gombeza, ku-, *to forbid.*

Gote, magote, *knee.*

APPENDIX

Gugu, magugu, *undergrowth, weeds.*
Gusa, ku-, *to touch.*

H

Habari, *news, message, story.*
Ha-ifai! *it is of no use! never mind!*
Haja, *request, need.*
Halafu, *afterwards, presently.*
Halali, *lawful.*
Hali, *state, condition, health.*
Hamna, *there is not, or are not, no.*
Hapa, *here, this place.*
Hapana, *there is not, no.*
Haraka, *haste.*
Haraka, ku-, *to make haste.*
Haramu, *unlawful, prohibited.*
Hari, *heat, perspiration.*
Haribu, ku-, *to destroy, spoil.*
Hariri, *silk.*
Hasira, *anger, wrath.*
Hasira, ku-, *to injure.*
Hatta, *till, until, even.*
Haya, *these.*
Haya! *Work away! Be quick! Come along!*
Hema, *tent.*
Hila, *device, stratagem, deceit.*
Hisa, *pardon, permission.*
Hodari, *strong.*
Hodi! *hello!*
Homa, *fever.*
Hua, *dove.*
Hujambo? *Are you well? How do you do?*
Huko, *there, at a distance.*
Huru, *free, not a slave.*

I

Ile, *that yonder.*
Illa, *except, unless, but.*

Illi, *in order that.*
Imba, kw-, *to sing.*
Imbu, *mosquito, mosquitoes.*
Inchi, *land, country, earth.*
Ingia, ku-, *enter, go or come into.*
Ini, maini, *liver.*
Inshallah, *if God will, perhaps.*
Inua, ku-, *to lift, lift up.*
Inzi, mainzi, *a fly.*
Ipi? *what?*
Isha, kw-, *to finish, come to an end.*
Ita, kw-, *to call, name, invite.*

J

Jaa, ku-, *to become full, fill, abound with.*
Jambo, mambo, *matter, thing, affair.*
Jana, *yesterday.*
Janga, *punishment.*
Jaribu, ku-, *to try.*
Jicho, plur. macho, *the eye.*
Jifu, majifu, *ashes.*
Jina, majina, *name.*
Jina lako nani? *What is your name?*
Jino, meno, *tooth, twist or strand of rope.*
Jisu, majisu, *a very large knife.*
Jiwe, majiwe, *a piece of stone.*
Jombo, majombo, *an exceedingly large vessel.*
Jua, majua, *the sun.*
Jua, ku-, *to know, how, understand, know.*
Jugo, *ground nuts, peanuts.*
Juma, *a week.*
el juma, *Friday, corresponding to our Sunday.*
Juma mosi, *Saturday.*
Juma pili, *Sunday.*

346

Juma tatu, *Monday.*

Juma 'nne, *Tuesday.*

Juma tano, *Wednesday.*

Jumla, *sum, total, addition (arithmetic).*

Juu, *up, the top, on the top.*

Juu ya, *upon, above over, on the top of, against.*

Juzi, *the day before yesterday.*

K

Kaa, ku-, *to. sit, dwell, stay.*

Kaanga, ku-, *to fry, cook with fat.*

Kabla, *before.*

Kahawa, *coffee.*

-kali, *cruel, dangerous, sour, sharp, severe.*

Kama, *as, as if, like, if, supposing.*

Kamata, ku-, *lay hold of, seize, grasp.*

Kamba, *rope.*

Kamili, *perfect, complete.*

Kana, ku-, *to deny.*

Kanga, *guinea fowl.*

Kaniki, *dark blue calico.*

Kanisa, plur. makanisa, *church.*

Kanzu, *long, shirtlike garment.*

Kapu, plur. makapu, *large basket.*

Karatasi, *paper.*

Karibu, *near, come near, come in.*

Karibu ya, *near by.*

Kasha, makasha, *chest, large box.*

Kata, ku-, *cut, clip, divide.*

Katika, *on, by, at, among, from, in, about.*

Kauka, ku-, *to get dry, dry.*

Kazi, *work, labor, employment.*

Kelele, makelele, *noise, uproar, shouting.*

Kem? *How much? How many?*

Kengele, *bell.*

Kero, *trouble, disturbance, uproar.*

Kesho, *to-morrow.*

Kesho kutwa, *the day after to-morrow.*

Khabari, *news, information.*

Khalas! *the end, finish! there is no more.*

Khamse, *five.*

el Khamse, *Thursday.*

Khamsini, *fifty.*

Kiapo, viapo, *ordeal, oath.*

Kiatu, *shoe, boot, sandal.*

Kiazi, viazi, *sweet potato.*

Kibaba, *measure for porters' posho.*

Kibanda, vibanda, *hut, hovel, shed.*

Kibanzi, vibanzi, *splinter, small piece of wood.*

Kibao, vibao, *shelf, small plank.*

Kiberiti, viberiti, *matches.*

Kiboko, *hippopotamus.*

Kifaru, vifaru, *rhinoceros.*

Kifungo, vifungo, *button.*

Kijana, vijana, *youth, boy or girl, son or daughter.*

Kijiko, vijiko, *spoon.*

Kijito, vijito, *small stream, brook.*

Kikapu, vikapu, *basket.*

Kikombe, vikombe, *cup.*

Kile, *that, yonder.*

Kilemba, vilemba, *turban.*

Kilima, vilima, *hill.*

Killa, *all, every.*

Kima, *monkey.*

Kimaji, *damp.*

Kimanda, *omelette.*

Kimbia, ku-, *run away, flee.*

Kimbiza, ku-, *to make to run away, to put to flight.*

Kingalingali, *on the back.*

Kinge, *too little.*

Kinoo, vinoo, *whetstone.*

Kinu, vinu, *wooden mortar, mill.*

347

Kioo, vioo, *glass, mirror.*
Kipande, vipande, *piece, instrument.*
Kipele, vipele, *pimple.*
Kipini, vipini, *handle, hilt.*
Kipofu, vipofu, *blind person.*
Kiroboto, viroboto, *flea.*
Kisa, visa, *cause, reason.*
Kishoka, vishoka, *hatchet.*
Kisibao, visibao, *waistcoat.*
Kisima, visima, *a well.*
Kisiwa, visiwa, *island.*
Kisu, visu, *knife.*
Kitabu, vitabu, *book.*
Kitanda, vitanda, *bedstead, couch.*
Kitana, vitana, *comb.*
Kitanzi, vitanzi, *loop, button-loop.*
Kitendo, vitendo, *action.*
Kiti, viti, *chair, seat.*
Kitu, vitu, *thing.*
Kitunguu, vitunguu, *onion.*
Kitwa, vitwa, *head.*
Kiu, *thirst.*
Kivi, vivi, *elbow.*
Kivuko, vivuko, *ford, ferry, crossing place.*
Kivuli, vivuli, *shadow, ghost.*
Kizibo, vizibo, *stopper, cork.*
Kiziwi, visiwi, *deaf person.* .
Kizungu, *a European language.*
Kofi, makofi, *the flat of the hand.*
Kofia, *cap, hat.*
Kokoto, makokoto, *small stone, small piece of stone.*
Kombe, makombe, *large dish.*
Kondoo, *sheep.*
Kongoni, *hartebeest.*
Koo, makoo, *throat.*
Kororo, *crested guinea fowl.*
Koru, *water buck.* .
Kosa, ku-, *to make a mistake, do wrong, blunder.*

Koti, *coat.*
Kubali, ku-, *accept, acknowledge, approve.*
-kubwa, *large, great, chief.*
Kufuli, *padlock.*
Kuku, *hen, fowl, poultry.*
-kukuu, *old, worn out.*
Kule, *there, far off, yonder.*
Kulee, *yonder, very far off.*
Kumbuka, ku-, *to remember, ponder over.*
Kumbusha, ku-, *to remind.*
Kumi, makumi, *ten.*
Kunde, *beans.*
Kungu, *mist, fog.*
Kunguru, *crow, raven.*
Kuni, *firewood.*
Kunja, ku-, *to fold, wrap up.*
Kupe, *tick, cattle tick.*
Kusanya, ku-, *to collect, gather, assemble.*
Kutt, ku-, *to meet with, see, find.*
Kutu, *rust.*
-kuu, *great, chief, noble.*
Kwa, *with, for, on account of.*
Kwake, *to him, with him, to our, at his or her house.*
Kwako, *to or with thee, to or at thy place.*
Kwamba, *if, as if, though, that.*
ya kwamba, *that.*
Kwangu, *to or at my house, to or with me.*
Kwanza, *beginning, at first, formerly.*
Kwao, *to or with them, at or to their place.*
Kweli, *true, sincerely, the truth.*
Kwetu, *to or with us, to or at our place.*
Kwiba, or ku-iba, *to steal.*

SWAHILI–ENGLISH VOCABULARY

L

La, *no.*

La, ku-, *to eat, consume, wear away.*

Labda, *perhaps.*

Laini, *smooth, soft.*

Lakini, *but, however.*

Lakki, *a hundred thousand.*

Lala, ku-, *to sleep, to lie down.*

Lazima, *necessity, it is necessary.*

Leo, *to-day.*

Leso, *handkerchief.*

Leta, ku-, *to bring, send, fetch.*

Lewa, ku-, *to become drunk.*

Lia, ku-, *to cry, weep, cry out.*

Lima, ku-, *to cultivate, hoe.*

Linda, ku-, *to guard, watch, keep.*

Lindi, malindi, *pit, deep place.*

Lini? *When?*

Lisha, ku-, *to feed.*

Liwa, ku-, *to be eaten, worn away. consumed.*

Lozi, *almond.*

Lulu, *pearl.*

Lumba, ku-, *to make a speech.*

M

Maagano, *contract, agreement, covenant.*

Maasi, *rebellion.*

Madevu, *beard.*

Mafuta, *oil, fat, grease.*

Mafuu, *crazy, cracked.*

Magugu, *weeds, undergrowth.*

Mahindi, *Indian corn, maize.*

Majani, *grass.*

Maji, *water, liquid, juice, sap.*

Majibu, *answer.*

Makasi, *scissors.*

Makosa, *fault, mistake.*

Mali, *goods, property, riches.*

Mamba, *crocodile.*

Maneno, *language, message, business.*

Mapatano, *agreement, conspiracy.*

Mapema, *early.*

Mapigano, *liking, pleasure, love.*

Mapululu, *wilderness.*

Marra, *sometimes, at once.*

Marra moja, *once, at once.*

Marra nyingi, *often.*

Mashua, *boat, launch.*

Masikini, *poor, a poor person.*

Maua, *flowers.*

Mavi, *dung, excrement.*

Mawe, *stones, stone.*

Maziwa, *milk.*

Mbali, *far off, separate.*

Mbega, *colobus monkey.*

Mbele, *before, in front, farther on.*

Mbele ya, *in front of.*

Mboga, *vegetables.*

Mbuyu, mibuyu, *baobab tree, calabash tree.*

Mbuzi, *goat.*

Mbwa, *dog.*

Mchafu, *filthy.*

Mchawi, wachawi, *wizard.*

Mchele, *cleaned grain, especially rice.*

Mchunga, wachunga, *herdsman, groom.*

Mchwa, *white ants.*

Mdomo, midomo, *lip.*

Meli, *ship, mail steamer.*

Mrima, *the mainland, especially the coast.*

Meza, *table.*

Mfalme, wafalme, *king.*

Mfuko, mifuko, *bag, pocket.*

Mfupa, mifupa, *bone.*

Mgongo, migongo, *back, backbone.*

Mguu, miguu, *leg, foot.*

Mia, *hundred.*

APPENDIX

Mimi, *I, me.*
Mingi, *many.*
Miwani, *spectacles.*
Mjeledi, *whip.*
Mji, *town, city, village.*
Mjinga, wajinga, *simpleton, fool.*
Mjusi, wajusi, *lizard.*
Mkate, mikate, *cake, loaf.*
Mkeka, mikeka, *fine sleeping mat.*
Mkia, mikia, *tail.*
Mkono, mikono, *arm, hand, sleeve.*
Mkubwa, *great.*
Mkuke, mikuke, *spear.*
Mkuu, wakuu, *great man, chief.*
Mlango, milango, *door, gate.*
Mle, *there within.*
Mlevi, walevi, *drunkard.*
Mlezi, walezi, *nurse, children's nurse.*
Mlima, milima, *mountain.*
Mlinzi, walinzi, *guard.*
Mna, *there is within, or is there?*
Mnazi, minazi, *cocoanut tree.*
Mno, *exceedingly, excessively.*
Mnyampara, *caravan headman.*
Mnyororo, minyororo, *chain, chain-gang of prisoners.*
Moja, mamoja, *one, same.*
Moshi, mioshi, *smoke.*
Moto, mioto, *fire, heat.*
Moyo, mioyo or nyoyo, *heart, mind, will, self.*
Mpagazi, wapagazi, *caravan porter.*
Mpaka, mipaka, *boundary, limit.*
Mpaka, *until, as far as.*
Mpira, *India rubber.*
Mpishi, wapishi, *cook.*
Mpofu, or pofu, wapofu, *eland.*
Msafara, or safari, *caravan.*
Mshahara, mishara, *monthly pay, wages.*

Mshale, mishale, *arrow.*
Mshipi, mishipi, *belt, girdle.*
Msiba, misiba, *calamity, grief.*
Mstari, mistari, *a line.*
Msuaki, misuaki, *tooth stick.*
Msumeno, misumeno, *a saw.*
Mtai, *scratch, a slight cut.*
Mtama, *millet.*
Mtego, mitego, *trap.*
Mti, miti, *tree, pole, wood.*
Mto, mito, *river, stream—pillow, cushion.*
Mtoto, watoto, *child.*
Mtu, watu, *person, man, somebody.*
Mtumbui, mitumbwi, *canoe.*
Mtungi, mitungi, *water-jar.*
Mtupa, mitupa, *euphorbia tree.*
Mua, miwa, *sugar cane.*
Muhindi, wahindi, *Indian Mussulman, corn plant.*
Mume, *male.*
Muungu, *God.*
Mvita, *mombasa.*
Mvua, *rain.*
Mvuke, *vapor, steam.*
Mvulini, *in the shade.*
Mwaka, miaka, *year.*
Mwalimu, waalimu, *teacher.*
Mwamba, miamba, *rock.*
Mwana, waana, *mistress, matron.*
Mwavuli, miavuli, *umbrella.*
Mwendo, *going, gait, journey.*
Mwenyi, *having, possessing.*
Mwezi, *moon.*
Mwiba, miiba, *thorn.*
Mwili, miili, *body.*
Mwinda, wawinda, *hunter.*
Mwisho, miisho, *end, conclusion.*
Mwitu, *forest.*
Mwongo, wawongo, *liar, false person.*

Mzee, wazee, *old person.*
Mzigo, mizigo, *burden, load.*
Mzinga, mizinga, *big gun, cannon.*
Mzungu, wazungu, *European, white man.*

N

Na, *and, also, with.*
Nami, *and I, or with me.*
Nao, *and or with them, it.*
Nawe, *and thou, with thee.*
-na-, *sign of the present tense.*
Na—na, *both—and.*
Naam or na'am, *yes, I am here.*
Na, kwa, *too, with, together.*
Nafasi, *space, room, time, opportunity.*
Nanazi, mananazi, *pineapple.*
Nane, *eight.*
Nani? *Who?*
Nasibu, *luck, fortune.*
Nazi, *cocoanut, fully ripe nut.*
Ncha, *point, end, tip, strand.*
Ndani, *within, inside.*
Ndani ya, *inside of.*
Ndege, *bird, omen.*
Ndio, *yes.*
Ndizi, *banana, plantain.*
Ndoo, *pail, bucket.*
Nena, ku-, *to speak, name, mention.*
-nene, *thick, stout, fat, complete.*
Neno, maneno, *word, thing.*
Ngoja, ku-, *to wait, wait for.*
Ngoma, *drum, native dance.*
Ng'ombe, *ox, cow, bull, cattle.*
Ngozi, *skin, hide, leather.*
Nguo, *cotton, cloth, clothes.*
Nguruwe, *pig, swine.*
Nguvu, *strength, power, authority.*
Ni, *is, are.*
Nina, *I have.*

Nini? *What?*
Ninye, *ye, you.*
Njaa, *hunger, famine.*
Nje, *outside, forth.*
Njia or Ndia, *way, path, road, means.*
Njoo, *come.*
-'nne, *four.*
-nene, *fat.*
Nuele or Nyele, *hair.*
Nuka, ku-, *to give out a smell, stink.*
Nungu, *porcupine.*
Nunua, ku-, *to buy.*
Nuru, *light.*
Nusa, ku-, *to smell, scent.*
Nuss, or nusu, or nussu, *half.*
Nyama, *meat, animal, beasts.*
Nyani, *ape, apes.*
Nyasi, *grass, reeds.*
Nyati, *buffalo.*
Nyika, *wilderness, plains.*
Nyinyi, *you* (plur.).
Nyoka, *snake, serpent.*
Nyota, *star.*
Nyuki, *bee.*
Nyuma, *at the back, afterwards, behind.*
Nyuma ya, *behind, after.*
Nyumbo, *wildebeest, gnu.*
Nyumbu, *mule.*
Nyundo. *ham-ner.*

O

Oga, ku-, *to bathe.*
Ogopa, ku-, *to fear, be afraid.*
Oka, ku-, *to bake, cook.*
Okoka, ku-, *to be saved, to escape.*
Okota, ku-, *to pick up.*
Omba, ku-, *to pray to, beg of, beseech.*
Ona, ku-, *to see, find, feel.*

Onana, ku-, *to meet.*
Ondoka, ku-, *to go away, get up, break camp.*
Ongeza, ku-, *to increase, add to.*
Onja, ku-, *to taste, try, examine.*
Onyesha, ku-, *to show.*
-ororo, *soft, smooth.*
Osha, ku-, *to wash.*
Ota, ku-, *to dream, to grow.*
Oza, ku-, *to rot, spoil, go bad.*

P

Pa, ku-, *to give, present with.*
Paa, *gaselle.*
Pafu, mapafu, *lungs.*
Pahali, *place, at the place.*
Paka, mapaka, *cat.*
Pale, *there, that place.*
Palepale, *just there, at that very spot.*
Pamba, *cotton.*
-pana, *broad, wide.*
Panda, ku-, *to mount, get up, climb, ride, go on board or ashore.*
Panya, *rat.*
Papa, *shark.*
Papayi, mapapayi, *papaws, common kind of fruit.*
Parafujo, *screw.*
Pata, ku-, *to get, reach, succeed, happen to.*
Patana, ku-, *to agree.*
Pembe, ku-, *horn, corner,*
Penda, ku-, *to like, love, choose, prefer, wish.*
Pepo, *spirit, wind.*
Piga, ku-, *to strike, beat, flap, shoot.*
Piga hema, ku-, *to pitch the tent.*
Piga kelele, ku-, *to shout.*

Piga mbio, ku-, *to run, gallop.*
Piga teke, ku-, *to kick.*
Piga na, ku-, *to fight.*
Pika, ku-, *to cook.*
Pili, *a large kind of snake.*
Pilipili, *pepper.*
Pima, ku-, *to measure, weigh.*
Pindua, ku-, *to turn over, upset*
Pipa, mapipa, *barrel, tub, pipe.*
Pita, ku-, *to pass, excel.*
Pofu, *eland.*
Polepole, *gently, moderately, quietly.*
Pombe, *native beer.*
Ponda, ku-, *to pound, crush.*
Ponya, ku-, *to cure, save, rescue.*
Posho, *rations, food.*
Potelea, ku-, *to perish, be lost.*
Pua, *nose.*
Pumzika, ku-, *to rest.*
Punda, *donkey.*
Punda milia, *zebra.*
Pungua, ku-, *to diminish, waste.*
-pya, *new, fresh.*

R

Rafiki, *a friend, friends.*
Rakhisi, or rahisi, *cheap.*
Rangi, *color, paint.*
Rasassi, or risassi, *bullet, cartridge.*
Rathi, *satisfied, content, blessing.*
-refu, *long.*
Roho, *soul, spirit, breath, life.*
Rudi, ku-, *to return, correct, keep in order, punish.*
Rudisha, ku-, *to make to return, to give back, repay.*
Ruka, ku-, *to fly, leap.*
Ruksa, or ruhusa, *leave, permission, liberty.*
Rungu, *club, mace, knobstick.*

S

Saa, *hour, clock, watch.*

Saa ngapi? *What o'clock is it?*

Sala, masala, *question, prayer.*

Saba, *seven.*

Sababu, *cause, reason.*
  kwa sababu, *because of, because.*

Sabuni, *soap.*

Sadaka, *offering, alms.*

Sadiki, ku-, *to believe.*

Safari, *journey, voyage, caravan.*

Safi, *pure, clean, neat.*

Safiri, ku-, *to travel, set out, sail.*

Safisha, ku-, *to make pure or clean.*

Saga, ku-, *to grind.*

Sagai, *spear.*

Sahani, *plate, dish.*

Sahihi, *correct, right.*

Salaam, *compliments, safety, peace, greeting.*

Salama, *safe, safety.*

Samaki, *fish.*

Samli, *ghee, clarified butter.*

Sana, *very, much.*

Sasa, *now.*

Sasa hivi, *directly, at once.*

Sauti, *voice, sound, noise.*

Sawasawa, *like, alike, even, all the same, level.*

Sayidia, ku-, *to help.*

Sema, ku-, *to say, talk, speak.*

Serkali, *court, government.*
  mtu wa serkali, *a man in the government employ.*

Seta, ku-, *to crush.*

Shaba, *copper, brass.*

Shamba, mashamba, *plantation,*

Shauri, mashauri, *advice, counsel, plan.*

Sheria, *law.*

Shidda, *difficulty, distress.*

Shimo, mashimo, *pit, excavation, large hole.*

Shinda, ku-, *to overcome, conquer, beat, stay.*

Shindilia, ku-, *to load a gun.*

Shingo, mashingo, *neck.*

Shirti, *shirt.*

Shoka, mashoka, *ax.*

Shona, ku-, *to sew.*

Shtaki, ku-, *to charge, accuse.*

Shughuli, ku-, *business, affairs, engagement.*

Shusha, ku-, *to let down, land goods from a ship.*

Si, *is not, or are not.*

Siafu, *reddish ant, that bites fiercely.*

Siagi, *cream, butter.*

Sifa, *praise, character, characteristic.*

Sifa, ku-, *to praise.*

Sijambo, *I am well.*

Sikia, ku-, *to hear, listen to, obey, understand.*

Sikitika, *sorry, sad.*

Sikitikia, ku-, *to be sorry for, pity.*

Siku, *day, days.*

Simama, ku-, *to stand up, stop, be erect, cost.*

Simba, *lion, lions.*

Similla! simille! similleni! *make way! get out of the way!*

Sindano, or shindano, *needle.*

Sisi, *we, us.*

Sisi sote, *all of us.*

Sita, *six.*

Sittini, *sixty.*

Siwezi, *I am not well.*

Socks, *socks.*

Soko, masoko, *market, bazaar.*

Soma, ku-, *to read, perform devotions.*

353

APPENDIX

Soruali, *trousers*.
Ssafi, or safi, *pure, clean*.
Starehe! *don't disturb yourself, don't get up!*
Sufuria, *cooking pot*.
Sukari, *sugar*.
Sumbuka, ku-, *to annoy, to be annoyed*.
Sumu, *poison*.
Sunni, *advisable, meritorious*.

T

Taa, *lamp, lantern*.
Taajabu, ku-, *to wonder, be astonished*.
Tafuta, ku-, *to look for, seek, search for*.
Taka, ku-, *to want, wish for, ask for*.
-tamu, *sweet, pleasant*.
Tandika, ku-, *to spread the table*.
Tanga, matanga, *sail*.
Tangu, *since, from*.
Tangu lini? *Since when, how long ago?*
Tangulia, ku-, *to precede, go before*.
Tano, or tanu, *five*.
Taraja, ku-, *to hope, expect*.
Tasama, ku-, *to see, look for*.
Tatu, *three*.
Tatua, ku-, *to tear*.
Tawanya, ku-, *to scatter*.
Taya, *jaw, jawbone*.
Tayari, *ready*.
Tazama, ku-, *to look, observe*.
Tega, ku-, *to set a trap, snare*.
Teketeza, ku-, *to burn, consume*.
Tele, *plenty, abundantly*.
Tembo, *elephant, also palm wine*.
Tena, *afterwards, again, further*.
Tende, *date, dates*.

Tengeneza, ku-, *to finish off, put to rights, fix*.
Thaifu, *weak, infirm, bad*.
Thalathini, *thirty*.
Thambi, *sin*.
Themanini, *eighty*.
Thuru, ku-, *to harm, injure*.
Tia, ku-, *to put, pour*.
Tissa, *nine*.
Tissini, *ninety*.
Toa, ku-, *to put out, blow out*.
Toka, ku-, *to go or come out or away from, go free*.
Tokosa, ku-, *to boil, cook by boiling*.
Tombo, *quail*.
Tone, matone, *drop*.
Toroka, ku-, *to run away from a master or home*.
Tota, ku-, *to sink, be drowned*.
Tu, *only, merely, only just*.
Tufe, *ball*.
Tumaini, ku-, *to be confident, hope*.
Tumbako, *tobacco*.
Tumbo, matumbo, *stomach, belly*.
Tunda, matunda, *fruit*.
Tunza, ku-, *to care of, look after*.
Tupa, matupa, *file, bottle*.
-tupu, *bare, empty*.
Twaa, ku-, *to take*.
Tweka, ku-, *to raise, take up*.
Twiga, *giraffe*.

U

Ua, ku-, *to kill*.
Ubau, mbau, *plank*.
Ubishi, *joke*.
Uchawi, *witchcraft, black magic*.
Ufu, *death, the state of being dead*.
Ufungu, *relatives*.

354

Ugali, *porridge.*

Uguza, ku-, *to take care of a sick person.*

Uhuru, *freedom.*

Ukucha, kucha, *nail, claw, hoof.*

Ule, *that, yonder.*

Ulimi, ndimi, *tongue, heel of a mast.*

Uliza, ku-, *to ask, inquire of a person.*

Uma, nyuma, *a spit, fork, awl.*

Uma, ku-, *to bite, sting, hurt, ache.*

-ume, *male, strong.*

Umeme, *lightning.*

Una, *you have, thou hast.*

Una nini? *What is the matter with you?*

Unene, *stoutness, thickness.*

Unga, *flour, powder.*

Unguja, *Zanzibar.*

Upana, *width, breadth.*

Upande, pande, *a side, part.*

Upanga, panga, *sword.*

Upele, pele, *large pimple.*

Upepo, pepo, *wind, cold.*

Upesi, *quickly, lightly, fast.*

Upindi, pindi, *bow.*

Usiku, *night.*

Uvuli, *shade, shadow.*

Uwingu, mbingu, *heaven, sky.*

Uza, ku-, *to sell.*

Uzuri, *beauty, fineness, ornament.*

V

Vema or ema (pron. yema), *well, very well.*

Viberiti (plur. of kiberiti), *matches.*

Vilevile, *just those things, in like manner.*

-vivu, *idle, dull, slow.*

Vua, ku-, *to undress, to take across a river, to fish.*

Vuke, *steam, vapor, sweat.*

-vungu, *hollow.*

Vunja, ku-, *to break, ruin, spoil, change a piece of money.*

Vuta, ku-, *to draw, pull.*

W

Waka, ku-, *to blaze, burn up, burn.*

Wake, or wakwe, *his, hers, its.*

Wako, *thy, your.*

Wala—wala, *neither—nor.*

Wale, *those yonder.*

Wali, *cooked grain, especially rice.*

Wali, *governor.*

Wana, *they have.*

Wanda, ku-, *to have, hold.*

Wanda, nyanda, *finger, a finger's breadth.*

Wangu, *my.*

Wao, *they.*

Wapi? *Where? Which people?*

Waraka, nyaraka, *letter.*

Washenzi, *wild people, uncivilized people.*

Wasi, *rebellion.*

Watu (plur. of mtu), *people.*

Wawili, *two, two persons.*

Weka, ku-, *to place, lay, keep, delay.*

Weye! *you! it is you!*

Weza, ku-, *to be able.*
 siwezi, *I a sick, I cannot.*

-wili, or bili, *two.*

Winda, ku-, or winga, ku-, *to hunt.*

Wino, *ink.*

-wivu, *jealous, ripe.*

Wongo, *falsehood, lie.*

Wote, *all, both.*

APPENDIX

Y

Yabis, or yabisi, *dry, solid.*

Yakini, *certainly, certainty, it is certain.*

Yamkini, *possibly.*

Yayi, mayayi, *egg.*

Yule, *that, that person.*

Z

Zaa, ku-, *to bear, breed, bear fruit.*

Zaidi, or Zayidi, *more.*

Zaliwa, ku-, *to be born.*

Zamani, *times, long ago, formerly.*

Zayidi, *more.*

-zima, *sound, whole, healthy, complete.*

Zima, ku-, *to extinguish, put out.*

-zito, *heavy, difficult, severe, sad, clumsy.*

Zua, ku-, *to pierce, bore, invent.*

Zulia, ku-, *to invent, to lie, tell falsehood.*

Zulu, ku-, *to be crazy.*

Zumbua, ku-, *to find.*

Zunguka, ku-, *to go round, surround, revolve, wander.*

Zungusha, ku-, *to make to go round, to turn.*

-zuri, *fine, beautiful, good, handsome.*

Zuzuka, ku-, *to be bewildered, to lose one's head.*

INDEX

A

Aberdare Mountains, 5, 9, 301.
Abyssinia, 211.
Ainsworth, H. M. Commissioner, 272.
Albert Nyanza, 93.
American Museum of Natural History, collecting specimens for, 25-26.
Americano, 7.
Antelopes, 16.
  characteristics of, 152-153.
  diminishing herds of, 154.
  habitat of, 153.
  Hunter's, 16.
  roan, 160ff.
  sable, 165-166.
Arabia, 32, 184.
Asgar, 36, 37, 39.
Asiatic elephant, 52, 53.
Askaris, 22.
Athi Plains, 2, 197.
  game on, 2.
  hunting on, 4, 82, 169.
Athi River, 90, 154, 237.

B

Baboons, 9.
  destructiveness of, 222.
  habits of, 221.
Baker, Sir Samuel, 88.
Bantu race of negroes, 245.
Baringo, Lake, 8, 124, 237.
  district of, 174.

Barker, Mr., 81.
Barnet, Mr. and Mrs., 8.
Black snake (poisonous), 234.
Bongo, 6, 9, 16.
British East Africa, climate and topography of, 1.
  diminishing game of, 300, 303.
  game laws of, 13-19.
  hunting grounds in, 2, 5-12.
  rainfall in, 2.
  scanty population of, 254.
  seasons in, 13.
  variety of game in, 302.
Buffalo, 6, 9, 12, 15.
  appearance of, size of, etc., 104-105.
  Cape, habitat of, 103, 106.
  Congo, Abyssinian, Senegambrian and gray, 103.
  habits of, 106.
  hunting of, 107, 109.
Bush buck, 6, 9, 12, 17, 180.
Bush pig, 9.
  giant, 223.
  habits of, characteristics of, etc., 222.
Bustard, giant, size of, habits of, etc., 239.
  smaller species of, 240.

C

Cape buffalo, 6, 9, 12, 15, 103ff.
Cape Colony, 167, 173, 201.
Caravan, almost lost, 197ff.
Central Africa, 113, 181.
Chameleon, 235.

357

INDEX

Giraffe, 2, 7, 9, 12, 15.
  characteristics of, habits of, size of,
    etc., 75–77, 80, 82–83, 86.
  combat between lion and, 80.
  habitat of, 66–67.
  hunting of, 77, 83.
  lack of voice in, 77.
  peculiar gait of, 76. .
  two species of, 85.
Gnu, white bearded, 39, 167.
Gojito Mountains, 62.
Government officials, commendation
  of, 272.
Guas Ngishu Plateau, 15, 77, 86.
  climate of, 10.
Guaso Narok, 7, 9, 135.
  eland hunting on, 159.
  swamp on, 8.
Guaso Nyaro, 7, 135, 177.
Guinea fowl, 9, 242.

H

Hartebeest, 2, 4, 6, 9, 10, 11, 35.
  characteristics of, 192.
  Cook's (Coke's), 6, 9, 16, 17.
  diminishing numbers of, 197.
  first specimen of, 193ff.
  food of, 196.
  hated by settlers and hunters, 195.
  Jackson's, 9, 16, 17.
  meat of, 196.
  Neuman's, 15, 16.
  size of, habits of, etc., 194, 197.
  speed of, 195.
  where found, 193.
Headman of safari, 28.
Heron, 124.
Hippopotamus, 6, 8, 9, 12, 16.
  characteristics of, habits of, etc.,
    87–90, 91, 94, 101.
  destructiveness of, 101.
  first experience with, 90.
  geological distribution of, 87.
  habitat of, 87.
  method of escape of, from hunters,
    89.

Hippopotamus, names of, 88.
  photographing, 96.
  shooting, 97ff.
  size of, 88, 101.
  two species of, 87.
  white, 88.
Hornbill, 244.
Hunting grounds, 2, 12.
Hyenas, 9, 12.
  description of, habits of, etc., 212–
    215.
  howl of pack of, 216.
  increase in regular hunting grounds
    of, 215.
  man-eating, 213, 215.
  ravenous appetite of, 213.
  spotted, 212.
  striped, 211.

I

Iguana, 234.
Impalla, 6, 12, 16, 17.
  flesh of, 183.
  habits of, 181–183.
  size of, color of, etc., 180.
Ito, Marquis, testimony of, 269.

J

Jackal, 9.
Johnston, Sir Harry, address of, to
  Basogas, 271.
  government report of, 270.

K

Kanga, 242.
Kedong Valley (southern), 8.
  encounter with rhinos in, 141.
Kenia, Mt., 6, 35, 55, 201, 220, 223,
  301.
  hunting buffalo on, 109.
Kenia-Laikipia region, 154.
  game in, 9.
  length of, 5.
  return route from Rumuruti to,
    8–9.
  route to, 6.
  tour of, 5.

INDEX

INDEX

INDEX

THE END

Lightning Source UK Ltd.
Milton Keynes UK
UKHW020641060223
416537UK00012B/2483